D1523837

Market Socialism in Yugoslavia

CHRISTOPHER PROUT

WITHDRAWN

OXFORD UNIVERSITY PRESS
1985

Oxford University Press, Walton Street, Oxford OX2 6DP
London New York Toronto
Delhi Bombay Calcutta Madras Karachi
Kuala Lumpur Singapore Hong Kong Tokyo
Nairobi Dar es Salaam Cape Town
Melbourne Auckland

and associated companies in

Beirut Berlin Ibadan Nicosia
Oxford is a trade mark of Oxford University Press

Published in the United States
by Oxford University Press, New York

© Christopher Prout 1985

British Library Cataloguing in Publication Data
Prout, Christopher
Market socialism in Yugoslavia. – (Economies
of the world)
1. Yugoslavia – Economic conditions – 1945-
I. Title   II. Series
330.9497'023   HC407
ISBN 0–19–828286–9
ISBN 0–19–828287–7 Pbk

Library of Congress Cataloging in Publication Data
Prout, Christopher
Market socialism in Yugoslavia.
(Economies of the world)
Bibliography: p.
Includes Index.
1. Yugoslavia – Economic policy – 1945-
2. Yugoslavia – Economic conditions – 1945-
I. Title   II. Series
HC407.P77 1985   338.9497   85–10534
ISBN 0–19–828286–9
ISBN 0–19–828287–7 (pbk.)

Photoset by Enset (Photosetting),
Midsomer Norton, Bath, Avon
Printed in Great Britain by
Butler & Tanner Ltd, Frome

PREFACE

I was encouraged to write this little survey by Nita Watts and Michael Kaser. Both have been a constant source of good-humoured advice and encouragement. In the course of writing Chapter 4, a number of discussions with Saul Estrin proved invaluable. I am acutely aware of the debt I owe to the many distinguished American and Western European scholars and specialists in the study of Yugoslav economic and social affairs. Their names are too numerous to list, but their influence has been all pervasive and I have tried to acknowledge my debts as fully as possible in the Notes. At various stages of its production, Linda Cannon, Michael Timms and Kay Godfrey have had the thankless task of typing from a near indecipherable manuscript and I am extremely grateful to them. Mrs Godfrey also compiled the Index. I alone am responsible for any errors or omissions in the text.

CONTENTS

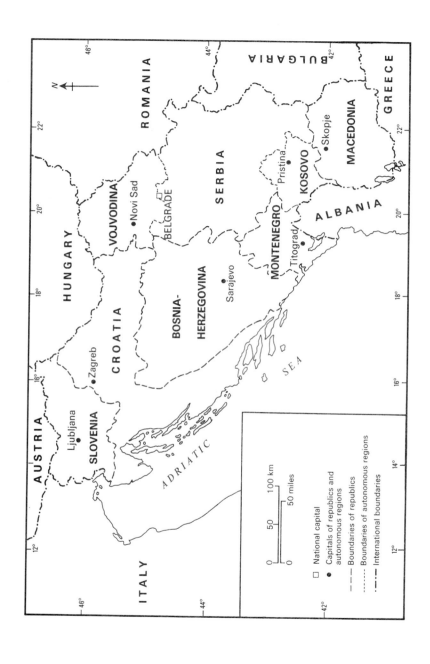

INTRODUCTION

Yugoslavia, the Land of the South Slavs, became a nation state in December 1918. It comprised the independent states of Serbia and Montenegro and a number of territories from the former Habsburg and Ottoman Empires. At its head was a Serbian monarch. Serbs, Croats, Slovenes, Macedonians, Bosnian Muslims, Montenegrans, Magyars and Albanians were the main ethnic groups represented in the new country. Serbs accounted for about 40 per cent, and Croats for about 25 per cent, of its 14 million inhabitants. The former Habsburg territories in the North, Croatia, Slovenia and Vojvodina, were wealthier and the more economically developed. But Serbians dominated the political system. Economic development between the wars was largely confined to the exploitation, by foreign capital, of the nation's plentiful mineral resources. Yugoslavia remained one of the poorest countries in Europe, with its peasant farming families constituting about 75 per cent of the total population. During this period its politicians were mainly preoccupied with inward looking nationality questions.

With the Axis invasion in April 1941, the kingdom collapsed and its territory was partitioned into a number of occupied areas more or less corresponding to ethnic divisions. There ensued a bitter and bloody struggle, part popular uprising against the hated invader and part civil war between the component nationalities. Out of all this emerged the victorious Partisans, led by Marshal Tito. At the end of 1945, the monarchy was formally abolished and Yugoslavia was declared a Federal People's Republic. The Federation contained six republics, Slovenia, Croatia, Bosnia–Herzegovina, Serbia, Montenegro and Macedonia, and two autonomous provinces, Vojvodina and Kosovo. The creation of these autonomous provinces reflected the political claims of the Magyar and Albanian minorities. Soon the Party also acquired a matching republican structure.

However, power in both State and Party was concentrated almost entirely in the hands of the federal authorities. In January 1946, a Constitutional Assembly adopted the Constitution of the Federal People's Republic of Yugoslavia which closely followed the 1936

Constitution of the USSR. Thereafter, Tito set out to model his country on Stalin's Russia. So matters might have remained had not Stalin and he fallen out. It was their bitter feud, culminating in Yugoslavia's expulsion from Cominform in 1948 and the subsequent Soviet blockade, that provoked Tito into adopting a new approach to economic and social development founded upon the complementary principles of debureaucratization and mass participation. Together, they constituted the ideological basis for Yugoslav market socialism.

The legal character of the self-managed enterprise was quickly established. Worker collectives, socially-owned industrial assets and surplus value accounting—the three ideologically inspired features which distinguished the Yugoslav firm from its Western counterpart—were all innovations of the early and mid-1950s. Price and foreign exchange controls were also relaxed. However, until the mid-1960s, stringent statutory limits were placed upon personal income distributions to generate high domestic savings for capital investment. Moreover, a substantial proportion of these savings were siphoned off by taxation and recycled through a network of national, regional and local investment funds in accordance with priorities laid down in successive Five Year Plans. Though Stalin's centralized and hierarchical system of economic management had disappeared, his economic strategy remained intact in Yugoslavia. Tito aimed, like Stalin, to achieve rapid industrialization of the economy through high rates of investment in manufacturing industry. Unfortunately, the strategy created imbalances in the rates of growth of production of finished and semi-finished goods, raw materials, agricultural commodities and infrastructure services. These imbalances caused severe current account payments deficits and inflationary pressures which were suppressed by the reapplication of price and foreign exchange controls.

The decentralization of decision-making in favour of the firm in the economic sphere was matched by a shift in political power in the State and Party structure from the federal government to regional and local authorities. Republics and communes used their emerging fiscal and monetary independence to pursue their particular interests by discriminatory taxes, subsidies and credits. Indeed, as the 1950s progressed, it became clear that decentralization to regional and local government was proving a more powerful influence on economic development than decentralization to the enterprise. Instead of allocating resources according to a blend of market forces and federally determined investment priorities, the system increasingly fragmented the economy into a series of republican and communal autarchies.

By the beginning of the 1960s, market forces were barely discernible beneath a morass of discriminatory interventions provoked either by macro-economic instability or by sectional self-interest. Support steadily grew for granting enterprises the freedom to make their own investment decisions and for increasing the exposure of the economy to world markets. Leading ideologists, such as Kardelj, saw the changes as a means of combating the threatened rebureaucratization of the economy of the republics and communes and of giving decisions over the deployment of surplus value to those who created it. The wealthier Northern republican leaderships backed them as a means of removing the power of a Serbian-dominated federal government to reallocate income earned in their territory to investment projects in the poorer Southern regions. The more liberally minded economists regarded them as essential both to a more efficient use of resources and to a pattern of development more in tune with the wishes of the consumer.

Not everyone in authority agreed and a power struggle ensued. Eventually, the proponents of decentralization prevailed and their views were reflected in a new Constitution and a series of legislative measures enacted between 1963 and 1965. By far the most important were those abolishing the social investment fund system and its concomitantly onerous burden of enterprise taxation. Commercial banks, owned by firms, were allotted the task of redistributing corporate saving. Significant changes were also made in the price and foreign exchange regimes to align domestic and world market prices. Henceforth, the self-managed enterprise, acting independently and in pursuit of profit, was to determine the amount and composition of production and investment and the pattern of income distribution, in response to national and international market indicators.

The sluggish adjustment of markets to their own new environment led to rapid disenchantment with the system that emerged from these measures. Hitherto, fiscal burdens and constant bureaucratic interference had given the enterprise no chance to demonstrate its effectiveness as an agent for economic efficiency. There is, now, little doubt in the minds of most Western observers, that its special character contributed to resource misallocations in the post-1965 economy. In particular, the absence of marketable equity shares—

and the correspondingly adverse implications for promotion, entry, exit, and merger, and for the range of financial assets that could be created by firms and financial intermediaries—had a negative effect upon capital mobility, product competition and, probably, the propensity to save; and the absence of a contractual wage had a similar effect on labour mobility, personal income differentials and, probably, on the degree of capital intensity, on the propensity of firms to hire and on inflation. Misallocations were further aggravated in the capital markets by the refusal of the authorities, at least until the beginning of the 1980s, to contemplate establishing a market rate of interest which reflected the scarcity of capital resources; and, in the labour market, by a legal regime which made it impossible to dismiss workers except for misconduct.

Despite the growing evidence of resource misallocation, the authorities were unprepared to modify the structure of the enterprise, although attempts were made to get round the problem in the capital market by the introduction of contractual substitutes. In fact, the most highly publicized symptoms of market imperfections, strikes and the accumulation of monopolistic powers by certain enterprises, provoked an intensification of self-management! The authorities regarded their emergence as evidence, not of poor capital or labour mobility, but of the excessive power of professional administrators in the firm. These administrators threatened, it was believed, to become an independent, expropriating class in precisely the same way as had the federal state bureaucrats two decades earlier. The solution they adopted was to retain the character of the self-managed enterprise but to reduce its scale. Accordingly, in 1971 the enterprise was replaced by the Basic Organization of Associated Labour (BOAL). The larger firms were divided up into a number of BOALs, each representing a distinct phase of the production cycle.

Although the structure of the self-managed enterprise was an impediment to performance, this aspect of the post-1965 system should be kept in perspective. Other considerations were also present which served to impede the operation of market mechanisms. One of these was the structure of the economy. Although the transition from planned to market growth reduced the absolute pressure on re-sources, the 1965 measures implied a radical change in the pattern of demand and a correspondingly radical reorientation in the produc-tion profile. The reorientation would have been challenging enough for a developed country with a well-established market system. But

Yugoslavia, despite its rate of industrial growth, was still, in 1965, a relatively underdeveloped, and extremely unevenly developed, economy, with an inadequate infrastructure, an under-exploited raw material sector, an agriculture largely based upon peasant farming, serious regional disparities in income and wealth, derisory financial markets and an uncompetitive industrial structure.

Moreover, the two economic factors which had most influenced the measures of the mid-1960s, fragmentation of the market by regional and local power centres and price and foreign exchange controls imposed by stabilization policies, persisted. Just as decentralization within the State and Party structure proved a stronger influence than decentralization to the enterprise in the decade before reform, so it did in the decade after. Regional and local authorities continued to control the disposition of resources through participation in the management of commercial banks. Moreover, the federal government, already weakened by its lost investment role, yielded further ground to the republics in the late 1960s. The reforms were not fulfilling the expectations of the Slovenian and Croatian leaderships and they sought greater autonomy in economic decision-making. They believed that the new system was still biased in favour of Serbia and the Southern republics. By the beginning of the 1970s, the federal authorities were incapable of taking any economic policy decisions of importance without the unanimous consent of the republics and autonomous provinces.

The exposure of the economy to increased world competition, chronic excess demand by firms for investment resources and the removal of statutory personal income controls, had an adverse impact on both the scale of the trade deficit and the rate of inflation. The fiscal system was unsuited for use as a weapon of demand management, and the absence of financial markets and a competitive rate of interest meant that monetary policy was not as effective as it might have been. Thus, the traditional short-term economic policy weapons normally used in a market economy were either unavailable or inadequate. Consequently, it proved necessary to continue to deploy a range of foreign exchange and price controls which created further distortions.

Dennison Rusinow, the distinguished authority on modern Yugoslavia, has described the decade after the 1965 reforms as Laissez-Faire Socialism.[1] By the early 1970s, it was clear that decentralization, in both the political and the economic sphere, had gone too far. Not only did the federal authorities have too little power but the republican authorities had too much. Tito's purges of the republican leaderships in 1971 and 1972, and the subsequent reactivation of the Party as a force in the management of social affairs, did much to restore authority to the federal leadership and coherence in federal policy making. But, from the point of view of economic management, the instruments of control were lacking. The federal government had considerably fewer powers of economic management than the average Western European government. The difficulty was that re-introducing pre-reform federal powers would contravene the fundamental ideological principles of the self-managed economy: debureaucratization and mass participation.

The solution finally adopted, and enshrined in the 1974 Constitution, was to implement the Five Year Plan by contractual techniques. Its investment targets were incorporated in over two hundred social agreements. These agreements were negotiated and concluded between trade unions, Economic Chambers and governmental authorities. Similar agreements were also reached on prices, personal incomes, and employment. Once this framework was established, firms tendered for the right to implement those parts of the plan to which they were commercially attracted. Subsequently, inter-firm self-management agreements were completed, binding firms to transact with each other in conformity with the terms laid down in the social agreements. There was no legal obligation on parties to conclude either social or self-management agreements except where a sector or branch was given a priority classification—which many were.

Unfortunately, the new system got underway at a time when the macro-economic situation was deteriorating sharply. Until 1973, export earnings were reasonably buoyant, although industrialists were finding it difficult to produce competitive goods of the quality required to penetrate hard currency markets. The phenomenal increase in hard currency invisible earnings, through tourism and remittances from the growing number of Yugoslavs working abroad, kept the current account in reasonable balance except when the economy became overheated. Following the oil crisis and the onset of recession in Western Europe, invisible earnings stagnated and Yugoslavia's percentage share of OECD markets fell sharply, leading to a cumulative current account deficit of $US2.2 billion for 1974–5.

Stabilization measures were rewarded with a modest surplus on current account in 1976. However, controls were soon relaxed and, for the next four years, the cumulative current account deficit was $US8.8 billion. The problem was exacerbated by the second oil crisis in 1979. From 1978 the authorities re-introduced deflationary measures. The gradual removal of excess demand pressures led to a much improved current account in 1981 and 1982. However, inflationary pressures, on this occasion, were not responsive to the traditional techniques of demand management. The rates of increase in the cost of living were 20, 30 and 40 per cent, respectively, for the years 1979–81 and showed no signs of abating. The seriousness of the crisis led to a radical downward revision of the targets contained in the Five Year Plan for 1981–5; and the need to seek the financial help and support of the International Monetary Fund and to reschedule its massive burden of hard currency debts severely constrained Yugoslavia's freedom of manoeuvre in economic policy making. Stabilization policy inspired quotas and other controls, moreover, inhibited the mechanisms of contractual planning.

Considering the handicaps—the legacy of war and occupation, the initial hostility of the Soviet Union, the problems of transition from a predominantly peasant-based agricultural to an urban manufacturing economy, huge differences in regional development levels, great ethnic diversity and constant institutional upheaval—Yugoslavia's economic achievement has been a substantial one. Between 1955 and 1980, social product and industrial production grew at annual rates of about 6 and 9 per cent respectively.[2] Annual fixed investment as a percentage of social product was remarkably high throughout the period. This performance was much better than the OECD average and on a par with that of Greece, Spain and Portugal, countries at a roughly similar stage of development. Domestic resources in Yugoslavia, moreover, played a much more important role than they did in these other countries which relied, to a far greater extent, on capital inflows and current transfers from abroad.[3]

Part One of this book deals with the development of economic institutions since 1945. Part Two examines the structure and performance of the capital, labour and goods markets since the mid-1960s reform. Part Three looks at the macro-economic framework. Given the scope of the survey and the space available, many important topics have been touched on only lightly, such as regional development, or ignored completely, such as agriculture. At the time of going to press, the latest year for which official statistics were available was 1982.

Part One

CHAPTER 1

THE ORIGINS OF MARKET SOCIALISM

1 Decentralization: the ideological basis

When the communist-led resistance movement became a constitutional regime at the end of 1945 it proceeded to adapt Yugoslav
society, as rapidly as possible, to the prevailing Soviet model. The
central objective was state ownership and control of the means of
production. In December 1946, the state acquired the more important manufacturing and all transportation, banking, and wholesale
concerns; and in April 1948 it nationalized the remaining manufacturing enterprises, the insurance industry, and most of the retail
trade.[1] Artisans alone were permitted to retain their undertakings on
a private basis, though the conditions under which they could do so
were carefully regulated. The control of these newly acquired state
assets was subjected to a rigorous system of centralized economic
planning and management. The Federal Economic Planning Law of
4 June 1946[2] established two hierarchies, one for formulating the plan
and the other for executing it. At the summit of both was the Federal
Planning Commission. Under the Commission, subordinate
planning authorities were established at the republican, district and
communal levels. The First Five Year Plan was divided into a series of
annual plans which themselves were subdivided into quarterly plans.
The execution of these plans was the responsibility of another hierarchy, with Ministries taking their instructions from the Federal
Planning Commission and passing them down through Industrial
Directorates to the enterprises. These instructions took the form of
legally binding regulations.

Despite the immediate and wholesale adoption of Soviet style
centralized industrial production planning, political conflicts
between the Yugoslav and Soviet Communist Parties soon developed.
Matters came to a head in the early months of 1948, and on 28 June
Yugoslavia was expelled from the Cominform.[3] The initial reaction of
the authorities was to re-emphasize the Stalinist features of their
system. At the Fifth Congress of the Communist Party held in the
following month no criticisms of Stalin were voiced; and, early in

1949, it was decided to collectivize agriculture. Moreover, collectivization in its early stages was pursued more vigorously than in most other Cominform countries.

The continued hostility of Soviet diplomacy, together with the increasingly harsh impact of the Soviet economic blockade imposed at the time of expulsion led, in the course of 1949, to the development by leading political thinkers in Yugoslavia of a critique of internal arrangements within the USSR. They believed that the intransigence of the Soviet Union towards Yugoslavia must reflect deep internal contradictions within Soviet society.[4] This critique blossomed into a more general analysis of the role of the state during the transition period from capitalism to socialism. It became known as the theory of state capitalism. Essentially, it asserts that state ownership and control of the means of production, indispensable at the beginning of the transition period, are only a first stage. Once all vestiges of capitalism have been removed, further progress requires that the state wither away. If it does not, and it showed no evidence of doing so in the Soviet Union in 1950, then there emerges a major contradiction in the transition process. Initially, surplus value is appropriated by the bureaucrats instead of the capitalists. Subsequently, bureaucratization develops into an independent system of its own which will manage the means of production so as to perpetuate its own control. Finally, bureaucrats become a separate class—state capitalists.

The logic of this argument with respect to the apparatus of Soviet style administrative planning recently established in Yugoslavia was unavoidable. If the retention of state ownership and control beyond their term of usefulness would imperil the chance of further progress towards socialism, it was incumbent upon the authorities to seek a new system of social regulation to implement the next institutional phase in the transition process. The basis for such a system was suggested to them by Edvard Kardelj in an article written in the middle of 1949.[5] According to Kardelj, the transition period requires that the organizational vacuum that emerges as the state withers away be filled by new institutional structures based upon mass participation. Change does not occur suddenly. As the organs of state bureaucracy phase out so the new participatory forms gradually replace them. For a substantial period the two forms coexist. Thus, at any given moment, the prevailing institutional arrangements are viewed as transient, a contemporary expression of a permanent and enduring drive towards the ultimate goals of socialism.

Both arms of the new ideology, debureaucratizationism on the one hand and mass participation on the other, pointed in the direction of decentralized economic decision-making. Legally the authorities were swift to divest the state of its rights of ownership and control over the means of production, thus abrogating the two fundamental characteristics of the Soviet system. On 28 June 1950, the Law on the Management of Government Enterprises by Workers' Collectives[6] pronounced the general principle that the right of management in any enterprise should be vested solely in its employees and prescribed the organizational structure, the Workers' Council, through which the employees, the collective, were to exercise this right. Moreover, in his speech to the Federal Assembly on the day prior to the passage of the new law, Tito stated: 'From now on, the state ownership of the means of production . . . is passing on to a higher form of socialist ownership.'[7] This 'higher form' involved a transfer of the ownership of the means of production from the state to society, a transfer subsequently enshrined in the Constitution of 1953.

In June 1950, however, the economy was still administered centrally. While Kardelj's theory of mass participation provided a solution for the internal management of enterprises, it offered no alternative economic *system* to administrative centralism. Such an alternative would have to find a way of making workers' control of surplus value in industrial enterprises compatible with the social ownerships of assets, or means of production, from which that surplus value derived. The received doctrine was that autonomous enterprises implied private ownership and control whereas social ownership implied state property and management. The way out of this ideological dilemma was supplied by Boris Kidric, Chairman of the Federal Economic Commission, in an article written in November 1950.[8] According to Kidric, social property managed by free associations of direct producers was the second stage of socialism following the first stage in which the state was both the owner and controller of the means of production. He called this second stage socialist commodity production, admitting that it was a step that Marx had not predicted.

During this new stage, relations between commodity-producing enterprises were freely entered into according to self-interest and were not the consequence of legally binding instructions imposed by decree. However, this did not mean that the rate of growth and pattern of development should be determined solely as a consequence of firms exercising their new right to its fullest extent. Since the subject-matter of their transactions was social rather than private property, the community had a duty to ensure that it was employed for a social and not for a private purpose. The practical difficulty that faced the authorities in the early 1950s, and continues to face them today, was to define the social purpose, and to elaborate institutions of social control to realize it, without maintaining that part of the bureaucracy so roundly condemned by the new ideology.

The new ideology also had far-reaching implications for the organization of the Communist Party of Yugoslavia, soon to be renamed the League of Communists of Yugoslavia, as the proceedings of the Sixth Party Congress, held in 1952, reveal.[9] Ideological emphasis on the role of participatory democracy made it impossible to justify an autocratic Party organization entrenched in every part of the state machine. But the difficulty was, as in the economic field, to democratize the Party without destroying its capacity to keep society moving in the right direction. The solution adopted in the Resolution and Statutes of the Congress proposed a democratically elected party, whose policies would be the outcome of free internal debate, divorced from the state apparatus and influencing the course of events in all spheres of social activity by persuasion. However, democratic centralism was retained. That is to say, policy decisions once taken by the leading Party organs were still binding on all members whatever position they had taken in the course of internal debate. Moreover, there was a clear rejection of any attempt to introduce a multi-party system.

So while the Party proposed to surrender its monopoly over political decision-making by divorcing itself physically from the state organization, it did not forgo its exclusive rights to political organization. Provided, therefore, that democratic centralism functioned effectively, it would invariably enjoy a great advantage over any would-be opponents. Following the Congress, immediate steps were taken to put its ideas into practice. Party cells established within the state structure were abolished and higher Party organs no longer had the authority to assign binding operational tasks to lower ones. This meant, in particular, that the Executive Committee of the Party, which replaced the Politburo as the chief executive organ, could no longer appoint its own nominees to direct the affairs of regional and local organizations. This separation and decentralization of the Party organizations was to have profoundly adverse effects on the cohesion of economic activity in the course of the following decade.

2 Decentralization: the first phase[10]

The system that emerged from these upheavals struck a balance between social control and market mechanism which the authorities were unable to maintain as the decade wore on. Until the mid-1950s limited, but within the limits real, freedom was given to markets to determine interest rates, commodity prices, production levels and even foreign trade patterns. Thereafter, they gave ground to an increasingly elaborate and discretionary system of social control; and by 1960 their role was almost unidentifiable. They were a victim, chiefly, of two forces. First, the diffusion of political and economic authority in Yugoslav society led to an increasing fragmentation of economic activity, characterized by a multitude of discriminatory interventions at republican and local levels. Second, the policy of rapid industrial growth, inaugurated by the First Five Year Plan in 1946, was untouched by the institutional upheavals of the early 1950s and created structural imbalances in the economy which had to be suppressed by direct controls on incomes, prices, and the balance of payments.

Social control

During the period of administrative planning, fixed production targets and prices were set for all inter-industry transactions. The incidence of profit and loss in an enterprise was purely arbitrary and of no significance in determining its future allocation of investment resources. It was simply an administrative unit at the foot of a state owned and controlled executive hierarchy, subject to the absolute discretion of the government authorities. This state of affairs lasted from the middle of 1946 until the end of 1951. Thereafter, the system was rapidly dismantled and, by the time of the new Constitution in 1953, the workers' collective had replaced the state *in law* as the manager and trustee of industrial resources in Yugoslavia. Henceforth, the ability of the workers' collective to decide on its own product range, investment programme, output level, and suppliers and customers on the basis of its own self-interest, could only be curtailed by the passage of legislation specifically derogating from these freedoms.

In fact, the system of social control subsequently established to 'guide' enterprises in their economic decision-making in conformity with the new ideology of socialist commodity production, limited their freedom in at least three ways. First, although the new planning system no longer stipulated legally binding production targets, it still required social property to be deployed in conformity with certain value targets laid down by an annual social plan. These targets, or 'basic proportions' as they were described, sought to define the size and pattern of the annual industrial investment programme by laying down the sums of money to be made available to each industrial branch from a particular federal, republican, or communal investment fund. Credits from these 'social investment' funds, replaced federal budgetary grants as the main source of investment finance for the enterprises.[11]

Second, the fiscal regime, which was the main source of finance for the new social investment funds, both reduced the financial resources available to individual enterprises to very modest proportions and sought to regulate their productive efficiency. The highest yielding levy was the turnover tax. Until 1961 it was levied as a single-tier charge upon the total value of finished goods. Thereafter, it was also imposed upon trade in intermediate goods. Apart from its revenue-raising role, it was chiefly used as an instrument of price policy. Rates differed, sometimes quite sharply, between industrial branches. Fiscal policy was also deployed to encourage patterns of factor employment conducive to productive efficiency. The tax on personal incomes, in order to discourage excessive distributions, was altered almost annually during the 1950s, usually in conjunction with changes in the accounting regulations for the appropriation of enterprise income.[12] The federal authorities strove to evolve a set of arrangements which both encouraged initiative and yet avoided inflationary pressures. After initial laxity, and the correspondingly extravagant response of workers' collectives to their release from administrative socialism, restrictions on personal income payments tended to be severe throughout the remainder of the 1950s. A capital tax was also introduced in 1954; although it was called an interest payment, the *kamnata na poslovni fond* or Interest Payment on the Business Fund was, in effect, a tax on net worth. It had both an ideological and an economic rationale. Ideologically, it represented the price that enterprises had to pay for being entrusted with social assets. Economically, it was designed to encourage the efficient allocation and utilization of capital resources in the absence of an equity market. In fact, it was never levied at a rate sufficiently high to reflect accurately the cost of capital in Yugoslavia.[13]

Third, even with respect to the appropriation of the modest amounts at their disposal, further legislation, together with certain legal factors, led to the perceptions of enterprise management about what was in their interest being modified, or even overridden, by the perceptions of the local communes and, to a lesser extent, other outside bodies. The growing authority of the communes derived both from the freedom given to them by the new social planning system and from their enhanced political position under the 1953 Constitution. Under the new planning system the federal authorities enjoyed direct control only over the allocation of resources in the federal investment funds. Republican and communal planning authorities and investment funds were no longer legally subordinate to their federal counterparts. It is true that the largest source of finance for such funds was direct allocation from the proceeds of federal taxes and federally regulated republican and communal taxes. But the republican and communal planning authorities were not obliged to pursue a particular investment policy with respect to such resources.

Moreover, the communes now enjoyed an enhanced constitutional status. Before 1952 local government units were at the base of a rigidly ordered pyramid exercising only those powers delegated to them by the federal government. The new ideology, with its twin objectives of debureaucratization and mass participation, infected the organization of the state no less than of the Party and the economy and led to a major reconsideration of the role of local government. The 1952 General Law on People's Committees[14] established the commune as the primary political unit in Yugoslavia and, most significantly for their rapid ascendancy in economic affairs, the 1953 Constitution gave them the power to legislate on all matters other than those specifically reserved to the federal and republican governments. In particular, they had wide discretion in imposing local taxes upon enterprises. Consequently, they often penalized relatively efficient enterprises by high taxation in order to finance the frequently ill-conceived and over-ambitious investment projects of other enterprises which better suited their local political ends.

The commune was also in a position to exercise substantial influence over the deployment of retained earnings. Enterprises were obliged to present their annual plans to the communal Council of Producers for approval and the Council made policy recommendations. These recommendations were almost always accepted. And where any project depended upon borrowed money for its successful completion, the influence of the commune was often conclusive since it usually acted as guarantor of bank loans. With regard to day-to-day operations, the commune was influential through its role in hiring and firing the enterprise director; this power, not surprisingly, tended to produce a directoral class sensitive to its wishes.[15]

Of particular significance was the part played by the commune in industrial market entry and exit.[16] The commercial objects of an enterprise were set out in its permit to trade. Attempts to diversify into areas not included in the permit could lead to immediate closure. And the scope for expansion even into permitted areas was limited in several ways. A firm established in one commune could only open a branch in another with the latter's permission—though the rule became less onerous towards the end of the 1950s when, as a result of the consolidation programme carried out in local government, the size of communal units increased. Moreover, although enterprises were legally entitled to establish other enterprises, in practice it was almost impossible for them to do so without the co-operation of the commune. The requirements were such—guarantees of initial working capital, adequacy of public utility availability, proper technically qualified management—that a firm could rarely have given them in good faith without the full support of its local authority. As to exit, enterprises could be placed in compulsory liquidation for inability to meet their pecuniary obligations. However, since the main creditors of ailing enterprises were either federal or communal banks, there was a tendency to petition in the courts only if it was official policy to do so.

Another source of influence over the enterprise, though less powerful, were the Economic Chambers established in 1954.[17] Each sector of the economy was represented by a chamber, membership of which was compulsory for all enterprises after 1958. Before 1958 their role was, in certain respects, similar to that of the commune but seen from a functional rather than a territorial perspective. Enterprises submitted their proposed production and investment plans to their chamber. Having scrutinized the plans, the chamber then made 'recommendations' with regard to production and investment policy, the main purpose of which was to avoid problems of under-production or over-production or excesses or deficiencies in capacity. As with the communes, these recommendations were not legally binding; and since communes and chambers 'recommended' from different perspectives, enterprise management sometimes had to choose between the two. Press comment and circumstantial evidence suggest that the communes had more success in imposing their views. Following legislation in 1958,[18] the chambers became less involved in investment and production planning and more concerned with the formulation and enforcement of federal economic legislation.

Enterprises with similar interests also grouped themselves into self-governing associations whose role should not be confused with that of the Economic Chambers.[19] These associations provided a forum for working out common technical, commercial and financial policies. Although they were forbidden to engage directly in commerce, their members, or certain sub-groupings of their members, were allowed to make joint credit applications, joint purchases and even joint use of each others' production facilities. Some members also adopted informal schemes of rationing raw materials. Such practices, frequently encouraged by communal or republican authorities, often had the effect of market-sharing or production-fixing.

On average, during the pre-reform period, over 35 per cent of the members of Workers' Councils were members of the League of Communists. Yet the average ratio of Party members to workers employed in the social sector was a mere 5 per cent. This pattern of influence was partly due to the predominant role of the unions in the Workers' Council election procedures.[20] But Party members were, in any case, under an obligation to involve themselves actively in the affairs of their work-place. It is extremely hard to generalize about their impact on enterprise behaviour. Prominent members of enterprises, communes, Economic Chambers and unions were all Party members yet their interests often conflicted. The Party itself was decentralizing during the period and sectional loyalties, as we shall see, came more and more to challenge federal ones.

Market mechanisms

Within this complex framework of social control, market mechanisms were intended to ration capital resources, to price commodities and to distribute foreign exchange. However, they did not last for very long. In an economy such as Yugoslavia's in the 1950s the chosen policy of rapid and comprehensive industrial growth was bound to create disequilibria. As the decade wore on, the symptoms of disequilibrium—high interest rates, rising prices, foreign trade deficits—were increasingly suppressed by direct intervention in the form of import, price and interest rate controls. As these controls multiplied, moreover, the increasing fragmentation of party political power gave regional and local authorities the scope to employ them for their own sectional ends.

Perhaps the most interesting initiatives took place in the capital market. Although the aggregate annual amount of planned investment and its sectoral allocation was a policy decision taken by the federal, republican and communal planning authorities, and the source of investment funds was the fiscal system, the distribution of funds as between enterprises *within* a sector was the responsibility of the banking system—initially the National Bank and, subsequently, specialized and communal banks. From December 1953 until the middle of 1956 a proportion of these intra-sectoral funds were allocated by competitive rates of interest. Since the funds allotted to each sector by the planning system were non-substitutable, a separate competitive rate was established for each industrial branch. Auctions were announced inviting enterprises to bid for funds and requiring them to state, *inter alia*, the size of the desired loan and the rate of interest they were prepared to pay for it.[21] The total demand for funds was then compared with the supply available and a market clearing rate established. Those who bid at or above the market clearing rate paid that rate whatever they had originally bid.

Unfortunately, enterprises were prone to offer higher rates of interest than they could afford, in order to make certain of exceeding the market clearing rate, with the result that the clearing rate regularly exceeded the expected rate of return on the investment of the funds bid for. Enterprises behaved recklessly in their drive to obtain as large a share as possible of the available resources. Having barely emerged from the status and mentality of government agencies, the consequences of 'getting the sums wrong' in a market environment had yet to make themselves felt. A number of measures were introduced in an attempt to foster more realistic loan applications by enterprises but with little success. The passage of the Law on Commercial Loans of July 1956[22] marked the failure of the system by making future enterprise applications for investment fund money dependent upon satisfying the banks upon a number of factors, such as expected rate of return on the investment, impact on foreign trade and the extent to which total financial requirements are supplied from own resources. In addition, the rate of interest at which banks on-lent investment fund resources was henceforth controlled by the Federal Secretary of Finance. He determined the maximum and minimum rates for the relevant category of loan, leaving it to the bank concerned to vary the actual rate within these boundaries.

As for commodity markets, by the end of 1952 the authorities had substantially liberalized consumer prices. After experimenting with a variety of consumer pricing techniques, the Price Law of 18 June 1952 established the general rule that enterprises selling consumer goods could charge what they wished unless the commodity in question was listed.[23] Subject to an announcement in the Official Bulletin, the Federal Executive Council, the leading state economic policy making organ, was free to add a commodity to the list if for one reason or another it was in short supply. Partial liberalization also occurred in the raw material and intermediate goods markets. However, by 1954 the country was experiencing serious inflationary pressures.[24] Workers' collectives in every industry were awarding themselves excessive wage increases, though the strength of rises was influenced by differing degrees of commodity scarcity. Moreover, the freedom of enterprises to establish their own prices for unlisted items led in the course of 1953 and 1954 to the emergence of a variety of monopolistic practices, both in the intermediate and final goods markets.[25] Certain enterprises were reported as holding goods off the market or even decreasing production in order to create artificial scarcities.

The situation was ideal for such behaviour because many sectors of the economy were insulated from foreign competition. Not only did the foreign exchange regime provide most industrial concerns with ample protection from abroad; but also the high priority placed upon imports of raw materials and heavy industrial equipment meant that foreign exchange was frequently unavailable for the purchase of competing manufactured consumer goods. At first the authorities encouraged the communes to exercise control of prices. However, the interests of communal authorities often conflicted with those of their federal counterpart since they favoured high levels of profit to enhance their local revenues. In 1955, therefore, the federal authorities introduced a comprehensive price control system. Since this system has survived more or less intact, discussion of its main features is reserved until Chapter 5.

During the period of administrative planning, all foreign trade transactions were carried out by specially selected state enterprises in accordance with the plan; an import or export licence was required for each transaction, and every commercial agreement affecting foreign trade had to be submitted to the Ministry of Foreign Trade for approval. The official rate of exchange of $US1 = 50 dinars (old) was of no commercial significance, the difference between domestic and foreign prices being made up from or paid into a Price Equalization Fund. Apart from retaining the power to announce monthly export quotas on goods in short supply, the new system abandoned the old regime of physical controls in favour of an elaborate network of exchange restrictions and import and export subsidies and taxes.[26] Its basis was a number of so-called currency coefficients. These were, essentially, factors by which the prices of imported or exported goods were multiplied before foreign currency was bought or sold in respect of them. A fixed exchange rate of $US1 = 632 dinars (old) applied to all such transactions. Thus export coefficients encouraged exports if they were greater than one and discouraged them if they were less; conversely, import coefficients encouraged imports if they were less than one and discouraged them if they were greater. The coefficients were, in effect, simply a form of import and export taxes and subsidies.

Initially the exporter was placed in a rather privileged position within this regime. Half of the foreign exchange proceeds of any export transaction had to be sold immediately to the National Bank at the official rate. The remaining half could be retained to purchase imports, be kept on account with a foreign bank, or be sold to the National Bank at the market rate which fluctuated around $US1 to 900 dinars (old). The attraction of retaining these resources to purchase imports was particularly strong for those items—such as manufactured consumer goods—which carried a high import coefficient. Since most enterprises exported or imported through one or another of about twenty-five to thirty specialist import–export firms, it was a relatively simple matter for the importer client of one of these firms to gain access to foreign exchange without having to apply through official channels and suffer the effect of an adverse coefficient. The loophole tended to exacerbate the already severe balance of payments problems by permitting the waste of valuable foreign exchange on the import of non-essentials. It was, accordingly, rapidly closed so that by the end of 1955 the exporter was compelled to sell 100 per cent of his foreign exchange earnings to the National Bank at the official rate.

By the middle of the 1950s, therefore, the coefficient regime applied to all foreign trade transactions. It resulted in a domestic price structure which bore little relation to world market prices. Indeed, increased foreign trade profitability for an enterprise became as much a function of the ability to influence the levels of particular coefficients in its favour as of improvements in efficiency. The purpose of the system was, of course, to encourage a pattern of foreign trade consistent with the investment objectives set out in the Social Plan. But it had the effect of isolating the domestic economy from international market forces and the competitive pressures that they tend to produce.

Even in the days before comprehensive price, interest rate and foreign exchange controls, there was a market mechanism in Yugoslavia only in the sense that some prices were not fixed but free to move. Those characteristics of an economic system which ensure that a market mechanism is endowed with a modicum of rationality—free entry and exit, mobility of capital and active restrictive practices legislation[27]—were either absent or barely evident. Intervention was needed to provide the necessary legislative framework within which market mechanisms could be nurtured and, ultimately, flourish. What mattered was not the fact of intervention but the ends it served.

Unfortunately, the interventions, or social controls as they were called, did little to advance the cause of such a market system. They served, for the most part, the interests of federal and, increasingly, regional and local industrial development policy. Scarce commodities, foreign exchange and investment funds were rationed by officials and those officials enjoyed wide discretionary powers. Indeed, the financial position of an enterprise depended largely upon its ability to influence them. The combination of price, foreign exchange and interest rate controls, and budget subsidy and taxation policy, produced a pattern of individual enterprise profitability which owed more to the ability to command official favours, either by virtue of the particular role an enterprise was seen to play in development strategy or through its political connections, than to industrial efficiency.

3   The 1961 measures

Whatever the shortcomings of the first phase of decentralization, the second half of the 1950s was a period of rapid economic growth in Yugoslavia. The targets of the Second Five Year Plan were achieved at the end of its fourth year, social product growing at an annual rate of 12 per cent and industrial output at 14 per cent. Towards the end of 1960, in addition to preparing the targets for the Third Five Year Plan of 1961–5 which was to start a year earlier than originally envisaged, the authorities drafted reforms in the banking, fiscal, and foreign trade areas.

These measures, though modest in themselves, were intended by their proponents as the first stage of a radical reform in the economy whose ultimate objective was to give the enterprise the decisive say in investment as well as production matters. From the middle of the 1950s, there was a drive by the more liberal party members to obtain a substantially greater degree of democratic participation in political, economic and social decision-making. In particular, they attacked the party bureaucracy and its tendency to put sectional before national interests. Liberal influence, and with it the momentum for further debureaucratization and increased democracy, grew steadily from the Seventh Party Congress in 1958. It was reflected in the First Programme of the League of Communists published in 1959 and the commitment to draft a new Constitution whose main task would be to assert strongly the role of self-government in all sectors of society.

Banking

In the field of investment allocation the role of the communal banks and specialized banks was substantially enhanced by the Law on Banks of 15 March 1961.[28] Until the beginning of 1954, the National Bank, through its branch system, had a monopoly of all commercial banking operations in Yugoslavia. The Law on Banks and Postal Savings of 28 January 1954[29] permitted communal authorities to establish their own banks both to engage in commercial banking operations and to control the implementation of the local budget within their respective territories. For the remainder of the decade the communal banking system grew alongside, and coexisted with, the National Bank branch system.

Specialized banks—the Yugoslav Investment Bank, the Agricultural Bank and the Foreign Trade Bank—were established in the mid-1950s to manage the federal investment funds.[30] The National Bank also gave them funds in order to extend credits on their own behalf. As a result of the Law on Banks of 15 March 1961, the National Bank ceased to perform commercial banking functions which, henceforth, became the sole prerogative of the communal and specialized banks. This represented an important decentralization of the banking function to the territorial units although, together, the three specialized banks still controlled over 65 per cent of the assets of the commercial banking system. The investment fund system itself remained intact for a further two years until its reform in 1963.

Enterprise accounting and taxation

Changes were also made in the enterprise accounting and fiscal regimes. In 1957 the Yugoslavs had reorganized the accounting practices of firms to bring them into line with the Marxian theory of value. Economic value added in any period—*ostvareni dohodak* or Realized Income as it was called in the accounts—was the difference between sales revenue and the cost of sales, the latter being calculated by adding the annual production costs of materials purchased, the annual allowance for fixed asset depreciation and the value of opening inventory, and subtracting the value of closing inventory. In other words, costs of materials purchased from other firms and depreciation of fixed assets were the only two costs recognized by the system. All other accounts charged against sales revenue were classified as *raspodela dohotka* or Appropriations out of Income. Since labour was held to be the source of all value it was entitled to appropriate all value added.

Although labour was allowed to *appropriate* all value added it was not permitted to *distribute* it all to its own use. To the extent that it had received assistance from other sources in accumulating value it was required to reimburse them for it. Thus, it was required to pay out of surplus value interest to banks that had extended credit to it, and taxes to the federal, republican and local communities that had granted investment funds and supplied public services. Thereafter, the collective was entitled to distribute the balance, called Net Income, between five funds: Fixed Capital, Working Capital, Collective Consumption, Personal Income and Reserve. Income appropriated to the Collective Consumption Fund could be employed either to purchase capital assets or to defray current expenses. Housing, education, holiday resorts, sports centres and medical facilities were the main activities to which the resources of this fund were devoted.

Once an appropriation out of Net Income had been made to one or other of these funds by the Workers' Council, no subsequent redistribution was permitted, except that the Fixed Capital Fund could be used to finance both fixed and working capital expenditure. At the beginning of 1961 the Fixed and Working Capital Funds were merged into one and renamed the Business Fund, making appropriations to fixed and working capital completely interchangeable. The restrictions imposed upon the proportions of Net Income appropriable to each Fund were also abolished.[31] Simultaneously, the progressive tax on Net Income was replaced by a flat-rate tax, thus increasing the resources available to collectives to distribute between the respective funds. However, the total annual Personal Income Fund appropriation was subjected to heavier local taxation. Shifting the incidence of enterprise taxation from Net Income towards personal incomes was intended to give collectives authority over a greater proportion of their value added and, at the same time, provide a strong disincentive for them to distribute it in the form of increased personal incomes.

Foreign trade

The main features of the foreign trade reform[32] were the devaluation of the dinar and the corresponding abolition of coefficients and the gradual replacement of quantitative restrictions by tariffs. As to the exchange rate, perhaps devaluation is an inaccurate description. The effect of the coefficient system had been to subsidize or tax particular sectors of the economy in accordance with policy-makers' preferences. Lying between the various rates employed previously, the new rate of $US1 = 750 dinars had features of both devaluation and revaluation.

On its own the change could have led to a fundamental realignment of foreign trade. However, in the previous year social sector enterprises became subject to customs levies which, hitherto, had been paid only by private citizens. In order to avoid the radical domestic price adjustments implied by the new exchange rate, the new tariffs were set to approximate the effect of the former differential exchange rates. For example, consumer imports were subjected to an *ad valorem* rate of 60 per cent, whereas semi-finished goods and raw materials were liable only to 10 per cent. Moreover, the import quota system was by no means dispensed with. Approximately 40 per cent of imports were subject to specific quotas, 20 per cent were controlled by the Yugoslav Investment Bank and 20 per cent required a general licence; the remaining 20 per cent were free. In order to avoid a drastic reduction in the incentive to export industrial goods, export premiums were introduced on a number of items.

Despite the premiums, tariffs and quotas, the reform did represent a fundamental change in the *approach* to foreign trade regulations. The previous system was in principle discriminatory. The new one accepted non-discrimination as its basis, subject to certain discriminatory features which were regarded by the authorities as temporary. The new approach, in particular the movement away from multiple exchange rates and towards customs duties, was connected with Yugoslavia's desire to become a full member of GATT (General Agreement on Tariffs and Trade); it had been an associate member since 1959. The changes were actively encouraged by the West and several Western trading countries, together with the IMF, pledged over $US275m. to assist the industrial sector in adjusting to the liberalized system.

4 Economic crisis[33]

The measures were passed in the context of a superficially impressive economic achievement. Their proponents believed that if the system worked well enough to meet the targets of the Second Five Year Plan in four years, burdened as it was by all the interventions of the late 1950s, how much better it would work without them. Not everybody agreed. In November 1960 the Federal Institute of Economic Planning published a draft of the proposed reforms and submitted it to a forum of economists.[34] The account of the discussion that took place demonstrates that there was substantial disagreement about the causes of recent economic success and the necessary ingredients for successful economic performance in the future. Critics were particularly concerned about the disintegration of national economic unity, the unequal rates of regional development and the prospect of excessive wage distribution that seemed to them likely to follow from such a degree of loosening of social control. Their cause was greatly strengthened by the sharp deterioration in the economic situation in the second half of 1961. By the end of that year Yugoslavia was in the throes of a major economic crisis, whose chief ingredients were an unmanageable balance of payments deficit and severe inflation. They were partly precipitated by the new measures but reflected problems that had an origin much deeper in the past. By liberalizing aspects of the system, the authorities simply revealed more clearly its structural instability.

The most unsettling feature of Yugoslavia's post-war development had been its current account balance of payments deficit. Between 1946 and 1961 the annual deficit was only once less than $US100m. and on no less than six occasions exceeded $US200m. Because of its political importance to the West, Yugoslavia had been able to extract a remarkable amount of help from Western creditors. However, the crisis of confidence when it did arrive at the end of 1961, was of peculiar severity. The unusually large deficit in that year was partly the result of the changes in the foreign trade system just described and the critics of decentralization made much of the nexus between decentralization and deficit. But the changed regime could not fairly be called a *cause* of the increased deficit. The partial removal of artificial incentives and constraints demonstrated how deep the structural imbalance in the trading account really was. In foreign trade, as in other sectors, the Yugoslavs had dealt with the problem of disequilibrium by the simple expedient of suppressing it. Undoubtedly, the irrationalities in the foreign trade system themselves had exacerbated the extent of the deficit. However, the chief culprit was the development strategy pursued by the authorities.

This strategy, inaugurated by the First Five Year Plan, involved the rapid expansion and diversification of the manufacturing sector at the expense of those sectors which were traditional exporters and whose immediate foreign exchange earning potential was far greater. The institutional upheavals of the early 1950s left this strategy unaffected; indeed, the system of social control was devised to ensure that it was preserved. Investment Fund allocations consistently favoured the manufacturing sector. The prices of most domestic raw materials and semi-manufactures were controlled and set at low levels, both to encourage industry to use them in preference to foreign alternatives and to keep domestic costs down. The low or zero profits that resulted from price control, together with the modest allocations made to them from investment funds, meant a low annual rate of investment for both sectors and, correspondingly, a slow annual rate of growth of production. This had two effects: first, industry had to turn to foreign markets for an unnecessarily high proportion of its raw material inputs. In doing so, it was assisted by the multiple exchange rate system which kept the costs of imported raw materials and equipment relatively low. Second, the low volume of production of certain raw materials denied the Yugoslavs valuable export earnings in foreign markets in which they were genuinely competitive. Low prices for agricultural commodities had a similar impact on investment, production, imports and exports.

The balance of payments effects of this strategy would not have been so disturbing had there been some indication that it was laying the foundations for a progressive improvement in the foreign trade account of the manufacturing sector with the hard currency areas. Yet, by the beginning of the 1960s, it was clear that it was not. The proportion of intermediate and capital goods in the total import bill from the hard currency areas increased steadily throughout the decade. New product development was often carried out on the basis of costly foreign licences which involved the use of the foreign partners' plant, spare parts and components, in addition to know-how and expertise. Accordingly, additional and permanent burdens were added to the import bill in circumstances where the benefits, in terms of increased export earnings or import substitution, were frequently small or uncertain. Although the proportion of finished industrial exports to total exports increased, a large part of this expansion was to bilateral trading account countries.

In singling out the industrial sector in this way the authorities were, of course, not only following in the footsteps of Soviet development policy but also in those of nearly all the developing economies in this decade. That was the generally accepted path. Moreover, the failures of the industrial sector could not be wholly laid against the door of development strategy itself. There were significant imperfections in the application of that strategy. Two of these are of particular note. Firstly, the federal government's approach to investment project planning, especially plant location, was too often influenced by extra economic considerations. The need to foster an industrial working class in areas where it was hitherto non-existent, to absorb a large and growing agricultural population which was underemployed, and to lessen the sharp economic inequalities between republics, all gave a distinct bias in federal policy towards locating new plant in Bosnia, Macedonia, Montenegro and the southern parts of Serbia. Secondly, the fragmentation of the investment planning system itself encouraged regional and local authorities to create self-sufficient economic units within their areas of responsibility. They sought as much investment funding for as wide a range of industrial ventures as possible whose production, once on stream, was protected at almost any cost.

This latter phenomenon came to be known as territorialism or particularism.[35] Restricting the sales of local raw materials, forbidding local firms to purchase elsewhere, limiting competition from outsiders—all illustrate the application of particularist policies. Usually, local enterprises were actively encouraged to produce as wide a range of products as possible. When this began to erode their competitive position or threaten their financial viability, the commune would quite simply step in and introduce regulations to protect them. The result was that the industrial structure of the country developed as a complex web of republican and communal monopolies, each one created and sustained by a labyrinth of privilege and subsidies granted by republican and communal legislation. Each republic built or expanded its own steel mill and several invested in automobile, electronic, consumer durable and chemical facilities of varying kinds in circumstances where their economic viability was highly dubious. The needless duplication and dispersal of production facilities meant that plant structure in many industries was conducive to optimizing neither horizontal nor vertical economies of scale.

Prestige, employment levels and tax yields all help to explain the addiction to particularism which had so deeply infected the economy by the late 1950s. But it would never have developed to the extent that it did had not the authority of the Party to discipline its sub-units been so severely eroded in the course of the decade.[36] It was a phenomenon distinct from nationalism—though clearly connected in circumstances where the allegation of particularism could be made against a republican unit. During this period, however, particularism was more usually associated with the behaviour of communes. With the growth of republican independence and rivalry, and the relative decline in the power of the commune after 1965, particularism and nationalism became rather less easy to distinguish.

After an initial surge, following the decentralization measures in the early 1950s, the authorities were able to limit the annual increases in the cost of living index to under 10 per cent until the early part of 1962, mainly through the strict controls on enterprise income distribution and through price control. Although price rises, the symptoms of inflation, were moderately well contained, the disease, in at least one form, was well entrenched in the interstices of the social investment system. The starting-point was the gap between the rapidly increasing industrial labour force and the corresponding rate of increase in the wage bill, on the one hand, and the relatively slow rate of increase in the production of consumer goods on the other. It was not until 1962 that the production index for consumer goods began to move ahead faster than that for capital goods. The consumer goods market, therefore, could easily absorb price rises. Prices were raised on a regular basis not by improving profit margins for the consumer goods enterprises but by raising the turnover tax on consumer sales. By so doing, extra funds were siphoned off to enhance the investment and budgetary resources of the republican and communal authorities. These funds were then applied to the financing of additional investment projects, in turn increasing the demand for capital goods and raising their prices. This meant that investment required even more financial resources to maintain previous levels—so once again taxes and the price of consumer goods went up. The system, therefore, fed on itself.[37] The state of chronic excess demand in both the capital and consumer markets also helps to explain the high demand for foreign consumer and capital goods which imposed such a drain on the balance of payments.

The authorities preferred to alleviate the symptoms through a more intensive application of price controls rather than attack the infection itself through fiscal and monetary policy. The diminishing control of the federal authorities over the social investment system made intervention through the fiscal system to check this tendency very difficult. Moreover, no attempt was made to pursue an active monetary policy at a time when there was an accelerating rate of increase in the money supply, in the form of short-term bank credit, to enterprises and consumer credit. Between 1952 and 1961 the money supply increased fourfold, mainly through the extension of short-term credits by the banking system to industrial enterprises seeking to supplement their long-term investment resources by using short-term money. Although open market operations were not feasible, the interest rate and reserve requirement weapons were available to the authorities but were not actively used.

Quite suddenly, in the first half of 1962, the rate of inflation accelerated very sharply. Devaluation, bad harvests between 1960 and 1962, above average personal income distributions following the 1961 fiscal reforms, together with an unchanged policy towards short-term credit, all appear to have contributed. The authorities acted swiftly. At the end of March administrative restrictions were introduced upon the volume of investment and tighter ceilings were imposed on the rate of credit expansion. In April, guide-lines were reintroduced on the distribution of Net Income as between Personal Income and other Funds, voluntary for the rest of that year but compulsory from the beginning of 1963; customs duties were also raised and price control intensified. By the end of 1962 over 65 per cent of the value of manufactured goods was subject to some form of price control.

5   The liberal case [38]

There is no doubt that the crisis that followed the 1961 measures strengthened the hand of the opponents of liberalization. As a consequence, the Executive Committee of the League of Communists became deadlocked over the issue of economic reform. Throughout the 1950s, Party discipline was increasingly undermined by the inability of the Executive Committee to get its decisions translated into effective action—the erosion of democratic centralism.[39] Now the fragmentation of the party structure had raised a problem of an entirely different order; its highest executive organ was unable to reach a decision at all.

The economic issue that divided the conservatives and liberals most sharply was the future of the social investment system and its corresponding fiscal burdens. This was critical not only in itself but as the centre of a wider, and more bitter, debate about the *locus* of economic power in Yugoslavia. The liberals advocated both the dismemberment of the system and the devolution of the power to make investment decisions to the enterprise and to a reformed banking sector answerable to the enterprise sector.[40] Their outlook was overtly founded upon an amalgam of Kardeljian ideology and a commitment to more liberal economic policies; but the mixture was flavoured with more than a pinch of sectional self-interest. The conservatives argued that liberalization would aggravate the present economic difficulties, hinder the pursuit of a national economic policy and threaten the political and cultural unity of the country.[41] Their support derived largely from those who had a vested interest in maintaining the status quo; that is to say from the local and regional Party bureaucracies interested in continuing to control the pattern of investment in their areas and the poorer republics hoping to continue to receive substantial federal support for their industries.

Ideological basis

Ideologically, the liberal proposal was squarely in line with the guide-lines for the social development of Yugoslavia laid down by the Seventh Party Congress. It marked a decisive step against bureaucratic elements in society and for democracy in industrial decision-making—the two targets which, together, form the ideological objective of the Yugoslav social revolution. Liberal ideologues believed that the prevailing economic system was detrimental to the achievement of both.[42] On the one hand, there was the diffuse bureaucratic web which implemented the Social Plan. On the other, there was the elaborate fiscal regime, sharply limiting the funds available to enterprises, and the power of communes to interfere in enterprise decision-making, which rendered derisory the right of the workers to determine their own economic destiny. Together these factors threatened the First Programme of the League of Communists of Yugoslavia and, indeed, undermined the social principles laid down in the 1953 Constitution. Hence the need to reaffirm the Programme and provide it with a firmer legal basis in the form of a revised constitution, the economic implication of which was a new definition of decentralization which depoliticized economic decision-making by transferring real power over surplus value to those who created it.

Economic basis

The conclusions of the liberal ideologists dovetailed neatly with those of the liberal economists. While accepting the importance of a rapid rate of economic growth, liberal economists took the view that the cost incurred by the consumer for the actual levels of growth achieved in the past decade had been too high.[43] Two factors were, in their opinion, responsible. First, they believed that the annual high rates of investment had impaired the incentive of workers to produce, thus adversely affecting industrial productivity. They argued that reduced rates of investment would mean higher rates of consumption which would, in turn, provide a major incentive towards harder work on the factory floor. Second, they believed that the distribution of investment resources, both between and within sectors, was irrational. This was partly the fault of the capital market as such. Apart from straightforward political interference by local bureaucrats, the deliberate application of differential interest rates and capital taxes was blamed for subsidizing certain industrial sectors by making capital arbitrarily cheap. But the problems went beyond the reform of the capital market. For the rational allocation of investment resources could not be separated from patterns of enterprise profitability which were themselves affected by price and foreign exchange controls in the goods markets.

The liberal solution was to leave the annual ratio of investment to consumption to be determined by the worker-managed enterprise. This was a radical policy recommendation; for previously the conflicting claims of consumption and investment had been resolved by political decision. Liberals accepted that a substantial increase in the level of consumption was inevitable. But they believed that the immediately adverse effect that this would have on growth would be at least partially offset in the future by a reduction in the marginal capital–output ratio. This would, in turn, result partly from the very fact of higher rates of consumption and their effect upon the incentive to work; and partly from the more rational allocation amongst investment proposals of such savings as were made. It was to achieve this latter objective that liberal economists advocated the abandonment of discriminatory intervention in the capital, goods and foreign exchange markets. They recognized that it was insufficient to exclude discrimination from one of these markets while retaining it in the others. This was one of the lessons learned from the investment funds' auction experiment of the mid-1950s and the foreign exchange reform of 1961. The combination of free domestic prices and open foreign competition would give rise to a rational pattern of enterprise profitability. This would, in turn, influence the capacity and inclination to invest by increasing or reducing the volume of own funds available. Moreover, enterprises wishing to supplement their own funds would have to compete for bank credit on equal terms.

The liberals placed particular emphasis on the importance of an open economy to the success of their policy. They recognized that domestic markets, generally speaking, were too small and too underdeveloped to perform an efficiency enhancing role if undisciplined by world market forces. In particular, foreign competition was seen as encouraging the cost consciousness of the Yugoslav enterprise—with respect both to the purchase of raw material and component inputs and to the propensity to invest in cost reducing production techniques—in order to deny the domestic market to competing imports and to penetrate hard currency markets with saleable exports. The result would be, it was hoped, a rational and internationally competitive industrial sector. But the policy had an important element of circularity. The open economy was to be the means by which industrial efficiency and competitiveness would be achieved; but, equally, industrial efficiency and competitiveness were the means by which the economy could be kept open, through creating and sustaining a healthy balance of trade. The two fundamental objectives of liberal economic policy, industrial efficiency and the open economy were, therefore, complementary, each one relying on the realization of the other for its own realization.

The link between international convertibility of the dinar and industrial efficiency had another dimension. Yugoslavia's desire to improve its ability to infiltrate hard currency markets, and generally to advance its economic bargaining power in the West, had caused it to seek membership of GATT. To achieve this aim it was compelled to liberalize its foreign trade and exchange regime so as to conform with GATT requirements. The foreign exchange reform of 1961 was the first major step in this direction. A further step, demonstrating the will and the capacity to achieve at least current account convertibility, was going to be crucial in convincing GATT members of the seriousness of its application. In making this further step the support of the Western banking community and, especially, the IMF was critical. It had already been forthcoming at the time of the 1961 reform and would be required again in the event of a further liberalization. This time, however, in view of the failure of the 1961 measures, it was almost certain that the bankers would require, as a condition of their support, a domestic economic programme which was consistent with the pursuit of convertibility; and, in particular, one which led to a radical transformation in the competitiveness of the industrial sector.

Despite the emphasis placed by the liberals on the role of market forces, they did not reject planning as such; only the bureaucratic intervention and arbitrary interference that had hitherto accompanied it. They objected not to the plan itself but to the way it was implemented. Although the workers controlled industrial wealth, they did not own it; and social ownership implied some kind of social planning. They favoured a predominantly market economy, therefore, not because of a sudden conversion to *laissez-faire* economics or to the doctrine of consumer sovereignty, but because it was considered a

better means of *implementing* the social objective of an efficient industrial sector than the methods already tried. Markets, including international markets, were to be the servants not the masters of socialist
society and adopted because, at this particular state of Yugoslav
economic development, they were seen as the most effective way of
promoting that society's economic objectives.

Although they intended to spell out the social objective in the form
of a Five Year Plan, they hoped it would be largely self-implementing.
Such interventions as had to be made in the markets would be
macro-economically motivated, applied *uniformly* in pursuit of stabilization. But discrimination or selectivity in the employment of policy
instruments on micro-economic grounds was prohibited.[44] A dilemma would, of course, arise in circumstances where the market
produced a pattern of resource allocation at variance with the socially
planned objective. In these circumstances the non-discriminatory
exercise of monetary and fiscal policy would be of little help. Yet the
reintroduction of differential treatment of enterprises or sectors would
fly in the face of the ideological and economic rationale of the reform.

Sectional self-interest

Liberal ideologues and economists tended to be Croation or Slovenian and their views received extremely strong support from the
leaders of these two republics. Some of this support reflected a
genuine belief in the logic and conclusions of the theoreticians. But, to
some extent, the arguments were acceptable because they advocated
an institutional solution that was attractive to these politicians for
other reasons. For example, as the most economically developed and
sophisticated of the republics they were much more likely to succeed
in a market environment, especially an open one, than their Southern
neighbours. Hence its adoption was likely to lead to a substantial
redistribution of income in their favour.

A further two of these 'other' reasons deserve particular mention
because of their importance in the reform debate. The first was the
impact of the social investment and federal budgetary system upon
the regional, as opposed to sectoral, allocation of investment resources. Northerners were incensed about the way in which savings
made by relatively efficient enterprises in the North were taxed and
transferred through the federal budgetary and social investment
system, to subsidize budgets and investment programmes in the

poorer republics. Since this practice was an integral part of federal economic strategy, dismantling the social investment fund system and emasculating the economic role of the federal budget would curtail or eliminate it. The second reflected the dissatisfaction with the status quo that went deeper than any single economic issue. Liberalization had implications for the structure of decision-making in Yugoslavia that were greatly favoured by the Slovenes and Croats. For it implied the weakening of federal power; or, more specifically, reduction in the ability of Belgrade to interfere in the economic and political affairs of these republics.

The importance of rapid industrialization in socialist economic theory, the notion that the able should subsidize the needy and the belief that the Northern republics had to some degree exploited their Southern neighbours before the Second World War, had all contributed to the regional bias in resource allocation after 1945. Resource transfer to the poorer areas had taken two forms.[45] One was by means of direct federal grant disbursed on the principle that, whatever their disparities in income and wealth, the inhabitants of these areas should receive the same educational and social privileges as their more fortunate neighbours. In practice the distribution of these grants was highly arbitrary and their disbursement unsupervised by the federal authorities. More often than not, they seem simply to have financed a regional or local budgetary deficit.

The other form was the fostering of a higher rate of industrial investment in the poorer areas. Unfortunately, the gestation periods for projects in these areas were far longer, and the rate of return on capital far lower, than for their Northern equivalents. Except for the years 1961–3, during which many of the Second Five Year Plan projects were completed, the per caput rate of growth of national income of the more advanced republics remained higher than that of Bosnia, Macedonia, and Serbia, though not Montenegro. By the late 1950s it was becoming clear that the policy of encouraging the more rapid development of the poorer republics was a failure. The donors viewed it as a reckless waste of scarce resources which would have been far more effectively deployed in the traditional industrial areas. The donees believed that the volume of industrial investments should have been matched by complementary investments in infrastructure and raw materials. They also believed that they had been subsidizing the Northern Republics by providing them with cheaply priced raw materials which enabled them to reap much higher industrial profits than they would otherwise have been able to do.

The main trouble was that 'aid' policy was built into the normal investment and budgetary procedures rather than regarded as a distinct phenomenon requiring special treatment. This meant that the debate about the regional allocation of resources called into question the whole social investment and budgetary system rather than just a separate agency whose responsibility it was to administer development finance.[46] The first step towards establishing a separate framework for industrial aid was taken in 1961. The Third Five Year Plan limited its aid content to completing projects begun during the life of its predecessor and set aside a 'fund' for this purpose. However, the money was apportioned out of the Federal Investment Fund and administered by it. So, although isolated conceptually, aid remained institutionally and financially an integral part of the federal social investment system. In 1961 the Federal Executive Council Report to the Federal Assembly contained a recommendation by Kardelj that an autonomous Development Fund be established, financed out of the federal budget, through which long-term programmes of aid could be formulated outside the federal social investment frame-work.[47] The recommendation became the focus of considerable inter-republican controversy.

Concurrent with the debate about resource allocation was the connected, but wider, debate about the distribution of power in Yugoslavia between federal and republican bodies. During the 1940s and early 1950s, there was a general acquiescence by the republics in the constitutional arrangements. Memories of the resistance, Russian hostility and the genuine attempt by the regime to find a solution to the nationalities problem in the 1946 Constitution all contributed to the consensus. However, from the mid-1950s this consensus began to erode, a process which had much to do with the disintegrating party structure. The 1953 Constitution, unlike its predecessor, did not accord sovereignty or the right of self-determination to the con-stituent republics and virtually dispensed with the Chamber of Nationalities. Sovereignty and self-determination were of symbolic significance and the Chamber of Nationalities had wielded little power; yet their demise created a grievance. A more tangible complaint related to the allocation of legislative and executive powers. On the face of it the republics should have benefited from the debureaucratization provisions of the 1953 Constitution. But the federal authorities sought to ensure that the policies pursued by them were uniform, particularly with regard to social, educational and cultural policy. Although the republics were empowered to pass laws supplementary to federal Basic Laws, the federal government tended to draft its Basic Laws in such detail that there was no scope to vary them. Moreover, in matters of 'general interest' the federal authorities retained the right to issue binding instructions to republican and local administrations.

In short, the dissatisfaction of the Northern republics had made them strong proponents of the liberal cause. The increased autonomy of the enterprise, implied by the developing concepts of self-management and belief in the efficiency enhancing role of the market, was a powerful weapon to use in the service of curbing federal authority. The opponents of liberalism united under the leadership of Rankovic, head of the secret police. His support derived, as already indicated, from two sources, both of which felt threatened by the proposed political and economic changes: the local and regional bureaucracies that controlled the pattern of investment in their areas through the social investment funds; and the poorer republics that received substantial federal subsidies through the federal budget and the social investment funds. The two categories of support had a common concern in preserving both the high annual rate of investment in industrial assets and the elaborate interlocking budgetary and quasi-budgetary mechanisms that financed it.[48]

6   The reform measures

The 1963 Constitution

The new Constitution was ratified in 1963.[49] It provided the basis for far-reaching changes in the decision-making structure in Yugoslavia in two important respects. The first of these was to supply the legal authority for the institutionalization of the ideological changes initiated by the Seventh Party Congress. It asserted strongly the role of self-government in all sectors of society and, accordingly, widened the principle of self-management from the industrial sector to other fields of social endeavour such as education, health and social welfare. The notion was that each sphere of economic and social activity should operate outside the budget as a so-called 'community of interest', exclusively responsible for its own management and unaffected by outside interference. It was a further stage in the process of debureaucratization and participatory democracy. On the one hand, it implied a radical reduction in the influence of the traditional budgetary mechanisms, particularly at the level of the commune; on the other, it signified a much wider participation by the average citizen in economic and social decision-making than heretofore.

The principle of exclusivity provoked complementary changes in the Federal Assembly.[50] It was reorganized into six chambers, four of which were functionally rather than territorially based. The deputies to the Federal Chamber itself were elected by universal suffrage from territorial constituencies. Deputies to the four functional chambers— Economic, Education and Culture, Social Welfare and Health, and Political Organization—were chosen from limited electorates in whose name they were to act. Lastly, each republic sent ten representatives and each autonomous province five representatives to the Chamber of Nationalities. To give as many people as possible the opportunity to serve and to prevent the development of entrenched interests in political power, no member could sit for two consecutive terms in the same chamber and members of republican and provincial assemblies could not sit in the Federal Assembly unless it was in a representative capacity in the Chamber of Nationalities. It was also forbidden, except in the case of Tito, for anyone to hold high office simultaneously in the government and in the League of Communists.

The second major change in the structure of authority wrought by the 1963 Constitution was to enhance the power of the republics. The liberal architects of the constitution, who had utilized Slovene and Croatian discontent with the prevailing political and economic structure to add weight to their own case, were now obliged to make important concessions to the demands of these republics for greater autonomy.[51] First, the Statement of General Principles recognized the right of each republic to self-determination and secession. Second, republican legislative powers were enhanced. Article 119 contracted the boundaries of exclusively federal law-making authority and even empowered republics to legislate *within* these boundaries had the federal authorities not already proposed to do so. A new Constitutional Court was established to adjudicate upon the legality of republican and federal laws in the light of these changes. Third, Article 226 stated that republican representation would be considered in determining the composition of the Federal Executive Council, though such a practice had already emerged *de facto*. Finally, Article 110 empowered the republics, by agreement, to establish common organizations to act jointly on matters in order to realize common interests.[52] Together these changes provided the Northern republics with a firm platform from which to launch a further assault on federal authority in the following years.

The budgetary system

Two legislative enactments of major importance soon followed the passage of the 1963 Constitution, one affecting the budgetary system and the other the social investment funds. Both reflected the new constitutional principle of autonomous self-management in economic and social activities and each qualified it, in accordance with Article 27, so as to allow for an element of aid for the poorer areas. In both cases the aid or subsidy element was clearly identifiable, instead of being buried in the interstices of the main system. The first of these, the Basic Law on Financing the Socio-Political Communnities, was passed in 1964 and came into force at the beginning of 1965.[53] The law restricted the role of the socio-political community budgets to financing administration and, in the case of the federal government, defence. Responsibility for all other public and social services was transferred to an appropriate 'community of interest', managed by private citizens and financed by *doprinosi*, or Contributions, levied on enterprise Personal Income Funds. Thus to represent the common interest of citizens in education, educational communities of interest were established whose main source of revenue was the educational contribution levied on the Personal Income Funds of enterprises located in their area. The rule was, therefore, that members of a community, that is the users of the services rendered by that community, met its expenses. It was a rule designed to eliminate the elaborate network of cross subsidization which had been such a feature of the social services sector of the budgetary regime during the previous years, mainly as a result of the direct grant system. But there was one clear exception to it. Republics whose combined republican and communal per caput budgetary revenue was lower than average were to be subsidized by those whose combined revenues were higher than the average.

Social investment funds

The demolition of the social investment system began at the end of 1963. The Federal Investment Appropriations Law, passed in December, abolished the Federal Investment Fund and distributed its assets between the Yugoslav Investment Bank, the Yugoslav Bank for Foreign Trade and the Yugoslav Agricultural Bank.[54] At the same time the republics and communes were permitted, but not obliged, to transfer the assets of their social investment funds to regional and local banks. A year later, under the 1965 Banking and Credit Law, they were required to so act.[55] Corresponding changes were made in the fiscal system. In 1964 the Net Income Tax for certain categories of enterprise was abolished.[56] With the mandatory abolition of the remaining social investment funds in 1965,[57] the Net Income Tax was abolished and, henceforth, taxes on enterprises fell exclusively on Personal Income Funds. For the first time the state had ceased to tax directly the value added by the collective. At the same time all restrictions on the distribution of Net Income as between the Personal Income and Investment Funds, removed in 1961 but reimposed again in 1962, were lifted. From now on, the proportion of Net Income ploughed back into the business, and the form in which it was ploughed back, was to be exclusively for the enterprise to decide. Quite apart from fulfilling the self-management objectives of the new constitution, the demise of the investment regime was the inevitable consequence of the republican dispute. By the early 1960s, the economic interests of the two camps differed so sharply that consensus about the objectives of investment planning and development strategy was no longer possible.[58]

Unlike its companion law on budgets, the Federal Investment Appropriations Law was silent on the question of a replacement for the social investment system. Indeed, throughout 1963 the whole topic of investment was so highly charged that almost certainly no proposal would have been acceptable to both sides. It was not until after the Eighth Party Congress in December 1964, when the political dispute was resolved in favour of liberalism, that a solution was found. It was, in principle, similar to that adopted for the financing of social services. The general rule was that enterprises finance their investment programmes either from retained earnings, whose volume would be immeasurably enhanced as a result of the fiscal reforms, or from bank loans obtained competitively from a reformed banking system. The self-managed enterprise, in other words, should be financially self-sufficient or pay the market rate for borrowed resources. The toughness of this rule was moderated by the establishment of the Federal Fund for the Accelerated Development of the Lesser Developed Regions on a similar basis to that advocated by Kardelj, in order to assist enterprises in the less developed areas. As with the new formula for federal budgetary assistance, the aid or subsidy ingredient in industrial investment was now to be clearly distinguished and identifiable from the normal rule of self-sufficiency.

Banking and credit

The Banking and Credit Law, which came into force on 1 April 1966, introduced two far-reaching changes in the operation of the capital market. First, it abolished the territorial limitations that had, hitherto, been placed upon the banks. Henceforth, all banking institutions were entitled to establish branches and compete for business in any part of Yugoslavia. Second, it devised a formula for the ownership and control of banks. Until 1965, banks had been owned or controlled by the federal, republican or communal authorities, now described, collectively, by Yugoslavs, as the socio-political communities. Extending self-management to banks had always been a thorny problem ideologically because enterprise funds (surplus value) deposited therein would be controlled (expropriated), thereafter, by workers (bank employees) who had not created them. The solution adopted by the law owed more to the new communities of interest than to the worker-managed enterprises. Henceforth, the users of a bank's services, the enterprises, and to a very limited extent the socio-political communities, rather than the workers in the bank, would control its affairs. Indeed, more than that, they would be entitled to found banks and retain a financial interest in them.

Potential users were entitled to found an investment or commercial bank provided a minimum of twenty-five of them agreed to put up the capital sum laid down in the law. The bank, once established, was to be managed by the founders, who could vote in proportion to their capital investment, save that no founder could have more than 10 per cent of the votes. Socio-political communities could join in as founding members but collectively could never control more than 20 per cent of the votes. The Workers' Council of a bank, which had no influence on business or credit policy, could hold no more than 10 per cent of the votes. At any time, therefore, enterprises controlled no less than 70 per cent of the votes directing the affairs of the bank. As to ownership, each founder member was issued with a certificate recording the amount of its investment. The certificates were registered securities, could be transferred to another enterprise and yielded an annual dividend out of bank profits.

The law broke new ground in a number of ways, two of which, especially, are of note. First, the founder of a bank was entitled to retain a financial and management interest in it after it had opened for business. This was entirely at variance with the practice in the enterprise sector where the founders relinquished any managerial and financial interest as soon as the new firm's plant was constructed and production was 'on stream'. Second, enterprises were issued with shares which were, in limited respects, transferable.

Less developed regions

Article 27 of the 1963 Constitution stated that the economically under-developed republics should receive 'resources from the Social Community to allow their more rapid economic development and the creation of a material base for social services'. This Article was the one important qualification to the general constitutional doctrine of self-sufficiency and autonomy. It supplied the legal authority for both the federal budgetary subsidy and the Fund for the Accelerated Development of the Lesser Developed Regions established in February 1965 to provide development finance. Although a federal body, the Fund was to be administered and financed autonomously. Its Governing Board comprised one representative from each republic and six members elected by the Federal Assembly. It was financed out of a levy on social sector enterprise Net Income of 1.85 per cent. The Board was empowered, *inter alia,* to formulate plans to aid the underdeveloped areas, to disburse its budgetary resources on more favourable terms than would be obtainable from the banking system, to give technical assistance and to raise loans within the country and abroad for its aid programme.

Implementation

It was not until the resolution of the political debate between liberals and conservatives in December 1964 at the Eighth Party Congress that the reform gained expression as a coherent social and economic philosophy. What finally emerged had the appearance of an inevitable development from what had gone before; though, had the balance of influence tipped in favour of the conservatives, this would not have been so. It was the progressively deteriorating economic climate in the course of 1964 that precipitated the resolution of the debate. The restrictive measures imposed in the early part of 1962 moderated the rate of inflation over the next eighteen months and reduced the current account balance of payment deficit from $US217m. in 1961 to $US48m. in 1962 and $US80m. in 1963. From the end of 1963, however, the rate of inflation increased alarmingly and the balance of payments worsened; in the event the current account deficit for 1964 was $US203m. so that, once again, default on external debt obligations seemed inevitable in the absence of substantial Western financial support.

The fact that such support was unlikely to be forthcoming, or at least sufficiently forthcoming, in the event of a retreat from liberalism was undoubtedly a factor persuading waverers to opt for reform. But the passage of the new Constitution, the demise of the social investment funds in 1963 and the budgetary legislation in 1964 indicate that events were already favouring the liberals. It is likely, therefore, that the economic crisis only affected the timing of reform.[59] In the event it was a further eighteen months before the new system was fully implemented. The continued antagonism of some party leaders to liberalization led to their failure to enforce the new legislation in the territories for which they were responsible.[60] Opposition was particularly marked in the Executive Committee of the Serbian League of Communists. It was not until autumn 1966, after Rankovic had been removed from office, that the Serbian Central Committee purged their own Executive Committee.

By the end of the first quarter of 1965 the structural basis for the new system had been laid. The new roles for enterprises, sociopolitical communities, communities of interest and banks had been clearly defined. What remained was to supply the market environment to direct the decisions of these actors towards achieving the complementary objectives of industrial efficiency and dinar convertibility. Such an environment was provided, or rather intended to be provided, by the price and foreign exchange legislation passed at the end of July 1965.[61] The purpose of the domestic price reform was to eliminate the negative consequences of the previous scheme by realigning domestic prices both in relation to each other and in relation to the world market. The average increase in prices was planned to be in the order of 25 per cent, but there were marked inter-sectoral variations in the proposed rates of increase: for example, agricultural prices were scheduled to increase by over 30 per cent and raw material prices by 25 per cent, but manufacturing industry by only 8 per cent. In order to align the new average domestic price level with world market prices, the dinar was devalued from $US1 = 750 (old) to $US1 = 12.50 (new), the average level of customs duties was cut from 23 per cent to 10 per cent and export premiums were abolished. Together, it was hoped that the changes would establish ratios between production costs and sales prices which would stimulate industrial rationalization along the lines that the liberal reformers had advocated.

Stabilization measures were introduced towards the end of 1964 and at the beginning of 1965 in order to create stable macro-economic conditions for the new system, and were regarded by the authorities as an integral part of the reform.[62] They were also prompted by the need to impress foreign creditors with the seriousness of their intention to get on top of their economic difficulties. Expenditure limits were imposed upon certain categories of fixed investment in an effort to divert enterprise savings into working capital and so reduce the demand for short-term bank credit. A variety of credit controls were also introduced: in particular, central bank reserve requirements were increased, repayment terms for consumer and industrial credit were stiffened and companies seeking long-term loans for investment purposes were required to commit a higher proportion of their own funds to the project in question. Lastly, price restraint was extended. Even the new price levels and relativities introduced by the July 1965 legislation had to be sustained by controls of one sort or another.

7   The mid-1960s measures in context

The measures in the mid-1960s were intended to inaugurate a new system in which worker-controlled enterprises, acting independently and in pursuit of profit, determined the magnitude and composition of annual aggregate industrial production and investment and decided the pattern of income distribution in the industrial sector in response to market indicators. The reforms, in effect, shifted the motive force in the economy from the socio-political communities to the firm. Already endowed, to the extent that ideology permitted, with the attributes of managers and shareholders, the workers' collectives now assumed the additional role of entrepreneur. At the same time the measures transformed, at least in theory, the economic environment within which the new entrepreneur was to seek his profit. They were intended, after the initial stabilization measures, to release the product and factor markets, such as they were, from the labyrinth of selective interference and give them the opportunity to develop their own adjustment mechanisms—though they also blunted important weapons available to the authorities for the maintenance of macro-economic stability.

Given the dimensions of the break with the past that this implied, it is remarkable how much the fundamentals of the new order owed to the achievements of the early and mid-1950s. Social ownership, the principle of workers' self-management and the structure of the enterprises, the principle of free pricing and the freedom of industrial enterprises to enter into foreign trade transactions were all established principles by the end of 1953, though often derogated from in the later 1950s. Moreover, by the end of 1957, wages as a contractual item had been abolished and by 1961 the principle of non-discrimination in foreign trade had been introduced. The capital market alone owed its character to the events of the mid-1960s. Apart from the innovations in the capital market, the reform measures are significant, institutionally, not for what they created but for what they removed.

CHAPTER 2

REFORM AND REVISION

The economic and social system forged by the measures of the mid-1960s was to last no more than a decade. The Constitution of February 1974, and the proceedings and resolutions of the Tenth Party Congress held in the following May, both confirmed important changes in industrial organization and formulated new rules for investment planning which were implemented at the beginning of the 1976–80 Social Plan. These changes were based upon a novel decision-making unit, the *osovni organizacije udruzenog rada* or 'basic organization of associated labour' (BOAL), and on a new system of planning through social and self-management agreements. Animated by a revitalized and recentralized party, these institutional innovations were welded into a social scheme which amounted to a redefinition of self-management and market socialism. The redefinition involved a retreat from the spontaneous approach to economic and political development that had been the theme of the Eighth Party Congress and the mid-1960s reforms. Self-management was not abandoned. On the contrary, its importance was re-emphasized both ideologically and by the elaborate institutional arrangements in support of it set out in the new Constitution. But henceforth the decision-making process within self-managed bodies was to be protected from anti-socialist influences by the active intervention of the Party.

The central defect of the measures of the mid-1960s was their failure to satisfy the economic expectations of those who had initially supported them. The behaviour of decentralized factor and product markets during this period not only did not induce the kind of structural changes expected but also contributed to an era of unprecedented macro-economic instability. Chapters 3, 4, 5 and 6, respectively, investigate the operation, performance and evolution of the capital, labour and product markets and the macro-economic framework in which they performed. Serious though they were, however, economic difficulties were not the only ones that faced Yugoslavia in the years following the reforms. The country also underwent ideological and political upheavals, the responses to which themselves helped to shape both the economic philosophy and the institutional arrangements ultimately adopted at the Tenth Party Congress and in the new Constitution of 1974. These upheavals, and the responses to them, are the subject-matter of this chapter.

1 The transformation of the enterprise

The structure of the firm

The Law of 28 June 1950[1] declared the workers' collective to be the sovereign body in the Yugoslav enterprise. It had to debate and approve the articles of association and any changes in them and vote by referendum on matters which involved merger or the sale of assets. The articles might also have required that the collective vote upon other matters of a fundamental nature. In practice, the majority of powers arising under the articles were exercised by the Workers' Council which was elected biennially by the collective from amongst its members. Day-to-day management was conducted by a professional administration headed by an enterprise director. To supervise the commercial operations of the director and his technical staff, the Workers' Council elected a management board. Unlike the Councils, which usually met about once a month, management boards met frequently. To prevent this becoming an elite, members of the boards had to be re-elected each year and could only stand twice in succession. Moreover three-quarters of them were required to be directly concerned with production.[2]

Since the legislation applied equally to collectives whose membership numbered 30[3] or 30,000, it is not surprising that the authorities were unwilling to lay down a detailed participation code binding on all firms. In the course of the second half of the 1950s a number of larger firms subdivided their collectives into economic units, each corresponding to a distinctive phase in the production cycle.[4] Indeed, schemes of this sort proliferated to such a degree that, in 1961, the Law on Economic Units was passed to introduce a degree of uniformity.[5] No limit was imposed upon the number of workers in any unit, its size being determined by technical rather than manual factors. However, it had to be small enough to need few supervisors and to enable each member to participate fully in the decision-making process. Economic units were delegated powers by their enterprise Workers' Council. Their governing body was a monthly meeting of all members which, in turn, was entitled to delegate functions to executive subcommittees. The only legislative limit on the degree of decentralization was that it should not be so excessive as to inhibit the responsibility of the Workers' Council for the overall control of business policy. By 1965, most enterprises with collectives exceeding 1,000 members had at least one tier of economic units.

The reform measures left these institutional arrangements untouched. However, it soon became apparent that the mere removal of state bureaucracy from enterprise affairs was insufficient to guarantee participatory democracy in industrial decision-making. The alienation of collectives from control over their means of production and surplus value seemed to be taking on more subtle and insidious forms. The growing number of strikes, together with evidence derived from sociological investigations,[6] convinced the authorities that major contradictions existed within the structure of the enterprise itself. Accordingly, they embarked upon a series of initiatives culminating in the replacement of the enterprise, both as the primary vehicle for industrial democracy and as the fundamental legal and economic decision-making unit, by the BOAL.

The alienation of the collective[7]

There was a substantial increase in the number of *obustava rada* or work stoppages in the years immediately succeeding the reforms. Essentially unofficial strikes, they had no constitutional or other legal status in Yugoslavia. They were neither approved nor forbidden. The absence of any legislative treatment is explained by the socialist doctrine that strikes are an exclusively capitalist phenomenon, reflecting the innate tensions and contradictions of capitalism and impossible in societies where the means of production are owned and controlled by workers who would, in effect, be striking against themselves. This argument seemed to apply, *a fortiori*, in a socialist society which was self-managed.

Work stoppages in Yugoslavia take on a very different form from their Western counterparts. According to a study made in the years immediately following reform,[8] nearly two-thirds of them involved less than one hundred workers and only 11 per cent more than three hundred. Most were of very short duration; over 75 per cent lasted a day or less and only 5 per cent more than four days. As a mode of protest they were usually opposed by enterprise trade union representatives who, nevertheless, frequently supported their objectives. About 60 per cent of them in fact achieved their stated objective.[9] Concessions were usually made very quickly which helps to explain why the average duration of work stoppages was so short. The anxiety of management and trade union officials to terminate them swiftly was probably the result of the complete absence of any official guidance as to the line they should take. Faced with this uncertainty, and the fact that the occurrence of a stoppage itself indicated some managerial inadequacy, those in charge usually felt the best course was to resolve the dispute at all costs. Sanctions against the instigators could be, and on occasion were, taken after the event.[10]

The overwhelming majority of stoppages concerned the level or distribution of personal incomes.[11] During 1966 and 1967 a large number of firms were in serious financial difficulties as a result of the severe credit squeeze of those years. Some stoppages were undoubtedly intended to bring the plight of a particular enterprise or group of enterprises to public attention; or, at least to influence a wider audience than the decision-makers in an enterprise.[12] But the evidence reveals that 80 per cent of the stoppages involved a grievance at least partly against an individual or group within an enterprise.[13] The small size of most stoppages also tends to confirm the localization or specificity of motive. However, commentators differ about the origins of these conflicts. Some regard them as the result of a communication gap; others see them as evidence of the growth of a new form of class conflict between production workers and professional administrators.

Proponents of the first view concluded that most stoppages occurred because of a failure of communication between the decision-takers and the ordinary workers.[14] When things are going well and money is plentiful, so the argument goes, the average worker is likely to be satisfied without more. The real test of participation comes when times are not good. During a period of low pay, when the worker is anxious about the future, he needs careful nurturing and reassurance if he is to remain co-operative and not become disenchanted. The representative organs, therefore, must ensure that the reasons for their decisions are thoroughly understood by every member of the collective. Unfortunately, many representative organs are dominated by professional administrators and technocrats who do not appreciate the need to explain and justify their policies to the mass of workers. Work stoppages, accordingly, express the frustration of members of the collective at unexplained and seemingly arbitrary reductions in their income or welfare.

Not everybody agreed with this point of view. One writer claimed that had the workers been better informed about the position of the enterprise, they would have been more likely to strike.[15] Another found that over 70 per cent of the stoppages broke out before the protesters had exhausted the channels available within the enterprise for settling disputes.[16] This could be taken to indicate a failure to communicate with the decision-makers by the workers. But an earlier inquiry, which found the equivalent percentage to be only 46 per cent,[17] suggests two alternative explanations. One was a growing disenchantment with the established grievance settlement machinery. Workers may, increasingly, have regarded the strike as the only effective way of getting a fair hearing. The other was that the high rate of success that stoppages enjoyed, and the speed with which they achieved their aims, made them a relatively more attractive way for the dissatisfied worker to communicate with management.

Other writers believed that work stoppages provided evidence of growing class conflict in industrial society. Jovanov, for example, discovered that 74 per cent of all protesters participated in stoppages which were limited exclusively to manual workers.[18] Moreover, in over 70 per cent of all stoppages involving 60 per cent of all protesters, the conflict appears to have been with the administrators within the representative organs rather than with the representative organs as such. Indeed 85 per cent of all stoppages included at least one member of a representative organ.[19] In an earlier study Jovanov found half of the strikes exclusively against the administration, but only 5 per cent exclusively against the representative organs.[20] The suggestion is that a new class, the enterprise administration, had emerged and was expropriating surplus value, just as first the private capitalist and, subsequently, the state bureaucrat used to do. It followed that the production workers were also being forced into the role of a distinct class. Their sense of identity was probably reinforced during the years immediately after the reform by the generally depressed economic conditions which hit this class of worker the hardest. But there is no evidence to be found amongst the statements issued by protesting groups that they regarded themselves as members of an oppressed class. Indeed, the willingness of production workers to oppose each other is more than apparent from the number of stoppages which involved one economic unit protesting against the favoured treatment received by another.

A large number of studies were carried out on the structure of decision-making in the Yugoslav enterprise in the years immediately following the reforms.[21] Broadly speaking, they conclude that directors, department heads and technical experts had a very high degree of influence upon the decisions of the representative organs both at the enterprise and at the economic unit level.[22] In law, the administration could only propose and execute. It was for the representative organs to decide. But, as these studies reveal, the power to propose could be deployed so as to fetter the power to decide. Although it was the self-management organs that made the final choices, the alternatives from which they chose were formulated and documented by the director and his technical staff. Often the evidence on the relative merits of competing proposals was too complex for the production worker to understand. It could be presented in such a way as to make a particular option appear to be something which, in reality, it was not. Generally speaking, the control over, and grasp of, technical information proved an extremely powerful weapon in the hands of the administration.

However, the extent to which administrators had become an independent class in the Yugoslav economy by the end of the 1960s is difficult to assess.[23] As a group they were set apart, both educationally and vocationally. They shared a reasonably uniform educational background and owed their position to their technical or managerial abilities. It is not difficult to see how the combined effect of these factors would have led them to adopt a similar approach to the optimum technical and commercial requirements for running an enterprise. However, they were also members of a hierarchy at the summit of which was the general director. In the last resort they did what he said. And although he was often, though not always, a man of similar background, the responsibilities of his post, and the pressures to which he was subject, required him to take a range of matters into consideration when making a decision far wider than that of his subordinates.

Legally, the general director served two masters. He was appointed by the Workers' Council after public advertisement and short-listing. Nominating committees composed of both commune and enterprise representatives undertook the short-listing procedure. Therefore, he was obliged to the enterprise by the terms of his contract of employment. At the same time, by virtue of statutory law, he was an agent of the commune and bound to ensure that each decision made by the representative organs was in accordance with federal, republican, and local laws and regulations.[24] Indeed, he was authorized to refrain from executing any decision which was *ultra vires* the general law or the enterprise statutes. In addition, the general director was subject to a number of extra-legal pressures from socio-political bodies external to the enterprise, especially the commune.

Perception studies placed a low value on the degree of influence of the socio-political bodies on enterprise decision-making in the decade after reform.[25] But this conclusion is not very helpful because, in this case, influence was exerted through the personality of the general director rather than directly upon the representative organs. Of particular importance was the influence that the commune could wield over the election and re-election of the general director to his post. The nominating committee habitually put forward the name of a single candidate to the Workers' Council. The latter could reject it. But they could only appoint an alternative from a further nomination by the same committee. Indeed, one well-informed commentator is reported as saying, with regard to the appointment of the general director, that the heads of the commune and Party executive usually had the last word.[26] Election and security of tenure apart, it is hard to generalize about the strength of communal influence. Much depended upon how reliant an enterprise was upon a communal authority for obtaining outside finance. Although a large part of the communes' financial power had disappeared with the abolition of the social investment system, they still wielded some influence through their involvement in banking and development finance. Much, too, revolved around the interplay of personalities.

Over one third of the administrators questioned in a sample survey believed that the population at large regarded the post of general director as being primarily socio-political.[27] This doubtless had something to do with his relationship with the commune; and with the fact that many general directors had previously been assembly deputies or held other socio-political offices. But the association must also have been fostered by the growing involvement of general directors in socio-political institutions. The main reason for this was that enterprise members increasingly tended to elect administrators, especially general directors, to the various economic bodies at communal, republican and federal levels. For example, in the 1969 elections to the Economic Chamber of the Federal Assembly, 93 out of the 120 deputies were administrators, 80 of whom were general directors. To

the extent that general directors were part of the socio-political establishment, the idea that enterprise and socio-political objectives
necessarily clash needs, at least some, modification.

Constitutional amendment 15

Whatever their individual titles, by the second half of the 1960s
business administrators had come to be regarded as a distinct and
powerful group in Yugoslav society. In pre-reform days, such
strictures as were expressed about administrators usually concerned
the acts of particular directors; criticism was limited to local press
campaigns and the occasional intervention by the communes or trade
unions. It was not until the enterprise itself became the most potent
force in economic society that the powers of administrators, generally,
became a political issue.

The most articulate opponents of the administrators came from a
group of ideologues known as socialist humanists.[28] Their analysis of
the reasons for the emergence of a managerial technocratic elite went
far beyond an investigation of the defects in enterprise decision-
making. They saw it as the inevitable consequence of the introduction
of autonomous enterprises and decentralized market mechanisms.
These, they argued, granted collectives effective property rights in the
means of production and encouraged them to compete against each
other for the sole purpose of acquiring more wealth. In this process,
the role of the business managers and technocrats was indispensable
because they were trained to make enterprises better equipped for
competing and acquiring—hence their growing economic and social
power. It followed that the socialist humanist solution involved a
transformation of the system itself. They sought a rededication to the
ideals of social ownership of wealth and of equality of income. For
them, making alterations to management structures alone was merely
scratching the surface of the problem. Many of the criticisms and
policy recommendations were adopted by the student movement and
contained in their Manifesto of 4 June 1968.[29] They were also echoed
in some of the resolutions passed by the Sixth Conference of the
Trades Union Congress of Yugoslavia (TUCY) later in the same
month, especially in regard to personal income equality.

The position of the ideological establishment was considerably less
extreme.[30] It believed that at this particular stage of economic and
social development a market system was the best means of achieving

Yugoslavia's industrial objectives. Undesirable in principle, inequalities in personal incomes were an inevitable price to be paid for enhanced productivity. If ideological concessions had been made in the field of property rights they were modest and essential to the effectiveness of the capital market. In this context the enhanced status of administrators was welcomed by many as evidence of a more professional approach to industrial management. That said, however, the establishment remained unerringly committed to the two ideological forces that had shaped Yugoslav institutions since the early 1950s: debureaucratization and participatory democracy. No better evidence of the threat to these fundamentals could be provided than the post-reform escalation in work stoppages. Pre-reform stoppages could be explained by the bureaucratic interference of the socio-political communities in enterprise affairs. The reforms purported to remove those. It followed that either the system had developed new contradictions, or the old ones were returning in a more subtle form.

To satisfy their own ideological requirements, and to cut the ground from under the feet of the more radical proposals made by the social humanists and others, Constitutional Amendment 15 was passed in December 1968.[31] The Amendment, with its two provisos, gave collectives almost complete freedom to formulate their own management structures. It superseded all existing enactments respecting the organization of the enterprise, in effect repealing both the law of 28 June 1950 and the 1963 Constitution, Articles 91–4. Henceforth, the enterprise statutes, and resolutions validly made under them, determined the composition and powers of, and the election procedures for, the self-management organs and their administration. The two provisos were, first, that the Workers' Council, or a body which performed a similar function, must be preserved. And, second, that administrators should be appointed and dismissed solely by the Workers' Council or its equivalent—thus excluding all socio-political involvement through the management nominating committees. But there was no longer any obligation to retain a management board; and all the requirements of Article 93 of the 1963 Constitution with regard to the terms of appointment and powers of the general director and his staff no longer applied. Indeed, Amendment 15 made no mention of the administration except to state that it should be responsible solely to the Workers' Council.

Of course, there was nothing to prevent enterprises from preserving the old arrangements. But, in the course of 1969, a large number of them redrafted their statutes to introduce new organizational forms. Nearly all the new drafts appeared to have left the position and powers of the general director much as before. Moreover, far from abolishing the management board, the tendency was either to retain it or to replace it by a number of executive boards each with a specialist technical, planning or financial function. Since the requirement that 75 per cent of the management board consist of production workers no longer applied, the new board or boards were composed of a high proportion of administrators. Often the electorate for appointments to one board was another board. Indeed, the management boards of the large merged enterprises were sometimes composed solely of the directors and heads of department of their component factories and divisions. What is more, these patterns appear to have repeated themselves in the economic units.

Amendment 15 had, in short, backfired. Instead of leading to more democratic structures and greater worker participation it had had quite the opposite effect. One reason seems to have been the widespread financial *malaise* in the enterprise sector at that time which influenced many collectives into conceding more power to professional management. In view of the aversion to risk of workers and the overwhelming obsession with personal income levels revealed by the sociological surveys of the late 1960s, this reaction is not so surprising. In the last resort greater financial stability was more attractive than greater democracy. Another reason, applicable to the larger firms, appears to have been the need to develop more effective means of functional and territorial co-ordination between different divisions and plant. It is, indeed, hard to escape the conclusion that enterprises had taken the opportunity provided to bring their organizational arrangements more into line with the exigencies of modern managerial efficiency.

These developments were soon under fire from both the League of Communists of Yugoslavia and the Trades Union Congress of Yugoslavia. On 14 October 1969, at the end of the Fifth Plenum of the Central Committee of the League, the delegates stated that workers' self-management was threatened by 'bureaucratic and dogmatic aspirations, the technocratic tendencies of administrators and diverse other attempts to slow down or even hinder its development'.[32] Similar accusations were made by the Trades Union Congress which began a determined campaign against the recent organizational changes. The first move was made on 15 November when Dusan Petrovic, their President, issued a press statement condemning the proliferation of executive boards and the way in which they were usurping the function of the Workers' Councils.[33]

In the middle of December, the Trades Union Congress addressed a letter to the Federal Assembly requesting that it provide an official interpretation of certain aspects of Amendment 15. The Assembly referred the matter to its Constitutional Commission. The Assembly was by no means entirely in sympathy with the trade union position. As might have been expected from their background, a number of deputies to the Economic Chamber accused the Congress of being totally one-sided; and the Social Welfare Chamber, while condemning bureaucratic and technocratic tendencies, emphasized the importance of professional management to technical and commercial advancement.[34] On 5 June 1970, almost six months after the request, the Assembly passed a formal resolution on the application of Amendment 15.[35] The Resolution did little more than spell out and reassert the philosophy behind the Amendment, which was to give each collective the freedom to develop its own management structure rather than have it imposed from outside. Indeed, inherent in this philosophy was the notion that no specific recommendations on organizational structures could be made, since to make them would be to limit the freedom of the collectives to devise their own. The unions, in so far as they wanted the Assembly to place limits on this freedom were, in effect, asking it to do something illegal by virtue of the constitutional status of the Amendment. The legislative enactment of new organizational rules binding on the collectives, therefore, had to await a further revision of the Constitution.

Constitutional amendment 21

This revision was forthcoming exactly a year later, in June 1971, in the form of Constitutional Amendment 21. The new Amendment accorded constitutional status to one of the resolutions adopted by the Second Congress of Self-Management held in Sarajevo in the early part of the previous month. The Congress had been convened with the declared objective of reviewing the two decades' experience of self-management and making recommendations for its improvement. In particular, it was hoped to devise a comprehensive Self-

Management Code. It included delegates from all social sector activities and from all the socio-political communities and the 27 resolutions finally approved covered almost every aspect of contemporary economic and social importance in Yugoslavia. The Congress itself sat for a mere three days, 5–7 May. But its steering Committee had taken nearly two years to arrive at draft resolutions acceptable to all participants.

The period of preparation for the Second Congress coincided with the crisis over Amendment 15. The failure of the Federal Assembly to act decisively in its favour led the Trades Union Congress, increasingly supported by the Party establishment, to press for further constitutional change. Consensus was reached on what form this change would take through the process of drafting for the Second Congress of Self-Management. What finally emerged was a commitment to convert the economic unit from being a vehicle for attaining a modest degree of decentralization in the larger enterprises into the fundamental unit of industrial organization in the Yugoslav economy. Clause 2 of Amendment 21 states.[36]

The basic organization of associated labour is the fundamental unit of associated labour by which the workers . . . regulate directly and equally their working relationships. . . . They have the right to transform any part of an enterprise or similar work organization whose performance can be measured either by market criteria or assessed in some other way independently into a basic organization of associated labour. The members of a basic organization of associated labour which is part of a work organization have the right to detach themselves from it and become an autonomous unit. . . . The income realized in whatever form by the basic organization of associated labour belongs entirely to that unit.

The only reservations were that the creation or separation of a BOAL 'must not damage the rights of workers in other BOALs nor the interests of the enterprise itself', and that the right to disburse personal income would be regulated by the system of self-management and social agreements, itself a product of the June 1971 constitutional changes.

At the beginning of 1971 there was a total of 6,713 enterprises in Yugoslavia with representative organs, of which 4,896 had no economic units, 1,331 had them at one level, and 127 had them at two levels.[37] Assuming that economic units had been introduced into the vast majority of enterprises whose manufacturing cycle or plant composition would reasonably allow, the new Amendment seemed likely to affect something in the order of 1,500 of them. Some were quick to conform with the new requirements. But many more were reluctant to comply. Despite strong pressure, especially from the trade unions, a large number of enterprises made no move to introduce BOALs. They argued that such an organizational change would produce excessive disintegration, perhaps to the point of anarchy, in industrial organization. Union leaders claimed that, far from leading to anarchy, the BOAL system was essential to the achievement of full social integration in the industrial sector; that the reason for the unwillingness of enterprises to make the relevant changes was the existence, in their midst, of a number of powerful bureaucratic and technocratic groups who were opposed to them because they would destroy their power base; that the destruction of these groups was necessary to prevent the expropriation of the worker from what was justly his; and that the best means of destroying them was to implement the terms of the Amendment as soon as possible.[38]

The post-reform system was exceptionally ill-equipped to formulate and implement economic and social policy to support or modify the reform measures. The deficiency, moreover, grew more acute as the need for swift and decisive action became more pressing. It derived from the progressive fragmentation of the political fabric of the country which had already reached serious proportions by the time of the mid-1960s measures. To the Party leadership, widespread non-compliance with Amendment 21 was one more example of the growing loss of authority of the federal organs of the League of Communists and, indeed, of federal institutions generally. They believed that the real opposition to change came from *within* the Party, from the republican Party hierarchies who worked hand in glove with leading administrators in the bigger enterprises to promote their territorial economic interests irrespective of the interests of the nation. The successful implementation of Amendment 21, therefore, went beyond the issue of participatory democracy. It became a major factor in the struggle for power within the League of Communists itself.

The pattern of institutional change within the Party during the late 1960s made central decision-making impossible without a consensus amongst the republican Party leadership. By the Ninth Party Congress, held in 1969, it had been decided that the republican Party congresses should precede the Federal Congress, draft their own political platforms and name their own delegates to the federal representative organs. These organs, now restructured to consist of an Annual Conference of 285 delegates, a collective Presidency responsible to it of 40 members, and an Executive Bureau to service it of 15 members, were all composed on the basis of strict republican proportionality, regardless of population or Party strength.[39] A similar pattern was being established in federal legislative and executive organs. Constitutional amendments in 1967 and 1968 increased the powers of the republics within the Federal Assembly. The Federal Chamber was abolished by Constitutional Amendment in 1968 and replaced by an independent Chamber of Nationalities whose deputies were required to adhere strictly to the views of the republican assemblies that had nominated them. There were 140 representatives, twenty from the assembly of each of the six republics and ten from the assembly of each of the two autonomous provinces. Legislation introduced by the other constituent chambers of the Federal Assembly had to be approved by the Chamber of Nationalities. This gave the republican assemblies considerable influence over the whole range of federal legislation.[40]

This state of organizational deadlock fostered the contemporary illusion that Yugoslavia was becoming a genuinely liberal society. This was especially encouraged by the behaviour of the Federal Assembly which, from the middle of 1964, frequently subjected Federal Executive Council legislative proposals to contentious debate and even amendment. But the atmosphere had, in fact, no connection with the advent of general pluralism.[41] The critics of these legislative proposals were members of the same party as their advocates. They were responsible not to the people but to the regional and local Party officials who nominated them. Conflict occurred in the legislature simply because the Party was no longer a single unit. Democratic centralism was a broken reed. Discussion of a wide range of critical and highly contentious policy issues, previously discussed behind closed doors in federal Party caucus, now became public as deputies canvassed the economic and social interests of their respective republican Parties. Nor were republican Parties themselves entirely free of internal dissent. There were many contested seats for the 1967 and 1969 federal elections and the press often reported conflicts between Party members at the communal level.[42] Federal deadlock, moreover, enhanced the illusion of liberalism in another way. It prevented any positive action being taken against the more outspoken non-party critics of the current state of Yugoslav society.[43]

The trend towards republicanism, already reflected by institutional changes in the League of Communists and the Federal Assembly, was acknowledged and formalized by further constitutional amendments passed, along with Amendment 21, in June 1971.[44] These reconstructed the remaining federal institutions on a practically confederal basis. Following the example set by the League of Communists two years earlier, Amendment 35 established a collective Presidency. It was composed of three members from each republic, two from each province, and Tito. Twenty two members, excluding Tito, were elected by their representative republican and provincial assemblies to serve a term of five years. From their number, a President and Vice President were to be elected by annual rotation. Amendment 36 exempted Tito from the rotational principle. The Federal Executive Council and the Constitutional Court were also restructured on the basis of republican parity.

Amendment 20 granted the republics primary authority over all matters not expressly designated by the Constitution as federal. The matters so designated were national defence, foreign policy, individual and national rights, foreign trade and exchange policy, monetary policy, measures necessary to guarantee a 'unitary market' and, where necessary to prevent substantial disruption to the economy, the power to limit the taxing authority of republics and communes.[45] The Federation was also stripped of most of the fiscal powers that it retained after the 1965 reforms. The interest charge on enterprise Business Funds and the federal direct tax on private incomes were both abolished. The yield from the federal turnover tax henceforth accrued to the republics. Only customs duties, together with a few other minor sources of income, remained to it. Although it continued to be responsible for the administration of the Fund for the Accelerated Development of Underdeveloped Regions, the republics henceforth financed it. Indeed, from now on the federal government relied on republican contributions and on borrowing to finance most of its activities. Even the exercise of many powers for which it was still constitutionally responsible required the consent of the six republics and two autonomous provinces. A list of the economic subjects upon which the Federal Assembly could act only with their agreement included the Five Year Plan, monetary policy, foreign currency and trade matters and, indeed, the federal budget itself.[46]

The high point of the erosion of central authority was reached during the second half of 1971. From having been its warmest supporters in the early 1960s, the Croats had come to regard the reform system, and especially the banking and foreign currency regime dominated by the great Serbian banks and foreign trade enterprises, as a vehicle for their own exploitation.[47] On the evidence, their view is hardly surprising. In 1970, Serbian banks controlled nearly two thirds of the nation's banking assets—whereas Croatian banks were responsible for merely one sixth. Moreover, Serbia's foreign trade enterprises had an annual turnover, that year, of about 23,000 million dinars compared with Croatia's 2,000 million dinars. Yet Croatia generated, at that time, 30 per cent of Yugoslavia's industrial production and 35 per cent of its foreign exchange earnings.[48] The Croatians believed that the Amendments would change nothing. This was partly because unanimity between the republics was necessary to effect any sort of economic change; and partly because the Amendments did not provide for the kind of changes in the banking and foreign exchange sectors that they wanted. Unless these sectors were radically reformed, the devolution of economic authority effected by the Amendments would be meaningless. This belief led to growing pressures within Croatia to obtain the power to make its own economic policy.

At first the Croats had not been alone in their objections to Serbian economic hegemony. The Slovenes and the Macedonians, in particular, shared their point of view. However, as Croat demands for virtual economic independence became steadily more uncompromising, their allies deserted them. The problem was that the Croats were now incapable of analysing any economic issue in other than nationalist terms. Moreover, an influential group of members of the Executive Committee of the Croatian Party appeared to be lending some support to the *Matica Hrvatska* nationalist movement.[49] This movement had already had an unprecedented political success earlier in the year by capturing control of the Croatian students' Federation; and in December 1971 it organized the students' strike in Zagreb in support of fundamental change in Yugoslavia's foreign exchange system.

Tito was now sufficiently concerned with the turn of events in Croatia to act decisively. The development of an organized political movement, whose focus of loyalty lay outside the party establishment and competed with it ideologically, was unacceptable to him. The Croatian party leadership was promptly purged of those who had sympathized with its objectives. Tito blamed the disaffection of the disgraced members of the Croatian party on the 'liberal' ideological development within the League. The main reason for this, he believed, was the decline of the doctrine of democratic centralism, a decline which he ascribed to the resolution of the Sixth Party Congress which had taken place nearly twenty years earlier.[50] Following the purges he began a determined campaign to reaffirm the cohesive role of the Party in Yugoslav society and reassert the principle of democratic centralism. In September 1972 the Executive Bureau of the League, by now reduced from fifteen to eight members, addressed a letter to the entire Party membership calling for greater unity of action and rededication to the principle of democratic centralism.[51] The new enemy was liberalism, the notion that permitting the free play of political and economic forces was the best way of resolving social conflict and establishing coherent policies. Quite the opposite had happened. Party members at all levels were called upon to reassert the role of the League in all aspects of social development. Members who did not implement Party decisions were threatened with expulsion.

Although the manner in which the Croats had expressed their point of view had provoked the purge, the substance of their complaints was not lost on Tito. Indeed many of their recommendations, for example on the foreign trade and banking regimes, were subsequently adopted. If liberalism had led to nationalism in Croatia, it had equally fostered 'technocratism' elsewhere. In the following months a number of other republican and provincial Party leaders, notably in Serbia, were accused of technocratism and removed from office.[52] The technocratism referred to in this case was the tendency of certain leaders to encourage the growth of, and the concentration of power in, large enterprises with the object of furthering the influence and prestige of their republics. They conspired to accumulate excessive economic power by the use of social property for private ends. There was no point in persuading enterprises to become more democratic when the political leaders of the areas in which they were situated were pressing them to move in precisely the opposite direction. It is not surprising, therefore, to discover that one of the chief specific charges made against the purged Party leaders was that they failed to ensure that the terms of Amendment 21 were complied with by the enterprises within their respective territories. Thereafter, Amendment 21 met with little opposition.

The BOAL

The process of breaking down enterprises into smaller industrial units was already completed or well under way by the spring of 1974 when a new Constitution was promulgated,[53] *inter alia*, incorporating and elaborating Amendment 21. The criterion for the establishment of a BOAL was that its financial performance could be assessed independently by market or other means. It followed that the number of members in any particular BOAL varied enormously. In *Beogradska Konfeksija*, for example, a clothing factory employing 5,600 workers, 20 BOALs were established. The largest of these, with a membership of approximately 700, consisted of the workers in the organization's 200-odd retail outlets; the smallest, with a membership of about 80, was the group of maintenance engineers. The size of BOALs in the production divisions ranged between 250 and 450 members.[54] Each BOAL included administrators and workers at all levels of skill. In most enterprises the practice was for existing economic units to convert themselves into BOALs by the simple expedient of changing their names and establishing their own system of representative self-government. The old enterprise was itself transformed into a *radna organizacije* or working organization (WO). The WO was a legal person but had no authority over the personnel or assets of a BOAL without its consent. The larger enterprise had, therefore, become a kind of federation of BOALs.

Each BOAL elected its own delegate to the central Workers' Council and the central management board of the WO to which it chose to belong. Being delegates to, rather than members of, these central bodies the representatives of the BOALs were obliged to act on instructions and could be recalled at any time. Moreover, any BOAL could withdraw from a WO, provided that it was not in breach of contract, either to join another WO, or even to operate independently if the nature of its work permitted it to do so. Legal sovereignty, therefore, now lay with the BOALs. Strictly speaking they were free to choose their own WO, to hire and fire their own workers, to change their own prices and distribute their own Net Income between the four funds in any way they wished. They were, indeed, under no obligation whatsoever to delegate any powers to central councils or boards. Such restraints that were placed on them in these matters existed because they had *consented* to their presence. In principle, this seemed to make a substantial advance on the previous system of economic units.

In practice there appear to have been few alterations in the way in which industrial units were managed or in the balance of power between centre and periphery. There seem to be several reasons for this. First, the completion of social and self-management agreements, as the next Section relates, placed important constraints upon their behaviour. The simultaneous introduction of the BOAL and the system of contractual planning was no accident. They were regarded by the authorities as complementary, indeed essential, to each other. The one guaranteed democratic decision-taking; the other ensured that the decisions taken formed part of a coherent technical and commercial framework. Hence the refusal by the authorities to accept the criticism that smaller units would lead to excessive fragmentation of the industrial structure.

Second, many BOALs formed part of a highly integrated manufacturing cycle. Although legally and financially independent, their technical dependence upon, and geographical proximity to, the preceding and succeeding stages in the cycle compelled them to conform with the production and investment policies of their neighbours. They had no alternative factories to integrate into and they were not viable on their own. For example, although each of the eight BOALs embracing the furnace, rolling mill and foundry stages of steel production at the *Boris Kidric* works was an independent accounting unit with its own self-management organs, they were all obliged to delegate investment and production planning to the central Workers' Council.[55] The delegation of production and investment policy to the central Workers' Council, moreover, usually led to a high degree of centralized personal income determination. The difficulty was that the degree of success or failure of a BOAL in complying with centrally determined plans might have had very little to do with the intrinsic efficiency of its members. A unit may recently have been the beneficiary of productivity enhancing investments; or a unit at an earlier stage in the production cycle may have failed to meet its own targets thus affecting the performance of subsequent units. In short, the degree of interdependence within the manufacturing cycle may have made it impossible to distinguish, accurately, the performance of one BOAL in isolation from the performance of another. Singling out and rewarding one unit as more efficient or more productive would have been liable to have caused friction if the unit really owed its success to others. This consideration did not, however, apply in different technical or commercial circumstances. Many hotels became BOALs forming part of a tourist complex organized as a WO. The advantages that membership of a WO brought in this case were economies of scale in borrowing, publicity, marketing and so on. But it was by no means impracticable for a hotel to choose to go it alone; or to join another complex even if this were some distance away.

Third, the multiplicity of BOALs in any WO almost certainly worked against the acquisition or retention of power at the periphery because of the difficulty of forming coalitions between BOALs that would be large enough and enduring enough to dominate the central Council and management committees. Indeed, the central organs could actively discourage the formation of such coalitions by playing off one BOAL against another. Fourth, despite the fact that it was now the periphery that delegated to the centre, and not vice-versa, the factors that previously made the influence of the administrators pre-eminent persisted. Technical and financial skills, together with the capacity to take an overall view of the WO's commercial situation, placed them in a strong position to persuade the representative organs to their way of thinking, despite the new constitutional prohibitions on their being members of such organs. Finally, it will be recalled that any BOAL inheriting assets which were subject to existing contractual arrangements was bound by the terms of that agreement. While a newly established BOAL was entitled to renegotiate its rights and obligations with respect to its prospective WO and associate BOALs, it could not repudiate or modify the terms of existing contractual obligations binding upon it, and to which outsiders were party, without their consent.

The Croat complaints against the foreign trade enterprises were not lost on Tito. The huge domestic financial resources that were generated from their foreign currency earnings had been used to merge with some enterprises or to provide credit on a contractual basis to others. Soon they were at the centre of a complex web of economic relationships influencing decisions over the deployment of large sums of socially-owned resources. They were the classic example of the much publicized phenomenon of the 'group ownership' of social property. They, like all other enterprises, were now subject to the new rules on BOALs; and, after 1974, their functions had to be performed on an agency basis whereby their services were supplied for an agreed fee.

Banks

The 1965 Banking Law was also revised, although the new rules took a number of years to evolve. The object of these new rules was to eliminate the excessive power that both professional administrators and socio-political communities were alleged to have acquired over the allocation of business bank resources.

Since the reforms, it was argued, substantial sums of 'anonymous financial capital' accrued to business banks. These funds were not earmarked for any particular purpose and were, therefore, available to lend to the most deserving investment projects. Interest rates never rose to a level high enough to clear the market. Because the demand for investment resources in Yugoslavia constantly exceeded their supply, bank administrators were accused of playing off their founding enterprises, competing for scarce loan resources, against each other. The accusations made against professional managers in banks were not unlike those levelled against their counterparts in industry. They had, it was argued, become an independent force in decision-making, capable of manipulating those to whom they were supposed to be subordinate. It was also alleged that bank administrators were working closely with industrial managers in the larger, multi-product enterprises. Between them, they were believed to have appropriated 'group control' over substantial amounts of social property. Measures were, therefore, taken, designed to make banks more accountable to their associated BOALs. In particular, they were no longer entitled to build up their own credit funds. They were obliged to disburse all earnings to their founders after appropriations to Personal Income and Reserve Funds.

The evidence on the allocation of resources by banks, discussed in Chapter 3, is not particularly helpful in proving or refuting this thesis. What is clear is that banks tended to limit their lending to projects in their own republic or commune; that some of these loans were made on the instructions of the republican or communal authorities; and that the republican and communal authorites were in a position to issue such instructions because a significant proportion of the resources available to business banks remained under their control. In complete contrast to the original intention of the 1965 reforms, the state actually retained an interest in the industrial investment system. The Bank and Credit Law of 1965[56] had obliged the socio-political communities to transfer the assets and liabilities of their former investment funds to a business bank of their choosing—in effect, making a gift to the new investment banking system of the net value of these funds. Early in 1966, however, this legislation was amended, giving the socio-political communities the option to reappropriate either the assets and liabilities themselves or their net value.[57]

If they chose the first option, the assets themselves, together with their associated liabilities, were expunged from the balance sheet of the relevant business bank and credited and debited to a separate investment loan fund. Like their pre-reform cousins these reconstituted funds had no executive staff. Their assets were managed by the business banks as agents for the socio-political communities. If the second option were chosen, the assets and liabilities of the pre-reform funds remained in the balance sheet of the banks concerned, their net worth being transferred from the credit fund of the business banks to an interest-yielding deposit account entry entitled, rather clumsily, Resources of Socio-Political Communities Earmarked for the Financing of Investment. The socio-political communities were entitled to stipulate how the business bank should employ these assets. In this case there was no need to re-establish distinct loan funds.

Most socio-political communities were quick to avail themselves of the terms of the revised legislation. The majority, including the federal authorities, chose the second option leaving the assets and liabilities of the pre-reform funds in the balance sheets of the business banks and acquiring earmarked deposits. However, in October 1969, the federal authorities cancelled their earmarked deposit account and switched the assets and liabilities of the old federal Investment Fund from the Yugoslav Investment Bank to a newly established investment fund named the Federal Fund for Financing Investment (FFFI). The change made no difference to the management of the assets, which continued to be deployed by the Serbian based Yugoslav Investment Bank on instructions from the federal authorities. The reversion to the old style fund did, however, allow the authorities to supplement its existing resources, consisting of the principal and interest payments from past loans, with a part of the revenue from the Business Fund levy. This reintroduced, in a modest way, and only at the federal level, the pre-reform practice of supplementing the resources of social investment funds by fiscal means.

Despite this small advance in federal influence, the FFFI did not last for long. Following the Constitutional Amendments in the middle of 1971, the assets and liabilities of the FFFI, save for those pertaining to the less developed regions, were devolved upon the republics. The assets comprising the principal and interest payments in outstanding loans to the less developed areas were transferred to the federal budget itself. The earmarked resources of the republican and communal authorities were transferred to the Regional National Banks whose lending policies were subject to close scrutiny by the National Bank. Moreover, socio-political communities were no longer allowed to become shareholders in business banks.

2   Market mechanisms and social control

The authorities had hoped, in 1965, that the autonomous operation of the markets would achieve the social plan objectives without their having to devise any mechanism of plan fulfilment beyond the provision of a stable macro-economic environment by conventional monetary and fiscal means. By the beginning of the 1970s, it was clear that their hopes would not be realized. Indeed, because of imperfections in the structure and functioning of the decentralized factor and product markets, and because of the dimensions of the macroeconomic disequilibria that accompanied and followed the reforms and the discretionary interventions that proved necessary to contain them, not only were planned targets not met but the hoped-for underlying changes in the economy, particularly in the basic industrial sectors, were not materializing.

It is revealing to note that the analysis by the 1976–80 Social Plan of the major economic weaknesses in Yugoslavia, written in the mid-1970s, is almost identical to that contained in the 1966–70 Social Plan, written in the mid-1960s.[58] Both refer to the imbalance in sectoral growth between the manufacturing, raw material and infrastructure sectors as the basic source of instability in the economy. Both dwell on the chronic regional income and wealth differentials. Both call for resolute action against territorial, sectoral and group sectarianism in the economy. Both urge transition towards an era of intensive development based on the strengthening of the qualitative factors of economic activity and away from the habit of extensive production practices manifested during the previous ten years. It is almost as if time had stood still.

It became widely accepted that some alternative mode of inducing structural change in the economy would have to be found. Despite the emphasis placed by the reformers on the role of market forces, they were not, as the previous chapter emphasized, opposed to planning as such; they rejected only the bureaucratic modes of implementation that had hitherto accompanied it. Ideologically, therefore, there was considerable unease about introducing an obligatory factor into the planning system. *Borba* summarized the central problem neatly in an article published at the beginning of August 1971:[59]

There is no country in the world that survives without basic levels of action on current development policies in the way that Yugoslavia does . . . We must solve the question of the role of the state. At present any mention of the state sounds like heresy; but Communists in favour of self-management are not against the state, they are only against an *étatist* state. The simplified idea of the withering away of the state is the root cause of the mistake.

Eighteen months later *Ekonomska Politika* expressed itself in much the same vein.[60] It believed that much of the hostility to the development of a system of plan implementation arose from the erroneous belief that there were only two alternatives for the economy—a legally binding federal plan or an entirely free market. Neither had produced a successful economic solution and both were ideologically unacceptable. In fact, it argued, the real choice was between the existing fragmented bureaucratic intervention and organized intervention based upon a new stage of self-management.

Social and self-management agreements[61]

The system of organized intervention that emerged is described in this survey as contractual planning to distinguish it from the more familiar categories of administrative and indicative planning. The idea was that self-managed institutions should evolve their own rules, rather than have them imposed from above, by concluding social and self-management agreements. This new approach to planning was revealed at the Second Congress on Self-Management and incorporated in Constitutional Amendment 21. It was later authorized by Articles 120–8 of the new Constitution. Social agreements, or compacts, were to be concluded between socio-political communities, trade unions and Economic Chambers at the intra- and inter-republican level, to establish general rules on a variety of economic policy matters to guide the decisions of BOALs and other work organizations in a particular sector or territory. Self-management agreements were to be concluded directly between BOALs and work organizations, and were primarily intended to co-ordinate their business policies within the framework of the social agreements. Both were to determine the context within which ordinary commercial contracts were negotiated and concluded.

Ideologically, the agreements had a number of attractions. They were free from the criticism that they reintroduced discriminatory bureaucratic intervention in economic affairs. At the same time, they had a strong flavour of participatory democracy. Initiatives derived from a variety of economic and social levels and not solely from an élite group of government officials. And the element of compulsion in them was carefully veiled. There was, as a general rule, no obligation to conclude social agreements. Moreover, no court existed to compel a party to a social agreement to comply with the agreement's terms; the contents of most social agreements contained broad policy directions which could only become operationally meaningful when filled out by the substructure of self-management agreements. The position of the work organizations, whose behaviour was the subject matter of social agreements, was rather different. They themselves were not a party to them though they might influence their content by lobbying their union, Chamber or republican representatives. To the extent, however, that the terms of a social agreement were subsequently incorporated into a self-management agreement by any firm, that firm was bound by them. Moreover, if a work organization refused to conclude a self-management agreement in conformity with the guidelines laid down by a social agreement, directives could be issued by the relevant socio-political community to compel it to conform. This power became Article 125 of the new Constitution.

A revised official interpretation of the role of market forces in the economy coincided with the introduction of contractual planning. It is well summarized by a contributor to the proceedings of the Tenth Party Congress who wanted:[62]

associated labour to gain control over the laws of commodity production and for society consciously and appropriately to guide and rectify market trends, thus diminishing the possibility of adverse influences being generated by the action of blind forces in socio-economic development and relations. The League of Communists must combat conceptions and tendencies to consider that market relations should be formed spontaneously and socio-economic problems can be solved by the markets automatic operation.

These views provide a very sharp contrast with those expressed at the Ninth Party Congress held in 1969. The prevailing mood of the second half of the 1960s was, as far as possible, to divorce the party from economic affairs. The self-managing community of production workers represented a phase of socialist endeavour based upon the 'free operation of economic laws'. This attack on spontaneity in market relations, only five years later, was connected with a wider attack on that phenomenon in social and political relations generally. The 1976–80 Social Plan referred in numerous places to the adverse effects of 'blind market forces', a reference to both the severe distortions and instabilities of recent experience, and the corresponding need for 'the conscious direction of market flows'. This was partly a veiled statement that the Party would involve itself more in economic affairs. But it was also a reference to the role that the Yugoslavs still saw the market as playing. Contractual planning, to summarize the 1976–80 Social Plan, sought to enable them to apply market criteria in a controlled environment, to avoid distortions and, on a long-term basis, to eliminate instabilities.

Five year social planning

Articles 69–74 of the new Constitution extended contractual planning to the investment policies of firms. These articles sought to link social and self-management agreements to the five-year social planning process. Their main purpose was to co-ordinate investment expenditure so as to avoid capacity duplication, perhaps the worst structural disease that afflicts the Yugoslav economy. Inter-firm competition was still regarded as desirable in this area but it was hoped that it would take place *before* the factories were actually built. In other words *ex post* competition in an actual market was to be replaced by *ex ante* competition at the project feasibility stage. The best project could be implemented and the others discarded.

The new system operated in the context of the 1976–80 Social Plan. It began with the enactment of a federal law authorizing the plan and outlining procedures and timetables. The principle was that all work and social units, through simultaneous negotiations, harmonize each others' initial objectives by successive approximation. BOALs and WOs and business associations sought to persuade the Economic Chambers to promote their particular sectors and projects. Economic Chambers sought to influence official thinking on industrial investment strategy. Meanwhile, the socio-political communities were assessing the investment proposals prepared by their respective planning institutes and seeking to persuade the trade unions and Economic Chambers of their merits.

When the negotiations between the trade unions, Economic Chambers of trade and socio-political communities were complete, the agreed investment targets were incorporated in some 240 social agreements—one for each of the thirty sectors in each of the six republics and two autonomous provinces. The object was to attain an *ex ante* balance which avoided both bottlenecks and duplication. Corresponding social agreements were then concluded on prices, imports and exports, personal incomes, employment and so on. Within the social agreement framework, and under the auspices of the Economic Chambers, firms in similar branches 'competed' for the right to implement particular parts of the programme. Subsequently, inter-firm self-management agreements were negotiated and concluded. According to Article 70, 'mutual obligations laid down in mutual agreements by basic and other organizations of associated labour . . . in order to realize a joint plan may not be rescinded or changed during the period of time for which the plan has been adopted.'

An important distinction is made in the legislation between priority and non-priority investment. In the course of the social planning procedure, certain sectors and branches were given a priority classification—they might, for example, have had great export or foreign exchange saving potential. The choice of sector was, itself, a matter for negotiation. There was a legal obligation upon socio-communities, trade unions, Economic Chambers and BOALs to conclude social and self-management agreements for priority sectors.[63] These agreements, moreover, were binding upon the banks associated with the contracting BOALs and WOs. They had an obligation to pre-empt resources for priority projects before they could contemplate lending elsewhere. By contrast, there was no legal obligation to conclude social agreements in non-priority sectors and branches though their conclusion was regarded as desirable.

Annual planning

Firms needed a stable macro-economic environment if they were going to realize their planned production and investment targets. One of the main reasons why the *laissez-faire* system failed to achieve its objectives in the decade after reform was because the economy experienced severe bouts of inflation and balance of payment deficits. Many of the problems derived from market imperfections. But the instruments available to the authorities to regulate money supply, aggregate demand, prices, wages, imports and exports were few and unsophisticated. Moreover, the timing and extent of their application was sometimes adversely affected by inter-republican disputes.

The macro-economic targets for the economy were established annually by the Federal Executive Council in an Economic Resolution which had to be debated and approved by the Federal Assembly. Until 1980 the targets and policies set out in the Economic Resolution were only recommendations. The annual aggregate growth, investment, consumption, production, price, incomes and balance of payments targets were consistent with the objectives set out in the Five Year Social Plans. Owing to the unsuitability of fiscal policy for aggregate demand management, the policy recommendations consisted, mainly, of a variety of monetary targets for the Yugoslav National Bank to achieve. Due to the inadequacy of the instruments of macro-economic control, the authorities were sometimes obliged to resort to temporary direct measures to bring a particularly severe bout of inflation or balance of payments deficit under control. Characteristically, these might include one or more of a wage freeze, a price freeze, credit quotas, cash deposits as a condition of receiving loans, and a freeze on federal investment. It must be emphasized, however that the federal authorities were only entitled to intervene directly on a strictly temporary basis to guarantee the unity of the market. As soon as the crisis was subsiding the measures had to be lifted.

Contractual planning increased both the number of economic variables which the federal authorities could legitimately target in the Economic Resolution and the policy instruments available to control them. Through social agreements, the socio-political communities, including the federation, were actively involved in formulating annual policies on wages and prices, imports and exports, borrowing and lending. They not only expressed their views about what these agreements should contain, but also participated in negotiating them. Moreover, once overall agreements were concluded and worked out in detail by a series of self-management agreements, they represented a political consensus amongst all contracting parties to realize their objectives. In effect, contractual planning enabled the federal authorities to intervene on a permanent basis in the formulation and implementation of macro-economic objectives in areas in which, hitherto, they could only do so in an emergency.

Federal decision-making

To succeed, contractual planning had to produce results on an inter-, as well as an intra-, republican level. Otherwise, there was a real danger that it would provide a roundabout means of evading the constitutional prohibition on republican policy making, rendering it impossible for the federal government to fulfil its constitutional obligation to guarantee the unity of the Yugoslav market. The first social agreements, concluded on personal income distribution in 1972, illustrate the problem. The republics agreed to negotiate intra-republican agreements on personal incomes only if each could devise its own system of regulation.

The Constitution of 1974, essentially, confirmed the changes made to federal institutions by the 1971 Amendments. The only substantial modification was to revert to a bicameral Federal Assembly with both houses selected in conformity with the principles of republican and provincial equality.[64] The Presidency, now reduced from twenty three to nine members, and the Federal Executive Council, retained their strictly proportional regional composition. Consequently, the success of the complex and delicately balanced structure of contractual planning at the federal level depended upon the success of those three institutions in obtaining inter-republican consensus on the major economic issues.

In 1974, the first inter-republican social agreements on employment and price policy were concluded. Both required republics and autonomous provinces to implement intra-republican social agreements consistent with their terms. From then on, inter-republican agreements on economic issues became easier to obtain. Undoubtedly, constitutional provisions to deal with cases of inter-republican deadlock provided an incentive to agree. Where the unity of the market, for example, was threatened by the absence of consensus, the Presidency could exercise autonomous legislative powers in the Federal Assembly and the Federal Executive Council could adopt measures binding on its republican counterparts.

The Presidency and the Federal Executive Council, however, were themselves institutions which depended upon inter-republican consensus to act. Improvements in inter-republican decision-making,

probably, owed more to a discreet institutional innovation at the time
of the 1971 Constitutional Amendments. A Co-ordinating Committee, and a number of specialist Sub-Committees, were established
to try and reconcile the conflicting economic interests of the republics
and provinces with the federal government's obligation to guarantee
a unified market. Their existence and role was confirmed by Article
357 of the 1974 Constitution. The President of the Federal Executive
Council chaired the Co-ordinating Committee which was composed
of the Presidents of the republican and provincial Exececutive
Councils. The Sub-Committees were chaired by the responsible
specialist minister from the Federal Executive Council and composed
of his republican and provincial counterparts.

The committees appear to have been fairly successful. Sometimes
agreements emerged only after lengthy and tortuous debate. But
members met in private and the way in which they achieved consensus was never revealed. Once a consensus was reached, perhaps in
the form of an unofficial draft legislative proposal, there was a
powerful incentive for the Federal Executive Council, the Federal
Assembly, and the Presidency to adopt it without substantial
amendment. Such proposals often represented a precariously
balanced Co-ordinating Committee compromise. Any amendment of
substance, therefore, might have jeopardized the proposal in its
entirety.[65]

Self-management, the state and the role of the Party

Despite the important contribution made by the Co-ordinating
Committee to greater coherence in federal decision-making from the
mid-1970s, the most crucial factor was internal change within the
League of Communists. No contrast between the mid-1960s and the
mid-1970s is more sharply etched than that concerning the role of the
League of Communists in the development of economic and social
forces in Yugoslavia. Following the reforms many leading party
ideologues, amongst them Kardelj, believed that the Party would
have to recognize that its views would not always be followed by the
representative organs of self-management.[66] To the extent that
members of those bodies were Party members they were, at any rate
in theory, bound by the doctrine of democratic centralism. But where
the Party was in a minority it should not attempt to interfere with

decision-making processes except by legitimate means of persuasion: that is by argument backed by evidence.

The doctrine of persuasion was a logical outcome of the separation of Party and state following the Sixth Party Congress. But it received particular impetus from the doctrine of 'exclusive' development enshrined in the 1963 Constitution: that is from the notion that distinct areas of social activity should be allowed to plan and operate their affairs free from external bureaucratic interference. The notion was, indeed, central to the entrepreneurial role of the individual enterprise ascribed to it by the economic reforms. Kardelj's views on the matter were also influenced by his concept of the nature of conflict within Yugoslav society at that time. He believed that social tensions were no longer attributable to conflicts of class but to conflicts of interest between different categories of consumer and producer. Indeed the four interest group chambers in the 1963 Federal Assembly, largely his brain-child, were a deliberate attempt to institutionalize and publicize these contradictions.[67]

It seemed but a small step from here to argue that the League had no monopoly power to determine the direction that socialism should take in Yugoslavia. Indeed, the decline of democratic centralism had led members of the same Party to express different views on this matter. Nevertheless, it was a monopoly that, in the last resort, Tito was not prepared to forgo as his reaction to the *Matica Hrvatska* affair indicated. Following the purges, Tito began to denounce the ideological position taken by the Party establishment on the role of the League in relation to self-management and to urge that the League adopt a more positive role in determining the pace and direction of economic and social forces in Yugoslav society. 'No one', he said in his final speech to the Second Annual Conference of the Ninth Party Congress in January 1972, 'mentioned the dictatorship of the proletariat. Many tend somehow to avoid it as they formerly avoided democratic centralism. But the dictatorship of the proletariat exists in our country as indeed it must'.[68]

In subsequent speeches and articles he, and members of the reduced and revitalized Executive Bureau of the League, developed this theme. Their main target was the 'spontaneity' theory of economic and social development which had characterized the decade following the Eighth Party Congress of December 1964. The theory was condemned for having overlooked, or underestimated, the class factor in Yugoslav society. The assumption has been made, wrongly, that

Yugoslav society was already classless and that existing levels of economic progress and social consciousness were adequate to support spontaneous democracy and self-management without the protection of the League. But the supporters of the spontaneity theory, by denying the right of the Party to interfere in self-management, had unwittingly fostered the revival of nationalism and class in the form of a techno-managerial élite controlling the economy and reprivatizing it through group ownership. If the relaxation of democratic central-ism had caused power to accrue to regional Party politicians, the theory of spontaneity had also caused it to pass to technocrats and administrators.[69]

This argument provides the key to the apparently contradictory emphasis on both self-management and a leading role for the Party which characterized the proceedings and resolutions of the Tenth Party Congress. Greater involvement by the Party was regarded as nothing less than a prerequisite of self-management since it was the only guarantee of protection from those who sought to usurp its role.[70] For example, the purges in Serbia were followed by a concerted effort to ensure that BOALs were introduced throughout the social sector. It is worth noting, however, that the purges and the subsequent creation of BOALs might also be said to have been an attempt to fragment powerful economic élites which had, hitherto, posed a threat to the Party. The re-emphasis on self-management at the same time as on Party discipline and control had the effect of dispersing all types of economic and social power other than the Party on as wide a basis as possible.

The difficulty in analyzing the consequences of this new relation-ship lies in the absence of almost any institutional initiatives to integrate the Party organization with self-management institutions. The President of the League was designated by the new Constitution an *ex officio* member of the collective Federal Presidency of Yugo-slavia—which was reduced in membership to nine, one member from each republic and autonomous province and Marshal Tito. 'By making this a constitutional principle', said Kardelj, 'we are, in fact, recognizing a reality in our society, namely that the leading ideo-logical and political role of the League of Communists is an essential factor of stability and cohesion in our society.'[71] Moreover, there were two other important sections of the new Constitution which enhanced the rights of outside bodies, themselves subject to Party discipline, to interfere in the self-management process. Article 104 restored the pre-reform position with respect to the election of industrial unit directors. They were, once again, appointed by the Workers Council from a list proposed to it by a committee containing equal numbers of representatives from the unit itself and from the communal assembly. And Articles 129–31, under the sub-heading Social Protection of Self-Management Rights and Social Property, gave general powers of interference in self-management organs to the assemblies of socio-political communities[72] and to so-called attorneys of self-management.

Article 129 stated the general proposition that the self-management rights of the working people should enjoy special protection. By Article 130:

If . . . self-management relations have become essentially disrupted, if serious harm has been caused to social interests, or if an organization or community does not fulfil its statutorily established obligations, the assembly of the socio-political community shall have the right . . . to dissolve the workers council . . . to nominate provisional bodies having statutorily defined rights and duties and temporarily to restrict the realization of certain self-management rights of the working people.

Moreover, according to Article 131:

Social attorneys of self-management, as independent agents of the social community, shall . . . institute proceedings before the assembly of the socio-political communities, the constitutional courts, or the regular courts for the protection of self-management rights of working people . . . or . . . for the annulment of decisions and other acts which violate self-management and social property.

The social attorney could institute proceedings on his own initiative and all self-management organs 'shall be bound to supply him with data and information needed for the performance of his function'. In short, he was a potent weapon in the hands of a recentralized party.

Tito's new views on discipline in the League are illustrated by the contents of the famous letter to Party organizations from the Executive Bureau, published in October 1972. It stressed the importance of, and placed a new emphasis on, democratic centralism and stated that severe measures would be taken against those who chose to follow their own path. By the middle of 1974 Tito was in charge of a Party organization that was more controlled than at any time since the early 1950s. This was remarkable in view of the confirmation by the 1974 Constitution of the 1971 amendments and the retention by the Tenth Party Congress of the decentralized League of Communist organization laid down by the Ninth. It was achieved, therefore, entirely by a transformed attitude to Party discipline and owed nothing to organizational change. What is equally remarkable, in view of the bitterness engendered by the inter-republican disputes of the early 1970s, is that these arrangements have survived him for as long as they have.

Part Two

CHAPTER 3

THE CAPITAL MARKET

To achieve the degree of structural change required in the industrial sector after 1965, it was essential that the capital market should mobilize and allocate resources efficiently. As Section 1 of this Chapter relates, ideological opposition to the introduction of the equity share placed it at a considerable disadvantage in fulfilling this task. No mechanism existed to shift funds from less to more productive uses and attempts to find a satisfactory surrogate met with only modest success. The absence of profit-related securities also helps, as Section 2 suggests, to explain the poor record of financial savings by households, though other factors were at work here, above all the low level of real interest rates. In most years, the rate of inflation exceeded the strictly controlled nominal rate of interest on time deposits. The low real cost of bank loans, whose nominal rates likewise remained subject to official control, together with the continued unwillingness of communal authorities to liquidate insolvent firms of any size, ensured that the post-reform capital market, like its predecessor, functioned in the context of a chronic excess demand for funds. The consequence, as Section 3 reveals, was that investment resources continued to be allocated between firms upon a discretionary rather than a market basis.

1 The equity problem

Assets and capital

The Constitution of 1946, modelled on the Soviet Constitution of 1936, divided property in Yugoslavia into three categories: state, co-operative, and private. The 1953 Constitution abolished that classification and recognized just two forms, social and non-social. Social property was not an established category in the sense that its predecessors had been. The Constitution itself, moreover, offered no help. It stated that assets designated as social were not capable of being owned in law by any individual or institution, but suggested no alternative scheme. It made no arrangements for vesting them and attached no rights or obligations to them.

The legal vacuum left by the new property classification in respect of industrial assets was filled by the enactment, in December 1953, of the Law on the Management of the Fixed Assets of Firms.[1] The new law circumvented the constitutional prohibition on ownership by granting to enterprises a so-called *jus utendi*, or right of use, over the fixed and working capital assets within their control. In fact, the new right gave enterprises powers over their assets which were almost identical to those enjoyed by Western corporations. They were free to produce, consume, buy and sell an asset. Although all inter-enterprise social sector purchase and sale agreements conveyed, in the subject-matter of the contract, a right of use rather than of ownership, the contractual terms, expressed or implied, were no more restrictive than if a right of ownership had been conveyed. Assets could be exchanged for other assets of any variety, whether tangible or intangible, provided their purchase was consistent with the registered objects of the enterprise in question. In particular, the exchange of tangible assets for cash balances was within the objects of any commercial enterprise. The only restriction on operations was that balance sheet values had to be maintained. As in normal Western company law practice, enterprises were obliged to maintain the value of their fixed assets, when diminished in the course of operations, by charging an appropriate amount for depreciation against current income. Less usual in Western practice was the requirement that reductions in book value caused by the sale of assets be replenished. However, this rule was frequently relaxed, both to help enterprises operating in declining industrial sectors and, in times of recession, to encourage price cutting to off-load hitherto unsaleable inventories of finished goods.

It has been suggested that there is an important distinction between the right to use and full ownership. Commentators have pointed, by way of example, to the inability of the collective to liquidate the enterprise voluntarily and share the fruits of liquidation or to raise capital by issuing shares to outsiders. However, such restrictions, which indubitably exist, do not relate to the relationship between the enterprise and its *assets* but to that between the enterprise and its *collective*—an entirely separate legal relationship which does not invoke the concept of the right to use.

The nature of *this* relationship is defined by the rights of the workers, both individually and collectively, in the annual income and net worth of the enterprise. The 1953 Constitution granted to the collective, indivisibly, the right of ownership (*not* the right of use) in enterprise income.[2] This right, it will be recalled, was subsequently reflected in the surplus value accounting system introduced at the beginning of 1958. But the Constitution granted no rights whatsoever in enterprise net worth. In the context of ideology the logic of this is not hard to discern. *Dohodak*, or income, is defined in Yugoslavia, as we have seen, as Marxian 'surplus value'. Accordingly, the authorities conferred upon the worker collectives full rights of ownership in income to eliminate any element of expropriation. But to have granted a proprietorial right in net worth, whether divisible or indivisible, would have meant reintroducing the legal ownership of share capital—in effect, reinstating an important form of capitalist expropriation. It would have entitled collectives, or individual members, to transfer rights in surplus value to outsiders who had played, or would play, no part in creating it. Once the collective reinvested a portion of distributable income, therefore, it lost all rights in it; although it had a right to decide on the distribution of any future income attributable to those reinvested assets because it had ownership rights in all surplus value.

The collective, therefore, had exclusive managerial rights in the enterprise by virtue of the Law of 28 June 1950 on Workers' Councils and exclusive property rights in its income by virtue of the 1953 Constitution and the subsequent rules on surplus value accounting. The possession of these rights enabled it to play the roles of entrepreneur, worker, manager and non-loan-capital supplier and to appropriate virtually all the returns that normally accrue separately to those who perform these disparate functions. But the collective had no power, as it were, to cash in on these rights. Because it had no property rights in net worth it could not convert them into, or transfer them for, financial capital. It could neither liquidate the enterprise in return for the financial equivalent of its surplus assets, nor could it transfer the enterprise to others in exchange for its value as a going concern. It was, indeed, the absence of rights in net worth which explains the absence of both a voluntary liquidation procedure and a market in equity capital. The collective, *qua* collective, was inseparable from its enterprise save in two sets of circumstances, both of which involved its disappearance. The first was where the collective voted to merge with another enterprise, in which case it became inseparable from the transformed unit; the second was where the enterprise was compulsorily liquidated, in which case any surplus assets reverted to the commune and the members of the collective were dispersed.

The inability of firms to issue their own shares or equity type securities was the reason for the paucity of financial assets in Yugoslavia. The only liability that firms could incur was debt. The only way to acquire extra assets, other than debts owed by other firms, was to plough back income. The system excluded the development not only of primary and secondary share markets but also of financial intermediaries such as mutual funds and investment trusts, which elsewhere invest in shares and whose liabilities provide an assortment of financial assets for investors with differing predilections towards risk and liquidity. The only intermediaries of any consequence in Yugoslavia were banks. The only asset they were entitled to hold, apart from cash, was fixed interest debt; and the only liabilities they were entitled to issue, apart from ownership certificates to member enterprises non-assignable except with the permission of the other members, were deposit accounts.

The absence of the marketable equity share follows, quite logically, from the ideology of self-management. But from the point of view of allocating financial resources in a decentralized environment it was a serious defect.[3] Physical capital and entrepreneurship were earning differential rates of return but the investor was paid a fixed rate of interest because firms and intermediaries were not allowed to create profit denominated liabilities. On the one hand, there was no structure of incentives, represented by a range of marketable assets differentiated according to risk, degree of liquidity and anticipated rate of return, to encourage the financial investor to balance the advantages of liquidity and security against those of a higher rate of return at greater risk. On the other hand, the end user, with expected high marginal productivity, had no means of competing for the extra funds he badly needed by bidding up their price. There was nothing, in effect, on the demand or the supply side to encourage financial capital to flow from low value to high value marginal product employment—to those areas where the return to physical capital and entrepreneurship was at its highest.

Investment partnerships

Considerable attention was paid to the equity problem almost immediately after the reforms, although the concern of the authorities was not to initiate a domestic share market but to attract foreign participation in Yugoslav industrial development on a permanent basis. They believed that the objectives of reform could be achieved only if their industries were consistently able to export to hard currency markets where standards were set by the technology of Western corporations. To meet these constantly changing and increasingly exacting standards it was essential to find a mode of co-operation which gave Yugoslav firms access to the most advanced technologies and know-how. In this respect, the traditional vehicle for technology transfer, the contractual licence involving the exchange of a carefully defined class of information for a fee, had serious deficiencies. The information itself had often become outdated by the time it was put to use. Moreover, undertakings to release details of improvements in a particular technology were of little value when the technology itself had become obsolescent.

In the course of 1966, the authorities formed the view that if Western companies were able to make project investments in either existing or new Yugoslav enterprises, whose financial yield was directly proportional to their profitability, they would be committed to improving the manufacturing efficiencies of their partners throughout the life of those investments. The difficulty was that the absence of ownership rights in net worth prevented enterprises, whether domestic or foreign, from either acquiring a financial interest in an existing enterprise or, indeed, retaining an interest in one they had promoted. Once a new unit was registered as a going concern the promoter was entitled to the repayment of its investment with interest. But there was no question of its retaining any managerial or income distribution rights in its offspring. Article 5 of the Law on Assets of Economic Organization (LAEO)[4] stated that, apart from the collective of the enterprise in question, 'nobody may acquire the right to effect distribution of the income of an economic organization nor any other rights affecting the management of an economic organization by giving assets thereto'. No clearer statement of the consequences of the two exclusive rights of the collective, the right to manage and the right to appropriate surplus value, could be adduced, though the effect of the Article may, equally, be deduced from the absence of property rights in net worth.

A means of circumventing this problem had been devised by the beginning of 1967 and became law in July of that year.[5] It permitted domestic enterprises to contract with each other, or in certain circumstances with a foreign enterprise, to form a business partnership whose assets were vested either in one of the domestic partner enterprises or in a new domestic enterprise established expressly for the purpose of holding and managing the partnership assets.[6] Whether the partnership assets were placed in an existing or a specially promoted enterprise, Article 5 of the LAEO continued to apply. That is to say, the assets of the partnership were vested completely in that enterprise, the management and income distribution rights remained solely with the collective of that enterprise and the rules with regard to its net worth were unaffected.[7] However, the partnership agreement was treated as a contractual liability of the enterprise, to which the partnership assets vested in it were subject.[8] These assets, therefore, had to be deployed by the enterprise in question strictly in accordance with the terms of the agreement. And the 1967 legislation entitled the partners to negotiate terms in that agreement granting them both managerial rights over, and financial rights in the income generated by, those assets. It is a curious fact, therefore, that since 1967, if two or more enterprises agree to pursue a common business objective and pool their resources to invest to that end, they can acquire managerial and financial rights in the completed project which are denied to the single enterprise acting autonomously.

It became the usual practice to constitute partnership assets as a separate accounting unit in one of the domestic partner enterprises. The partner in question simply bound itself contractually to guarantee that the unit carried out the tasks allotted to it under the agreement. But sometimes new enterprises were established to hold and manage partnership assets. Were the normal rules with regard to promoting new enterprises in Yugoslavia to apply, once the project was complete and on stream the partners would automatically lose all management control over, and rights in the income of, the partnership assets, unless they could persuade the new collective to re-adopt the terms of the partnership agreement. A new enterprise had no legal personality, and therefore no contractual capacity, until it was registered as a self-managed enterprise; and then its sole obligation, as we have learned, was to repay its promoter, at a fixed rate of interest, for any money advanced. To get round this awkward corner, the authorities amended the law so as to allow partners establishing enterprises for the sole purpose of vesting joint assets to dissolve those enterprises if they refused, on registration, to bind themselves to the terms of the partnership agreement.[9]

The new legislation imposed relatively few restrictions on the contents of partnership agreements. On management it said that the agreement *may* provide that the contracting parties exercise their rights through a joint body, the Business Board.[10] It was up to the partners to negotiate the composition, powers, functions and procedure of such a body. Normally partners, whatever the relative size of their investments, had an equal share in managing the partnership As to financial arrangements, shares in profit or loss were usually proportionate to the size of asset financing. But the partners could, in principle, adopt some other formula. Special accounting arrangements had to be devised to surmount the problem of defining profit presented by surplus value accounting. Broadly speaking, Western accounting rules were applied with profit calculated net of interest charges, taxes and personal income distributions. Partners were entitled to repayment of their initial capital investment, together with any supplementary contributions or reinvestments, at the end of the life of the partnership which had to be of a fixed duration.[11]

The value of the non-loan investment resources contributed to a partnership by foreign partners could not exceed 49 per cent of the total.[12] Under a conventional foreign investment regime, whose regulations relate to joint stock companies, the limit would have been understandable. There the managerial and financial interests of the foreign investor are directly proportional to the size of its equity investment. But this analogy bore no relevance to the Yugoslav case. In Yugoslavia the foreign investor did not receive an equity share. It simply provided certain funds and negotiated certain contractual rights with respect to those funds. There was no requirement that its managerial or financial entitlements should be strictly proportional to the relative size of its contribution to the value of partnership assets. Indeed with respect to management the usual practice was otherwise. The restriction, therefore, had only cosmetic value.

Foreign partners were excluded from banking, insurance, internal transport, trade, communal and social service activities unless the Federal Executive Council considered that such an involvement would contribute to 'a quick development of the branch of the economy concerned'.[13] Moreover, no agreement involving a foreign participant could take effect until it had been positively vetted and approved by the Federal Secretariat of Economics. The most important ground for refusal was where a partnership agreement 'does not provide for business co-operation aimed at increasing production, productivity and exports, the introduction . . . of modern techniques, technology and organization . . . or if it does not contribute to the advancement of scientific research in a domestic economic organization'.[14] This clause exposed the main motive behind the legislation.

These arrangements were not a satisfactory substitute for equity shares mainly because of the rules concerning assignment. Domestic partners were permitted to assign their contractual rights and obligations to another domestic entity subject to any restrictions laid down in the agreement.[15] Partners normally made conditions with respect to the reputation and financial viability of the prospective assignee and it was usual for the selling partner to grant first refusal rights to the other partners. The position with regard to foreign partners wishing to transfer their contractual interest was more complex.[16] Whether they wished to assign to a foreign or domestic enterprise they had to make a prior offer, in writing, to the domestic enterprise in which the partnership assets were invested. The latter had to accept or refuse the offer within sixty days. Should a foreign partner fail to comply with this requirement, its contractual interest could be compulsorily transferred by the Economic Court. In the case of both domestic and foreign partners, therefore, the restrictions on transferability were such as to inhibit the development of a market in partnership interests.

Securities

The passage of the legislation on investment partnerships provoked a wider ranging debate upon the desirability of allowing enterprises to issue profit-denominated securities. The tone of this debate was sharpened in 1971 when the Law on Securities was passed providing a legislative framework for the issue by firms of both variable interest rate bonds and profit-yielding transferable certificates of partnership assets.[17] According to the new law, enterprises might issue bonds whose yield depended on their profitability.[18] They would have to be redeemable and no management rights would attach to them. However, any firm in which the assets of a joint investment partnership had been placed would be allowed to issue a transferable certificate to any partner up to the value of their capital contribution. Unlike the transferable bond the certificate would carry with it rights to a share in management as well as profits.

The right to a share in management was a vital characteristic attaching to any marketable security in an economic system which had no contractual wage and whose corporate objectives did not necessarily favour the maximization of profit. The holder of a variable return bond, lacking any managerial rights, would be powerless to oppose a decision by the representative organs of the firm in which he invested to pay out exorbitant personal incomes or pursue a costly social welfare investment programme. Nevertheless, the transferable certificates had considerable drawbacks. They could only be transferred to other firms, or business banks, or socio-political communities. Unlike bonds they could not be subscribed by households. Restricting transferability to these categories, therefore, meant that the benefits of social sector productivity would be spread amongst a limited sector of society. Marketing to households would not, in any case, be practical unless the certificates could be subdivided into fractional values because it was rare to have more than two firms in an investment partnership. Investment partnerships were required by law to be of fixed duration and, therefore, like bonds these certificates would be redeemable.

Since the new law was only an enabling statute, considerable controversy ensued within the party circles as to whether this aspect of it should be activated by the issue of detailed decrees. Perhaps the most famous exchange of views occurred in the columns of *Delo* and *Komunist* in the course of 1972 between two leading Slovenes, Kardelj and Kavcic.[19] Kavcic, adopting a practical point of view, argued that large amounts of savings were accumulating in the household sector which were consumed on 'extravagances', such as foreign holidays, for want of a really attractive alternative. He believed that this money could be attracted towards industrial investment if firms could create an appropriate financial liability. 'Instead of going on holiday to the Fiji Islands', he suggested, 'and spending a million there, the person concerned could give that money to an enterprise dealing with capital investment which could give him interest *and perhaps even something extra in addition* depending upon the profitability of the investment concerned'.[20] Kardelj opposed Kavcic on the point of principle. Such a scheme, he asserted, did not fit in with the notion of self-management rights. He regarded individual shareholding, divorced from collective membership, as a form of exploitation of the labour of others. A series of autumn purges in that year which, as we have seen, marked the end of the liberal phase of post-reform development, not only saw the dismissal of Kavcic from office but also marked the end of public debate on the desirability of profit-related securities.

Transferability, strict profitability criteria, property rights on default, managerial rights and long maturities are probably necessary, if not sufficient, requirements for a viable equity-type security in a self-managed economy. Yet some or all of these characteristics would have eroded one or more of the ideological pillars upon which the social sector firm rested, namely, self-management, social property and collective rights in value added. It is true that the 1967 investment partnership legislation granted partners the power to negotiate similar rights in respect of partnership assets. But such rights were acquired by contractual arrangements entered into voluntarily by all parties including the firm in which the assets were to repose. It would have been a different matter altogether if such rights had become incidents of an item of intangible property to be enjoyed by whomsoever happened to own it. Then there would have been no agreement between the collective and the shareholder. Self-management rights and rights to social property and surplus value would have been converted into a financial capital sum to be bought and sold on the market: clear evidence that, once again, labour had become a commodity.

Much of the new law and most of the regulations made under it were concerned with fixed interest bonds. The issue of short- and long-term fixed interest securities by banks on behalf of both socio-political communities and enterprises had been permitted since 1961.[21] The Law of Securities greatly relaxed the conditions under which issues could be made. Bonds could be issued by social sector firms, communities of interest and socio-political communities, though social sector firms were only entitled to make an issue if their financial position met rather stringent criteria.[22] Banks could only issue them in very special circumstances with the permission of the Federal Executive Council. Such circumstances were usually likely to arise in respect of foreign currency issues. For example, in 1975 the National Bank was permitted to float a $50m. issue in foreign markets in its own name in order to replenish foreign exchange reserves. Any resident or non-resident, legal or natural, person could subscribe to any bond issue and could subsequently assign all or part of the bonds purchased to another such person. All bonds had to be redeemable; the ideological difficulties inherent in the perpetual right of a private citizen to income from a social firm were considered insuperable.

The first 'corporate' bond issue was made by *Cvrena Zastava* in 1969 when subscriptions were invited for a $78m. loan at 6 per cent, redeemable after four years. The first foreign exchange issue was by IMT, the tractor factory. They invited subscriptions in Deutsch-marks for bonds to the value of 15m. dinars, redeemable in three years with a yield of 10 per cent. So far, however, bond issues by firms have been few and far between and for modest amounts. Perhaps the biggest impediment to the development of an orderly new issues market in such securities was the absence of a secondary market which would have ensured immediate liquidity to the financial investor. Such a market could have developed if banks had been prepared to buy as well as sell bonds. But they were not willing to make a market in industrial bonds in the absence of a rediscounting guarantee from the National Bank. Moreover, as underwriters, they were unwilling to risk large or frequent new issues. In practice, to assist in marketing these bonds to the general public, certain 'sweeteners' were often offered, such as price concessions on the products of the issuing firm or concessionary credits. For example, IMT guaranteed to deliver its tractors on time to bond purchasers and its issue was heavily subscribed at least partly because of that undertaking!

Socio-political communities have issued bonds far more often and to a much greater value than firms, mainly to meet fiscal liabilities of various kinds. The decentralization of fiscal powers to the republics brought about by the constitutional changes of the early 1970s made the federal budget heavily dependent upon compensatory finance from the republics. The effect of this, because the compensation forthcoming was often insufficient, was to increase the size of the fiscal gap that had to be filled by financial means. Because of the frequency and size of these bond issues the household investor was not relied upon as a subscriber of any importance. The issues were placed, almost exclusively, with banks and social sector firms. Together with the issues of certificates of deposit and treasury bills, the bonds of socio-political communities are more relevant to the management of monetary policy than to the allocation of capital resources and are, therefore, discussed in Chapter 6.[23]

2   The structure of savings

The reform measures of the mid-1960s had a marked effect upon the distribution of National Income in Yugoslavia, reducing the share of the socio-political communities and increasing that of households and firms. This has had important implications for the sectoral structure of savings.

Socio-political communities

The decline in the savings of the socio-political communities as a proportion of total domestic savings, as Annex 1 demonstrates, reflected the declining role of social investment funds in the industrial investment process. The decline was not as rapid as the reformers had intended because, as we have already seen, the funds were reconstituted in 1966. Annual social investment fund savings equalled the increase in the net value of all reconstituted funds and earmarked deposit accounts during any year. Nevertheless, the absolute and relative contribution of these post-reform investment funds and accounts to total domestic savings was much more modest than that of their predecessors. Apart from the FAD, and to a modest degree until 1971 the FFFI, none of them was replenished from external fiscal sources. They relied entirely on the interest and principal repayments from past loans and deposits. As Annex 2 demonstrates, their share in total domestic *financial* savings was, at first, of greater significance since, unlike the household sector, they invested their entire savings in financial assets. But from 1971, the absolute decline in the value of their savings, together with the increased propensity of the household sector to invest in financial assets, led to a sharp decline in their contribution to total financial savings as well.

Firms

Interest in the savings performance of the firm has centred around the extent to which collectives, freed from pre-reform budgetary constraints, have been prepared to plough back resources under their control rather than pay them out in the form of personal incomes.

Annex 3, illustrating the ratio of Savings to Distributable Resources, demonstrates a declining propensity to save in the late 1960s followed by a partial improvement and levelling off in the early 1970s. Because of the introduction of social agreements in the course of 1972 the pre- and post-agreement periods are considered separately.

1965–1971. During this period the discretion enjoyed by collectives in distributing the financial resources under their control was legally unfettered. The figures do show a decline in the propensity of collectives to save out of available resources of just over 20 per cent between 1965 and 1970. There was an apparent recovery in 1971 but this is, at least in part, misleading. The replacement of the tax on the Business Fund by a compulsory loan to finance the FAD simply shifted these involuntary savings from the socio-political to the firm sector. The obvious inference to be drawn is a tendency amongst collectives to vote increasing proportions of the financial resources available to them for distribution to personal incomes. An attractive explanation would be to say that the propensity to save of the average worker is rather lower than that of the commune. However, over the same period, as Annex 4 reveals, households' propensity to save out of disposable income increased by over 40 per cent from 9.5 to 13.7 per cent. This phenomenon has excited considerable comment in Western academic circles and has been the subject of some pioneering work by Svetosvar Pejovich and Eirik Furubotn.[24] In a series of articles they have sought to demonstrate that the decline in the propensity to save by firms is explained by the peculiar nature of the relationship of the collective to the net worth of the firm.

One of the clearest statements of their thesis is contained in Pejovich's article, 'The Firm, Monetary Policy and Property Rights in a Planned Economy'.[25] He assumes that members of a collective have two alternatives with respect to that part of their income that they do not wish to consume. Either they allocate it to the Personal Income Fund and then lodge it in a bank time-deposit account. Or they plough it back into the firm to invest in income earning assets. In fact, the assumption is a simplification of reality because another option open to them would be to allocate the money to the Personal Income Fund and invest it in a small private sector venture, such as a taxi service, artisan's shop, restaurant or small hotel; but it serves well enough for purposes of illustration. Since members have full property rights in Net Income but none in net worth, once income is ploughed back into the firm and becomes part of its assets it cannot be reappropriated. The benefits members expect to derive from reinvestment, therefore, are limited to the enjoyment of a share in the extra income directly generated by such reinvestment while they remain members of the firm. But they lose all entitlement to the principal sum ploughed back. This makes it rather like an investment in an annuity for a fixed number of years with no recovery of capital. By contrast, members retain a right to their share of the principal sum appropriated to the Personal Income Fund and subsequently placed in a deposit account, as well as to the interest that it earns.

It follows from this that the rates of return on business assets required to make reinvestment at least as attractive an alternative as a time deposit will be far higher than the rate of interest on that deposit. How much higher will depend upon the average length of time that members expect to remain in employment with the firm—their investment time horizon. To take an extreme example, a sum of 100 dinars appropriated to the Personal Income Fund and invested in a savings account for one year at 5 per cent would require an annual rate of return on business assets of 105 per cent or more for an equivalent time horizon before preferences would shift to reinvest-ment, excluding considerations of risk. As the time horizon of the collective lengthens the required rate of return falls. For time horizons of five, ten, and fifteen years the rates of return on business assets that would make reinvestment at least as attractive as a 5 per cent per annum savings deposit would be 23, 13, and 9 per cent respectively. It is only at a time horizon of infinity that the required rate of return on non-owned business assets will equal the rate of return on savings deposits.[26]

The implication of this analysis is that self-managed firms will attempt to avoid self-financed investment unless either the expected rates of return on business assets are very high or the collective time horizon is very long. There are, in fact, grounds for believing that the average post-reform rate of return on business assets was fairly high. But rates, of course, varied from sector to sector.[27] As to the likely length of collective time horizons, commentators have taken differing views. Jan Vanek has argued that the time horizons of members in the average Yugoslav firm may have been long.[28] He believes that inter-firm labour mobility in Yugoslavia was low because of the impossibility of firing for other than disciplinary reasons, chronic unemployment and the social dimension of collective membership which often involved important benefits in terms of housing and education.

However, others are sceptical about this view and it is certainly a difficult issue upon which to generalize. Clearly, an important factor will be the age structure of the collective. For example, workers nearing retirement age would have been likely to prefer short-run personal income maximization. First of all they would have retired before any investment in the firm had fully paid itself off. Second, the fact that their state pension was based upon the average level of their personal income during the years immediately preceding retirement, meant that their pensions would have been lower to the extent that funds were diverted from personal income distribution to investment. The young appear to have been the most concerned with job security and greater equality of income distribution.[29] The first of these objectives, at least, was consistent with a modicum of reinvestment to retain competitiveness in the market. But empirical studies on this age group demonstrated a preference for private over collective saving.[30] The group most likely to have supported a reinvestment policy appears to be the more educated and skilled members in the middle stages of their careers. An important factor in predicting the savings behaviour of a particular collective, therefore, is likely to be the relative size and influence of each of these groups within it. The influence of the administration would also have to be taken into account. In short, the evidence on time horizons is inconclusive.

Furubotn and Pejovich, who take the view that the time horizon of the average collective is fairly short, advocate a change in the structure of property rights.[31] If workers were granted a transferable right of ownership in the net worth of firms the decision to plough back would be a simple matter of comparing the rates of return on business assets and time deposits, both adjusted for risk and liquidity. Such a step, given the strength of the ideological commitment to the indivisibility and non-transferability of net worth, was never a feasible option. But the solution to the problem, where it can be shown to exist, need not be so drastic. Some of the firms that did perceive the loss of right to the principal value of reinvested capital as a barrier to savings devised a simple technique for getting around the problem.[32] This involved distributing the sum to be reinvested as personal income to members and then borrowing it back from them, to be repaid either upon departure or as a lump-sum payment upon retirement. This was a simple contractual method for getting around the property rights dilemma.

While recognizing the likelihood of its existence, the magnitude of the Furubotn–Pejovich effect upon the savings performance of collectives remains, at any rate for the time being, a matter for speculation. Moreover, an important offsetting consideration was the need to provide a proportion of own funds as a means of raising bank loans for new investment. To the extent that income was distributed rather than ploughed back, firms had to borrow to invest. But, according to investment bank rules, borrowers had to finance a certain proportion of new assets from their own funds.[33] Therefore, a degree of self-financing was unavoidable. The higher the investment requirement the higher the self-financing requirement. Each dinar ploughed back, therefore, increased the ability of a firm to borrow at interest rates which may have been lower than the marginal productivity of capital.

A further offsetting factor, whose incidence is extremely difficult to measure, was the social pressure on firms, particularly the more prosperous ones, to curb their personal income distribution in the interests of both social justice and economic stability. Article 22 of the Law on the Assets of Economic Organizations stated that a Workers' Council was bound to consider, though not to comply with, a recommendation made to it by its communal assembly on income distribution. It was, in a sense, the failure of such social pressure to have sufficient impact on the behaviour of firms which led to its formalization in the early 1970s, in the form of social agreements.

Post-1971. In the course of 1972 social agreements affecting the income distribution policies of firms were introduced in all six republics. Their purpose was to achieve both greater macro-economic stability and a more just distribution of personal incomes with respect both to inter-firm differentials, dealt with here, and inter-worker differentials, dealt with in Chapter 4.[34] Their stabilization target was at the same time to reduce the 'cost push' effect of excessive personal income distribution and to alleviate pressures in the credit market by substituting self-finance for borrowed funds; these issues are touched on in Chapter 6.[35] Although techniques varied from republic to republic the social agreements all had the common objective of preventing excessive personal income distributions. Their effect was to require any firm whose distributable income per worker exceeded a certain norm to reinvest a progressively larger proportion of it.

The first Croatian Agreement, concluded in April 1972, may serve as a brief example.[36] Since the skill composition of each collective in the region differed, a common denominator had to be found to

measure the size of the labour force in each firm—the so-called
standardized work-force. This was a function of the number of
workers in the collective in question and the distribution of work skills
between them. Every worker in the collective was placed into one of
ten skill categories, each of which was awarded a coefficient or multi-
plier. These coefficients ranged from 2.533 for a D.Sc. to 0.667 for an
unskilled worker. Each of the ten coefficients was then multiplied by
the number of members in the collective that fell into its skill category
and the products summed to give the size of the standardized work-
force for the firm in question. The Agreement then laid down the
maximum levels of Gross Personal Income per standardized worker
(P/W) which a firm may distribute for any given level of Net Income
per standardized worker (Y/W). It took as base indices of 100 the
republican averages for each of these ratios. Thus for any given Y/W,
expressed as an index of its republican average, the agreement permitted the distribution of a maximum P/W, expressed as an index of
its republican average.

The annual republican social agreements on personal incomes
were made within the framework of the macro-economic targets set
out in the annual Economic Resolution. Following the normal pattern, there were about 240 operational agreements, comprising some
30 sectoral agreements in each one of the eight republics and provinces. Consequently, distribution ratios differed between republics,
branches and, indeed, firms within branches. A personal incomes
'floor' was provided by a guaranteed minimum net sum in each
republic. The general rule was that firms with above average personal
incomes per worker should allocate a higher proportion of distributable income to savings. This rule appears to have exacerbated the
inherent tendencies in the Yugoslav economy to both cost push
inflation[37] and excessive capital deepening.[38]

The statistical evidence, set out in Annex 3, suggests that the
agreements did not have a clearly identifiable impact upon the long
term aggregate savings behaviour of the corporate sector. The
explanation for this appears to lie in their increasing use by the
authorities for short term macro-economic purposes. In particular,
by seeking to influence the relative rates of increase in personal
incomes and prices, the authorities sought to regulate the level of real
wages. The annual target for changes in *real* wages came to assume a
central role in short-term demand management, especially in the

drive to control the level of consumer expenditure and the proportion of fixed investment financed out of own resources.[39]

Households and private producers

In spite of the poor opportunities open to prospective financial investors and the existence of a comprehensive social insurance system, the savings of households and private producers increased as a proportion of their disposable income from 9.5 per cent in 1965 to 18.1 per cent in 1981.[40] The increased share in Social Product of the disposable income of social and private sector workers explains part of the improvement. In the social sector, this resulted from the larger share of corporate value added in total Social Product and the propensity of collectives to pay out a bigger proportion of distributable resources in personal incomes. In the private sector, the post-reform rise in the prices of agricultural products and the development of private activity in the housing and tertiary sector were mainly responsible. Workers' remittances from abroad enhanced the incomes of households in both the social and the private sector. The positive attractions of real investment in private housing and financial investment in foreign exchange accounts were also important factors. Despite the reversal of the tendency of the disposable income of households to increase as a proportion of Social Product after the early 1970s, and the reintroduction of social control over the distribution of personal incomes in social sector firms, household savings continued to rise as a proportion of disposable incomes because, it seems, of the allure of the substantial net real returns on investment in foreign exchange accounts.

Whereas total household savings increased fairly steadily as a proportion of household income, the progress of the financial savings of households as a proportion of total household savings was much more uneven. Recession, and the more liberal attitude adopted towards private sector investment immediately after the reform measures, may explain the rather poor pattern of the late 1960s. The increasing attractions of foreign exchange deposits account for most of the rather better picture in the 1970s. But the overall performance was not particularly impressive.[41] As we have already noted, the decentralization of economic activity following reform produced a massive increase in the volume of savings by households but did not provide a corresponding range of financial assets and intermediary institutions to exploit them. Savers who preferred a high risk rate of return investment option were probably inclined to opt for the private sector.

Financial investments by households were made almost exclusively in currency or bank deposits. The pattern of investment is set out in Annex 5. Currency holdings were mainly determined by the volume of day to day household financial transactions and have been a fairly stable function of the variable. Sight deposits, which include time deposits for less than twelve months, proved a fairly attractive form of savings since these were quickly realizable and earned interest. They were also the usual vehicle for making the cash down-payment required to obtain consumer credit and, more generally, a means of relatively short-term accumulation for the purchase of consumer durables or holidays. Time deposits of twelve months and over proved an unattractive medium of investment. Their extra yield was insufficient to compensate for their lack of liquidity. The clearest trend in financial investment derives from the growth in value of foreign exchange deposits. This phenomenon is chiefly explained by the substantial export of labour during the post-reform years and the corresponding remittances of foreign currency earnings. The increase in the share of foreign exchange deposits in total financial investment was particularly marked in 1965, 1971 and 1979 because of the dinar devaluations in those years. Foreign-exchange-denominated deposits provided a satisfactory hedge against the danger of currency depreciation and offered a way of evading the restrictive system of foreign exchange controls.

It is extremely hard to predict what the effect would have been on the volume and profile of financial investment had the real rate of return on bank deposits been higher. The rate of return on bank sight and time deposits has been invariably negative, the combined result of high rates of inflation in the cost of living index[42] on the one hand and interest rate controls on the other. Until the end of 1971, legal ceilings on interest rates were imposed by the federal authorities. Since the passage of the Law on Credit and Banking Operations during that year,[43] the role of the federal authorities was limited to specifying the categories of deposit that banks or savings institutions could accept from individuals. Levels of interest rates and the conditions upon which deposits were made were, henceforth, determined by inter-bank agreements concluded under the auspices of the Yugoslav Bank Association and similar, conceptually, to inter-firm self-management agreements. What is striking about the statistics over the next decade is the relatively modest rise of interest rates following the removal of federally established ceilings. The rate of interest on dinar time deposits of households was 5 per cent from 1963 to 1968, 7.5 per cent from 1969 to 1972 and 10 per cent from 1973 to 1981. These rates, given the prevailing levels of inflation and demand for capital, seemed absurdly low.

There are a number of plausible reasons for such behaviour. One of these is that commercial banking policy was heavily influenced by the needs of founding members, who were at the same time their own banks' main customers. They stood to gain more from low interest rates as borrowers than from high interest rates as founders. Since it was in their interest to keep borrowing rates low, deposit rates had to be proprotionately lower. Indeed, the co-operative flavour of the banks' institutional structure made them behave more like service than profit-maximizing institutions—despite the criticism of financial capitalism that was levelled at them in the late 1960s and early 1970s. Of course, their position would have become more complicated if it could have been established that the interest elasticity of financial savings was high. Then the advantages that might have accrued from the increased volume of resources mobilized might have offset the costs that would result from an increase in the borrowing rate. Moreover, a greater volume of business and, perhaps, better margins could have meant more profitable banks, though higher interest rates could have brought with them lower demand for loans. There were also ideological objections to profits accruing to so-called non-productive organizations which strongly influenced the official approach to increased rates. And many firms facing losses or doing badly would have been faced with a crippling increase in their contract liabilities following any substantial rise in the nominal rate of interest. This would have meant, unless there was a corresponding change in the official attitude to bankruptcy proceedings, that they would have had to have been bailed out by the selfsame banks and the socio-political communities.

The 1981 Economic Resolution stated that interest rates should be raised to enable them to perform a more active role in the management of the economy.[44] At the beginning of 1982, there was the first move to put this new approach to work. In February, the discount rate of the National Bank was raised from 6 per cent to 12 per cent. The time deposit rate for household savers became 13 per cent.

Further increases took place at the beginning of 1983. The Central Bank discount rate became 22 per cent, the time deposit rates for households 28 per cent, and the long term commercial loan rate 32 per cent. These rates were maximum rates and they only applied to new contracts. Moreover, the rate of increase in the cost of living index continued to exceed the time deposit rate. Nevertheless, the increases suggest a new approach to interest rate policy. If this is so it will have far reaching implications, not only for the propensity to invest in dinar time deposits but also for the level of demand for, and the allocation of, capital resources, and for short term macro-economic demand management.

3   The allocation of resources

The reformers envisaged three sources of finance from which funds would be provided for social sector fixed investment. First, firms would plough back a portion of their Net Income and depreciation allowances. Their propensity to do so has just been discussed. Second, the banking system, redesigned by the 1965 Bank and Credit Act, would intermediate resources from low to high value uses. In both these cases it was expected that resources would be allocated as between competing claimants on the basis of strict market criteria. The objective test of capital productivity was modified by a third source of funds which was fiscal. This source was intended to appropriate resources for designated less developed areas according to profitability criteria which would reflect social as well as private costs and benefits. The effect of the reform measures, as Annex 6 indicates, was to raise the contribution of banks from less than 5 per cent to nearly 50 per cent of fixed asset financing by the beginning of the 1980s; and to reduce that of socio-political funds from 60 per cent to 2 per cent over the same period. The corresponding contribution of self-financing increased from about 35 per cent to 50 per cent. However, the inter-industry patterns of fixed investment financing showed quite large deviations from the average.[45]

Bank lending

Since the 1965 reforms, business banks conducted their lending operations in the context of a chronic state of excess demand for investment funds. Policy emphasis upon industrial modernization, the readjustment required to respond to a new pattern of incentives and, as we shall see in Chapter 4, the apparent predilection of the self-managed firm for capital-intensive modes of production, injected into the system a strong built-in demand for capital. Low or negative real interest rates on commercial loans,[46] aligned with the continued unwillingness of the communal authorities to liquidate insolvent firms of any size, only served to exacerbate these pressures. Moreover, the interest charge on the Business Fund was abolished at the end of 1970.[47] It followed that, just as in the pre-reform years, the marginal productivity of capital continued to exceed the cost of money and discretionary rather than market conditions determined the allocation of investment resources by banks as between competing bidders. At least three biases were discernible in the exercise of this discretion: the favouring of projects and support for ailing firms in their own territory, the preference for lending to 'basic' industries and the aversion towards risk.

The reforms failed to eradicate particularism. This failure undermined the official policy of industrial integration upon which the reformers placed so much emphasis. A few sectors, such as the automobile industry, were restructured, usually with the assistance of foreign capital and expertise. But, generally speaking, the pre-reform problem industries remained fairly static. One of the main reasons for this was that banks tended to support the existing industrial establishment in their own republics or communes—either by positively favouring local investment projects or by acquiescing in open-ended financial help to local firms when they were in financial difficulties. In a speech to representatives of the banking community in June 1969, President Tito stated:[48]

We are now only at the beginning of a process of integration which is mainly developing within republican boundaries. In the future it will be necessary to stipulate inter-republican integration. Circulation of capital should develop freely on the whole territory of Yugoslavia. There should exist no boundaries and capital must smash them away . . . Banks must assess more realistically the figures and data contained in investment programmes, because they are in a position to prevent the construction of parallel capacities, even at the price of encountering unpleasant arguments because of that. There should be an understanding of the need for the modernizing of our industry because without it we shall very soon find ourselves in a difficult situation.

He went on to give examples of industries such as steel, oil and chemicals where inter-republican co-operation was most needed.

One of the reasons for the particularist flavour of bank lending, as Annex 7 suggests, was the high proportion of total bank deposits which derived from the assets of former social investment funds—the so-called Earmarked Deposits. These constituted a substantial part of the long-term resources of business banks until the mid 1970s.[49] Each depositing commune or republic almost invariably required that its share of earmarked resources be re-lent within its own territory. Moreover, unlike the disposition of official resources before the reform, the placement of these funds was not subject to the discipline of even a regional plan. In addition, as indicated in the previous section, banks met with very modest success in attracting long-term domestic currency time deposits; and a part of those that they did attract were, in reality, obligatory down-payments in respect of loan facilities. However, even the untied resources tended to be allocated territorially. The explanation for this has probably much to do with the institutional structure of the banks themselves. Founder firms who were usually from the same republic, and sometimes from the same commune, were able to have first call on available resources leaving the remaining applicants to forage for what they could. Doubtless too, banks officials were encouraged by republican officials to pursue republican interests, a practice, as we have seen, which was roundly condemned in the course of the 1972 purges.

The impact of these tendencies would not have been so severe were the major banks willing to co-operate with each other on an inter-republican basis. Unhappily, they were not. A good example of this concerned the negotiations over the financing of a proposed aluminium complex in Bosnia, sponsored by *Energoinvest*, with potential Western partners.[50] The project had excellent foreign exchange earning prospects and financing its foreign exchange costs presented no problems. The difficulty was to find enough support from domestic banking sources to cover its domestic costs. The modest resources of the Bosnian banks and extra-budgetary funds were unequal to defraying a sum which was well in excess of $US100m. Unfortunately, there was insufficient support from the bigger domestic banks in the Northern republics to put together an inter-republican domestic financing package even though the project was considered to be of vital importance to the economic future of the country. At one stage the raising of a foreign loan to meet about $US40m. of the domestic financing gap was seriously considered—a step which would have reduced the value of the project's foreign exchange earning power substantially. Finally, the project got under way with the help of Soviet financing.

The second bias in lending policy was sectoral rather than regional. The continued influence of the socio-political communities ensured that particular industrial sectors or categories of firms were favoured at the expense of others. It was, for example, established federal policy to grant special treatment to 'basic' industrial sectors such as steel and chemicals. And, frequently, firms in these sectors appropriated far more resources than even the special concessions allowed because their financial situation was weak and the authorities felt obliged to support them.[51]

One other discernible bias in the behaviour of business banks was an aversion to risk. Their concern in making loans appears to have been much more to do with security than with profitability and, indeed, this is hardly surprising. Banks were required to fulfil both a commercial banking and a venture capital function yet they were restricted to investing in one kind of financial asset, the fixed interest loan. They had, therefore, no market incentive to channel their resources towards firms offering the prospect of a high return on capital. As with the household investor, there was no system of incentives to shift bank resources from low to high value uses. If a risk factor is introduced on top of the uniform rate of return then it is predictable that the banks will prefer the certainty of a modest rate of return to the chance of one. In the absence of differential rates of return to take account of risk, the rational bank is likely to deploy its resources in inverse proportion to the degree of risk. This was, indeed, a further reason why banks liked to place their funds in projects favoured by socio-political communities. Official participation was as good a security as they were ever likely to get for their investment in circumstances where they were never allowed to realize their security in liquidation as unsecured creditors.

From 1976, banks were subject to the new legislation on priority project financing.[52] About 60 per cent of planned production between 1976 and 1980 fell within its terms. The distinction between priority and non-priority projects introduced a fresh distortion into the Yugoslav capital market. Irrespective of whether a social agreement had been concluded with respect to a non-priority sector, it was a residual claimant on bank resources. Moreover, a portion of these residual resources was already earmarked to complete projects that had been begun before 1976. Banks were also subjected to constant pressure to make more funds available for so-called 'non-productive' uses, such as increasing the resources available to the Collective Consumption Funds of firms for housing and other social schemes. The pre-emption of residual resources for non-productive purposes caused increasing concern to the authorities who introduced measures to control it. Despite the obligatory nature of the rules with respect to priority project financing, it is interesting to note that there were considerable shortfalls in certain sectors—notably, transport, catering, oil, basic chemicals, gas, certain minerals, food processing and tourism.[53] Equally, some sectors—steel, non-ferrous metals, coal and machine tools—grew faster than planned. A contributing factor here was probably the relative availability of supporting foreign financing.

Trade credit

The state of excess demand in the capital market meant that the supply of net financial resources to firms was insufficient to meet the demand. One of the ways that firms attempted to overcome this state of affairs was to try and appropriate financial resources from each other. The medium chosen for this exercise was commercial credit. Annex 8 illustrates the importance of trade credit as a source of borrowed finance to firms. However, the asset and liability entries for direct credits in the social sector firms' accounts almost cancel each other out. As Annex 8 indicates, investment in trade credits was as heavy as borrowing by means of them.

Not all the blame should be laid at the door of excess demand.[54] Some commentators have placed part of the responsibility on the restrictive rules placed upon the deployment of cash resources by firms. Indeed, J. L. Rodic argues that this factor is the single most important cause of the excessive development of trade credits.[55] The requirement that reserve funds be held in cash, the need for cash deposits to obtain investment credits and the rule that to obtain most foreign credits an equivalent dinar sum had to be deposited for a period prior to receiving them, are some of the examples he gives of the ways in which cash resources were eaten up to no productive purpose. The growing practice of forcing firms to subscribe to the bond issues of socio-political communities, discussed in Chapter 6,[56] is a further example of the way in which cash resources were being siphoned away from productive use.

The disproportionate use of trade credit is usually referred to in the literature as the 'illiquidity' problem because it involved the accumulation of credit obligations to a value which exceeded the cash generated by business operations to pay them off within the period that they became due. Illiquidity has had at least two adverse consequences for the Yugoslav economy. First, it seriously undermined the application of monetary controls upon which the success of stabilization policy so heavily depended. The serious bouts of illiquidity in the mid-1950s, early 1960s, late 1960s, early 1970s, mid 1970s, and early 1980s all came in the wake of restrictive monetary policy, offsetting it by the compensating expansion of non-bank indebtedness. This aspect of the problem is discussed in Chapter 6.[57] Second, to the extent that less productive firms were able to appropriate resources from more productive firms through this medium, it was a cause of resource misallocation. As one correspondent put it, 'The poor collectives exploit the good ones which, therefore, have a large part of their working capital frozen in the form of claims on insolvent debtors'.[58]

The first illiquidity crisis in the post-reform period occurred between the second half of 1966 and the first half of 1968, at a time of severely restrictive monetary policy. During this period, enterprises still earned income on a cash, or receipts and payments, basis. If an enterprise had not received a cash payment for an invoiced sale it had not made a sale for purposes of its income statement. Thus, to the extent that sales were invoiced but not paid, value had not been realized and the amount available for distribution was reduced accordingly. Equally, until it had paid cash for its purchases it had not incurred an expense for income statement purposes. Since the accounting rules stated that personal income could only be met out of income realized on a cash basis in the current year of operation, firms were inclined to delay paying for their purchase of materials and components from other firms so as to maximize their cash resources. There was a strong disinclination, therefore, amongst sector enterprises to pay off their trade debts. Early in 1968 the situation began to ease following a reversal of monetary policy made possible by an improving macro-economic picture.

In 1969 an important accounting reform converted the assessment of Realized Income from a cash to an accrual basis. Annual sales were, thereafter, the sales invoiced during the year in question, irrespective of whether cash was actually received during that year. Cost of sales was charged on a corresponding basis. Realizing income on an accrual basis meant that meeting its trade debts did not affect the level of Realized Income of a firm, which was now determined by the dates of invoicing. The capacity to pay personal incomes, therefore, no longer depended upon the actual payments and receipts of cash. Accordingly, it was hoped that firms would no longer delay payment to other firms on the grounds that it would impair their ability to make personal income payments.

A restrictive monetary policy was reintroduced in 1970 and was followed by a worsening in the liquidity position of firms. As a result of the accounting changes, firms had the legal capacity to meet their contractual obligations; but they were frequently unable to obtain the cash to defray them. The problem was not lack of income but lack of bank credit to anticipate its availability in cash. Moreover, the new accounting system was being abused. Many firms were boosting the size of their Realized Income and, therefore, their borrowing power, by selling on very generous credit terms or failing to write down manifestly bad debts.[59] The average delay between sale and payment had, in fact, increased steadily since the introduction of the new cccounting arrangements, being 68 days in 1968, 76 in 1969, 82 in 1970, and 104 in 1971.[60] They were also reluctant to write down the value of unsaleable finished product inventory. They were living, in short, off what Finance Minister Smole once called 'fictitious income'.[61] The immediate reaction to the new crisis was to order multilateral debt clearing followed by blocking the accounts of net debtors.[62] However, recognizing the inadequate impact of these measures in the past, the authorities devised a more sophisticated approach to the problem. This new approach was reflected in the Law on the Social Accounting Service which was passed in August 1972 and which came into force on 1 January 1973.[63] Its purpose was to provide a special regime for illiquid firms which would be a surrogate for the Western remedy of liquidation, having its disciplinary effects yet avoiding its adverse social consequences.

Firms with net outstanding debts after clearing were obliged to issue acceptance certificates with limited maturities. Stiffer Reserve Fund requirements were demanded of such firms and the additional resources generated had to be applied to meeting the remaining debts. A most unpopular stipulation was that which compelled firms in default on accounts payable to limit their appropriations to personal incomes to 90 per cent of the 1971 average from 1 July 1972. Though this provision, unlike the others, was supposed to come into force in August 1972 it was delayed until 1 January 1973, largely because of the strength of the opposition shown to it by the Trades Union Congress.[64] Almost a year later, in December 1973, an even more stringent law was passed in respect of personal incomes, stating that debts to other firms must take priority over all other debts.[65] Hitherto, firms were required first to meet fiscal obligations, next personal incomes to a certain level, and only then debts on trade credit and bank loans. The old rule favoured greatly the chronic loss-maker because it rarely had sufficient funds to meet its accounts payable. Bank credit was usually exhausted by paying taxes, import duties and personal incomes.

The threat of new measures had a salutary effect upon the levels of trade credit in the second half of 1972, as Annex 8 reveals. So much so that it accounted for only 3 per cent of the borrowed resources of firms in 1972. However, it increased to 20 per cent of such resources in 1973 and by 1974 it had reverted to 1971 levels. The expansion on this occasion was accompanied by an unprecedented burst of stock accumulation amounting, in value, to about 50 per cent of fixed investment. There was now an acute awareness that far too high a proportion of income realized on the accrual basis derived from bad debts and unsaleable stocks.[66] It meant also that, because the level of Realized Income was exaggerated, so were fiscal liabilities whose excess payment proved a further drain on liquidity.

As early as 1971, the Federal Secretariat for Finance had produced a report blaming these factors for a major part of the illiquidity problem.[67] It recommended that every outstanding debt should have its book value reduced by 25 per cent for each ninety days that it was overdue; and that stocks should be valued at market price whenever it was lower than cost. Part of one of these recommendations was incorporated in the January 1973 measures.[68] It required that 25 per cent of the value of net receivables outstanding beyond ninety days be treated as a cost item in income statements. This was intended to make creditors more assiduous in collecting their debts. Many creditors, however, continued to believe that such measures were fruitless since they themselves had few sanctions in the event of non-compliance.[69] Perhaps the best was the threat to curtail essential supplies. For example, in the middle of 1971 INA, which was owed about 900m. dinars, threatened to stop fuel deliveries to delinquent firms such as *Electroprivreda* of Zagreb, whose particular debt exceeded 16m. dinars.[70] The Serbian power-generating corporation actually cut the supply of electricity to a debtor in order to collect an account receivable.

In January 1975 a more radical approach was adopted in the shape of a new accounting law which became fully operational in April 1976.[71] Three items were of particular significance. First, fixed assets were to be revalued at the end of each financial year if their value had grown by more than 10 per cent in the course of that year; and depreciation allowances had to be based upon these revaluations. Second, inventory appreciation was no longer treated as income available for distribution to personal income. Third, by stipulating that the income of a firm should be realized on the basis of goods sold and paid for, not goods sold and invoiced, the new law appeared to revert to the pre-1969 accounting system. At the time of its publication a debate ensued in order to determine what the words 'paid for' should, in practice, mean. The industrial lobby pressed hard for an invoice system with a thirty-day limit, but the authorities insisted on an upper limit of fifteen days, which was the definition of 'paid for' ultimately adopted. Inter-enterprise trade financed by a bank guarantee, irrevocable letter of credit or bill of exchange was not affected by this stipulation.

There was a severe contraction in the extension of inter-firm trade credit as a result of these measures. Indeed, so severe that the authorities permitted money supply to expand more rapidly than they had originally intended to compensate for the adverse effects on corporate liquidity. From the middle of 1978, however, when the National Bank reverted to a restrictive monetary policy to try and contain excess demand, inter-firm credits began to grow again. From 1979 to 1982, bank credit remained tight and real demand for consumption and investment goods fell. Yet, during these years, inter-firm credit accelerated sharply, helping to accommodate a high rate of inflation and an increase in nominal social product well above the increase in money supply. Once again, the absence of proper market disciplines proved fatal to efforts to restrict its growth.

The problem of illiquidity should be distinguished from the problem of insolvent or loss-making firms. The measures to control the excessive use of trade credit sought to distinguish net creditors from net debtors and impose sanctions on the latter to put their house in order. Firms who were unable to do so within a reasonable period, despite limits placed upon personal income distribution, were chronic debtors and therefore consistently eroding their asset position. Such

firms were traditionally subjected to account blocking. But the usefulness of this remedy was questioned in the early 1970s and other
solutions mooted. The issue of loss-making firms is discussed in
Chapter 5.[72]

Investment partnerships[73]

The main purpose of the investment partnership was to involve
foreign corporations in the industrial development of Yugoslavia.[74]
By 1980, approaching two hundred such ventures had been concluded. The foreign partners' capital contributions were modest and
almost all made in the form of know-how, technical services and
equipment. Nevertheless, these investments were only a fraction of
the total financial package that surrounded the partnerships. Bank
loans from domestic and foreign banks and suppliers' credit lines
financed the bulk of the equipment that constituted the project; and
many of the hard currency loans were forthcoming because of the
involvement of a Western corporation in the venture. Moreover, the
prime interest of the Yugoslavs, as we have seen, was not to attract
foreign capital.[75] It was, rather, to involve technologically advanced
Western firms on a long-term basis in the development or modernization of particular sectors of Yugoslav industry and to forge
permanent links with hard currency marketing outlets.

At first foreign corporations were slow to commit themselves. This
was partly because of the unfamiliar corporate structure of the Yugoslav firm and the complex notions of asset pooling and partnership.
But a more important obstacle seems to have been strictly financial:
the rules on profit transfer, capital repatriation and reinvestment
were too severe to tempt many potential partners to take the plunge.
The authorities, therefore, resolved to take a more liberal line. In
December 1969, an Amendment to the Law on Foreign Exchange
Transactions[76] substantially improved the conditions under which
foreign partners remitted their share of profits. Hitherto, investment
partnerships were subject to the retention quota rules, applicable to
all firms in Yugoslavia, which fixed the percentage of foreign
exchange proceeds from exports that enterprises were allowed to use
freely.[77] At that time the maximum rate was 14 per cent. Henceforth,
foreign partners were granted the right to remit profits up to the value
of 33 per cent of the annual hard currency export earnings of the joint
venture.[78] On 28 July 1971, just over eighteeen months later, a similar

concession was made in respect of capital repatriation.[79] From then on an amount up to the value of 33 per cent of the annual hard currency export earnings of the joint venture was available for capital repatriation to the extent that it had not already been appropriated for the purpose of remitting profits. Moreover, all or part of the unused standard retention quota available to the firm in which the pooled assets reposed could be used for a similar purpose. Foreign partners were also entitled to repatriate an amount up to the value of 10 per cent of the annual depreciation charge on the assets of the venture.

Repatriation was not the only matter dealt with by the 1971 measures.[80] Another important change was the abolition of the requirement that the foreign partner either reinvest 20 per cent of its share of profits or deposit this 20 per cent in a domestic account of a Yugoslav bank. Moreover, the circumstances in which a partnership could be terminated were extended to include a situation where the venture ran at a loss for two consecutive years. Of particular note, was the express guarantee made in the new regulations that no subsequent amendment to the law could worsen the conditions governing the investment of a foreign partner which existed at the time the partnership contract was registered. If the law were to be changed, the provisions of that contract, and the law valid at the time of its registration, would continue to apply if their terms were more favourable. In the mid 1970s, there was a sharp reduction in the number of new joint ventures registered. The redefinition of self-management and the enhanced role of the Party led to a much more restrictive interpretation of the existing joint venture legislation.[81] In 1978, a comprehensive new law was passed, mainly consolidating previous legislation but, in some respects, expressly confirming the new approach.[82] The general effect of the new provisions was to reduce the flexibility that was the hallmark of the earlier rules, thus reducing the attractiveness of joint ventures to foreign investors.[83]

Certain provisions are of particular note. First, the Federal Executive Council was now able to determine the minimum financial investment of the foreign partner. Second, the balance of power between the Workers' Council of the firm in which the joint venture assets reposed and the Business Board was shifted in favour of the Workers' Council. Third, registration procedures were made more complex. Fourth, agreements had to establish the maximum amount of profit to be distributed to the foreign partner. The permitted rate was determined by reference to a number of indicators such as the rate of profit prevailing in the relevant industrial sector in Yugoslavia, the profitability record of the domestic partner and the importance of the project to the Yugoslav economy. Should the foreign partner's share of the venture's profits exceed the limit, the excess was treated as repayment of capital. In the event of any loss, moreover, his capital was to be reduced by his share of the loss. In view of the further fall in foreign investor interest since 1978, the authorities have said that they will consider moderating some of the more restrictive measures.

The largest number of agreements were concluded by Italian and West German corporations. This is not surprising. Not only were Italy and Germany Yugoslavia's biggest Western trade partners; but they had also concluded a large number of industrial co-operation agreements and licensing arrangements with Yugoslav firms before and after the partnership laws were introduced. In fact, many investment partnerships were simply one further step in a business relationship which had been developing steadily for many years. Yet, even after the 1971 measures, there continued to exist a certain wariness on the part of foreign corporations. Foreign business men wishing to go beyond arm's length commercial relationships preferred industrial co-operation agreements as a medium of co-operation. Such agreements, often involving an elaborate network of sales, loan, licence, know-how and management contracts, were capable of providing most, if not all, of the features present in an investment partnership.[84] Yet, by adhering solely to contractual arrangements, they avoided all the complexities and prohibitions of the partnership legislation. Indeed, signing a partnership agreement was often the price that the foreign partner had to pay to conclude his licence, know-how or subcontracting agreement.

The requirement that partnerships should generate a substantial amount of foreign exchange meant that the range of industrial activities which could be the subject of such arrangements was extremely limited. The main sectors affected were transport and, to a lesser extent, pharmaceuticals. Foreign partners were naturally unwilling to allow the end-products of joint venture manufacture to compete with their own products in hard currency markets. They were more sanguine, however, about purchasing component parts from joint ventures to incorporate in their end-products. Motor manufacturers, for example, were happy to incorporate certain components produced in Yugoslavia into cars which they marketed in their own countries and in hard currency export markets. They would not, however, tolerate the sale of completed motor cars, assembled under licence in Yugoslavia, directly into such markets. Partnerships, therefore, proved suitable mainly for industrial processes which involved a fair amount of subcontracting. The foreign exchange requirement made foreign investment in many industries, such as steel and pulp and paper, unlikely. The relevance of the legislation would have been much wider if it had embraced ventures based upon import substitution; but the difficulty here was the familiar one of discovering a calculus which measured the foreign exchange contribution of such investments.

Official flows:[85] *The fund for the accelerated development of the lesser developed regions (FAD)*

The resuscitation of social investment funds at the republican and communal level in 1966 meant that a myriad of socio-political sources continued to provide investment resources for industry. These funds were not, as already indicated, independent bodies; they were merely special accounts whose affairs were managed by the banks on instructions from the relevant republican or communal authorities. They had no fiscal resources[86] and, therefore, grew slowly and their investment policies mirrored the interests of the territories in which they were situated. The FAD, however, was different. It was independently manged and fiscally financed and its overall investment policy was set out in the Social Plan.

The circumstances in which the FAD was established have already been discussed.[87] It began operations in 1966. The areas which qualified for its support were Bosnia, Macedonia, Montenegro and Kosovo. This was, in fact, the fourth time since the war that the area officially designated as underdeveloped had been altered. The First Five Year Plan (1947–51) accorded Macedonia, Montenegro and Bosnia this status. The Five Year Plan for 1957–61 added Kosovo but subtracted Bosnia because the latter had had a rate of per caput investment since the war that exceeded the national average. The 1961–5 Plan expanded the definition to include parts of Serbia, Croatia and Bosnia. The inclusion of South and South-West Serbia, southern and western areas of Bosnia, and the Lika, Banija and Kordun districts of West Croatia, extended the concept of underdevelopment to all republics except Slovenia. This was the only attempt made to look at the problem in other than strictly republican terms. Since the reform the less developed areas within the developed republics have been regarded as a problem to be tackled at the republican level.

Initially, the FAD was financed from federal resources including funds derived from the Tax on the Business Funds of Enterprises and from the repayment of credits made by the Federation to the less developed areas from 1961 to 1965. During the 1966–70 Plan, the FAD disbursed, annually, 1.85 per cent of the nation's Social Product as concessionary investment credits to the less developed areas. These credits were then on-lent to enterprises by their business banks on the same terms. In 1971, federal financing of the FAD ceased. Henceforth, each republic was made responsible for transferring a percentage of its Social Product to the FAD; for 1971–5, the rate was set at 1.95 per cent. Republics and autonomous provinces fulfilled this obligation for funds by compelling enterprises within their territory to 'lend' it to them. The size of the loan was calculated, like the abandoned Tax on the Business Funds of Enterprises, as a fixed percentage of the value of enterprise net worth.

The allocation of FAD resources as between the claimant regions was determined by the federal authorities for successive five-year periods. This practice was the only remnant of the pre-reform investment role of the federal government. The main criterion employed in arriving at a fair distribution was supposed to be the size of the difference between the per caput income of any particular underdeveloped region and the average level of per caput income for the developed areas. Thus, it was envisaged that Kosovo would receive the highest levels of per caput assistance because its per caput income level was the lowest in Yugoslavia—about one-sixth of that of Slovenia. In practice, the amounts that each republic, or in the case of Kosovo autonomous province, were to receive were the subject of intense inter-regional lobbying and the sums awarded did not always reflect the per caput criterion.[88]

Once the proportional entitlements had been established, the total sums generated by the tax or loan were shared out to the qualifying areas. Until 1971, the Fund distributed the funds to banks in those areas on highly concessionary credit terms: 1 per cent interest and 30 years maturity for highway projects, 2 per cent and 20 years for heavy industry, transport, agriculture and tourism, and 4 per cent and 15 years for all other purposes.[89] Intra-regional allocation was left to the discretion of the banks acting upon the advice of republican officials. But the ultimate loans to firms had to be made on terms which were correspondingly concessionary. After the introduction of compulsory loan financing through the republics, the Fund on-lent the proceeds to the banks on identical terms—that is at 4 per cent at 15 years plus a 2 year grace period. Its terms, therefore, were somewhat tougher. Moreover, the banks were allowed to determine the terms applicable to the ultimate borrower. In practice, however, they on-lent at the same concessionary rate.

One of the most serious obstacles to the success of the post-reform investment aid policy was the failure of the capital market to channel savings mobilized by banks and firms into the less developed areas in order to support the work of the FAD. Tito dwelt on this shortcoming in his speech in June 1969 to the Association of Bankers.[90]

When the underdeveloped and developed areas are in question, the banks should . . . invest their resources in such projects because the FAD cannot solve all their problems, either those of Kosovo, Montenegro, Macedonia or other regions on its own. If, for example, an enterprise from Macedonia wishes to get a credit from a Slovenian bank, let it go there and ask for that credit.

The inadequacies of the capital market in this respect were mainly the consequence of the general phenomenon of territorialization. But the problems of voluntary resource transfer from rich to poor areas were particularly marked because of the high-risk low-return combination that characterized many of the projects there. Moreover, a significant proportion of projects were in infrastructure or basic industry and, therefore, unsuitable for financing on commercial terms.

The 1971 Constitutional Amendments did nothing to improve the problem of inter-republican resource mobility. Indeed, the increased powers acquired by the republics at that time made the problem of territorialization, if anything, more acute. Moreover, the abolition of the FFFI,[91] and the corresponding phasing out of the federal role in the direct financing of infrastructure projects, was keenly felt. Of the total investment finance provided to the less developed areas during the 1966–70 Plan period, 27 per cent came from the FAD and a further 17 per cent from the FFFI.[92] This meant that during the years 1971–5 the less developed republics were, if anything, thrown back rather more on their own resources in order to supplement the work of the FAD. All the republics, developed and less developed, inaugurated programmes to encourage development in their most backward areas, either by direct lending to firms through regional extra-budgetary funds or by subsidizing interest rates on bank loans to them. Such programmes were, as might be expected, of relatively greater importance in the less developed areas. Not only was the need greater but the supply of spontaneous savings, both absolutely and relative to other sources, was less.

As to the operation of the FAD itself, both the choices of projects and the terms of lending seem to have been of questionable relevance to the nature and dimensions of the development problem.[93] A high proportion of the funds lent were deployed on a few highly capital-intensive industrial projects, particularly in the mineral and power sectors. This was a repetition of the pre-reform pattern. Between 1966 and 1969, 40 per cent of the funds accruing to Bosnia were used for six projects: two power plants, one oil refinery, one iron and steel works, a cellulose factory and a railway line. In Kosovo during the same period about 46 per cent was spent on a thermonuclear plant and mine.[94] Not only were the capital–labour ratios for these projects high; but because the projects were slow yielding and subject to price controls, and because social sector labour productivity was lower in the less developed areas, capital–output ratios were also high.[95] So the effect upon employment and growth of the investment effort in the less developed areas has been much less favourable than in the Northern areas. Moreover, despite the scarcity of capital and excess of labour in the Southern areas, the authorities continued to make FAD resources available to them on highly concessionary terms. Given the dimensions of their employment problem this seems hard to justify. Even if the FAD lending had remained on concessionary terms it would have been better, as the World Bank has suggested, if the investment banks in the region had re-lent the concessionary loans at a higher rate of interest and used the profits to provide output and employment-related subsidies.[96]

The policy approach towards the less developed areas adopted by the 1976–80 Plan was much as before. Save for Kosovo they were forecast to grow on average at 20 to 25 per cent faster than the country as a whole. Kosovo, it was hoped, would exceed the average by 60 per cent. As before, rapid changes in economic structure were proposed with the object of making industry the dominant activity in all regions. The FAD was again expected to contribute to about 30 per cent of total fixed asset investment there. During the planned period, firms were required to supply 1.97 per cent of their annual Realized Income to the fund. Of this 0.20 per cent was to go to Kosovo as a prior allocation. Of the remaining 1.77 per cent, 34 per cent was intended for Bosnia, 24 per cent for Macedonia, 12 per cent for Montenegro, and 30 per cent for Kosovo. The only change of significance concerned the way in which these resources were raised. In the previous planned period they had been accumulated entirely by means of a compulsory loan whose annual value was assessed as a proportion of enterprise net worth. Now firms were able to contribute up to 20 per cent of the value of their annual obligation, and in certain circumstances more, in the form of investment partnership arrangements.

CHAPTER 4

THE LABOUR MARKET

The average annual rate of growth of social sector employment in the fifteen years following the 1965 reforms was about half what it had been in the fifteen years preceding it; however, as Section 1 demonstrates, it was still well in excess of the average annual rate of growth in the size of the total labour force. Moreover, substantial emigration occurred during the period. Yet the competition for membership of a collective became more intense. This was because of the dualistic nature of the Yugoslav economy. By 1980, there were still almost three million peasant farmers whose productivity and earnings were very low compared with those of social-sector workers. As the material expectations of this group rose, the pressure to leave the land grew. The alternative options of persuading them to remain on the land either by changing the industry–agricultural terms of trade or, as Section 2 relates, by actively encouraging other forms of private enterprise, posed insuperable ideological difficulties.

Despite the absence of private ownership of productive assets on any scale, significant earnings differentials did exist in Yugoslavia. The notable difference between earnings in agricultural and non-agricultural and, to some extent, the more and less developed regions' households, was explained by the gap in labour productivity between private agriculture and the social sector. But there were also significant differences in labour productivity *within* the social sector itself which, in the absence of a contractual wage, led to quite remarkable intra-skill income differentials as between industrial branches. In contrast, average inter-skill differentials were suprisingly small. Indeed, it was not unknown for an unskilled worker in a prosperous branch of industry to earn as much as an expert in a weak branch. These matters are dealt with in Section 3.

1 Supply and demand

Growth of social sector employment

The lower annual growth rate in post-reform social sector employment was largely explained, as Annex 9 indicates, by the lower annual growth rate in social sector output. However, the decline in the rate of growth of output was not quite as marked as that of employment, the difference being accounted for by improved labour productivity. The especially rapid improvement in the rate of growth of labour productivity in the second half of the 1960s was accompanied by a spectacular rise in the proportion of capital to labour employed in the social sector. The trend was, in fact, well under way at the time of reform and was particularly marked in the industrial sector where increases were fairly general.[1] There was no discernible shift of investment resources into the more capital-intensive branches during this period. Indeed, if anything, the movement appears to have been in the opposite direction over these years. Sectors with, hitherto, relatively low capital–labour ratios seem to have made an important contribution to the overall increase. The trend was also mirrored in the productive behaviour of the transport and construction industries. From the early 1970s there was a substantial rise in the response of employment to increases in capital investment though this did not reflect a sudden conversion to labour-intensive production modes. Increases in the severity of the unemployment problem, together with the re-emergence of the Party as an important social force, led to growing pressure on social sector firms to improve their rates of hiring. It is impossible to isolate and give proper weight to the reasons for this spontaneous growth in capital intensity but it is helpful to dwell briefly on possible contributory factors.

Official development strategy. There is little more that can be said under this head beyond re-emphasizing that 'intensive' growth was the corner-stone of post-reform industrial policy. Great emphasis was placed on the modernization of plant and the acquisition of the most up-to-date equipment from Western markets.

Entrepreneurial labour.[2] The increase in the capital–labour ratio is consistent with an important theoretical deduction about the behaviour of self-managed firms. If it is assumed that they seek to maximise net income per worker and that they earn a positive entrepreneurial profit, then a propensity towards capital intensity can be shown to be inherent in the chosen technology of self-managed firms. That is, for any given output they will tend to employ more capital per unit of labour than the perfectly competitive capitalist firm.[3] For the purposes of comparison it is assumed here that a capitalist entrepreneur seeks to maximize his profit after payment of a fixed contractual wage for labour.

Any surplus that a capitalist entrepreneur earns after paying the market rates on the capital and labour that he employs represents his return for his skill and for the risk that he took; this may be called his return to entrepreneurship. It may also, of course, include a return to monopoly. The existence of the surplus does not in any way affect the cost of the labour and capital inputs he employs and, therefore, will not alter the relative levels of their employment in his production function. In Yugoslavia, however, there is no separate class of entrepreneurs who are entitled to employ labour at the market rate. Entrepreneurial profit is wholly appropriated by labour. It follows that earning any surplus attributable to entrepreneurship raises the cost of labour relative to that of capital. The rational collective will, consequently, choose a more capital-intensive technology than the capitalist entrepreneur.

It should be emphasized that the capital-intensive bias in the self-managed firm depends upon entrepreneurial profit being positive. If it is, or becomes, negative then the bias will be reversed. The cost of labour will become relatively less than that of capital and there will be a propensity towards a labour-intensive production mode. Thus, for the capital-intensive bias to persist in the economy as a whole, the net entrepreneurial profits of all self-managed firms must be positive. This is why, in long-run perfectly competitive equilibrium when entrepreneurial profits are zero, the self-managed firm acts in exactly the same way as the capitalist firm.[4] This is illustrated in Fig. 4.1.

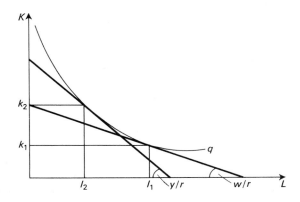

Fig. 4.1

K represents capital, L labour, q a production possibilities curve, r the rate of interest, w wages in a capitalist system, and y net income per worker in a self-managed economy. Given w and y, w/r and y/r represent the angles of the tangents drawn through the points at which the capitalist entrepreneur and the collective respectively are indifferent between employing an extra unit of labour and an extra unit of capital. The proposition is, quite simply, that where entrepreneurial profit $E = O$, then $y = w$ and the capitalist and the self-managed solutions are the same. But where $E > O$ then $y > w$ and the self-managed firm will shift say, from $l_1 k_1$ to $l_2 k_2$. Thus, where p equals the price of the final product:

$$E = pq - rk - wL$$

$$y = (pq - rK)/L$$

when $E = 0$

$$w = (pq - rK)/L = y$$

and when $E/L > 0$

$$y > w.$$

It is true, of course, that in the West the entrepreneurial function is usually performed by a supplier of capital to the firm. Why does this not have the effect of increasing the cost of capital and so introduce a labour-intensive bias to the capitalist firm earning entrepreneurial profits? The reason is that the capitalist entrepreneur has the option of borrowing capital contractually at a fixed price in the market place if it is cheaper. The price of his capital input is, therefore, determined exogenously. However, the socialist entrepreneur, the collective, does not have this option with respect to labour. The reason why earning a surplus increases the collective's cost of labour is not because it appropriates the entrepreneurial surpluses—the capitalist does so too—but because it cannot employ outsiders, or its own members, on a contractual basis.

The cost of capital. In Yugoslavia, the productive assets of self-managed firms are either self-financed or financed from borrowed resources on fixed interest terms—save in the rare case of investment partnerships. If the total present value of such assets is not paid for at a rate which reflects their scarcity, then collectives will tend to choose a more capital-intensive production technique. In fact both sources of finance were underpriced. In the case of self-finance this was due to the absence of an equity market together with the unwillingness of the authorities to devise a fiscal surrogate, which would have had the effect of charging own funds at a price which reflected their scarcity.[5] The rate of tax on enterprise Business Funds, abolished in 1971, was inadequate in this respect.[6] As to borrowed funds, the average nominal rate of interest was well below the probable market clearing rate. This underpricing was aggravated by inflation, by the low cost of capital goods, and by the absence of penalties for unprofitable investment decisions which made it unnecessary to discount the expected rate of return on prospective investment projects for risk.

It is assumed, for the purpose of illustration, that the opportunity cost of self-finance is consumption forgone. Only those business assets, therefore, whose marginal productivity is higher than, or equal to, the subjective discount rate of the collective in question will be self-financed.[7] Because time horizons vary from collective to collective, the proportion of self-finance forthcoming for any given demand-for-capital schedule will vary. The collectives will seek to borrow financial resources for those assets whose rate of return falls between the subjective discount rate and the market rate of interest from borrowed resources. But since the price of borrowed resources is below their market clearing rate, demand for them exceeds their supply. Insufficient intermediated resources are forthcoming to create enough business assets to reduce their marginal productivity to the artificially low price of financial capital. The return per unit of capital, therefore, is higher than the rate of interest. It follows that collectives that supply and borrow capital resources earn a rate of return on them. In the case of self-financed resources this rate of return is measured by the difference between the rate of return per unit of physical capital employed and the rate at which the old business tax or, after 1971, the new obligatory loan is levied on the business fund.[8] In the case of borrowed resources it is measured by the difference between the rate of return per unit of physical capital employed and the rate of interest.

In effect, part of the rate of return on capital accrues to the collective in the form of a monopoly rent. This is illustrated in Fig. 4.2. Here, K is a demand-for-capital schedule. I_3 represents the desired amount of physical capital at the prevailing rate of interest. The

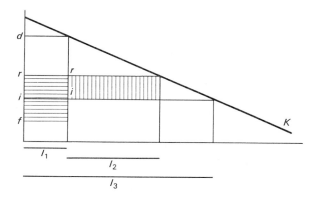

Fig. 4.2

subjective discount rate, d, determines the amount of investment, I_1, which is self-financed. Given the condition of excess demand in the market for borrowed funds, I_2 is the additional amount of investment achieved from the resources actually obtained; r is the rate of return on I_1 and I_2. The return accruing to the collective from self-financing is measured by the horizontally shaded area rI_1-fI_1, the sum deriving from the difference between r and f where f is the rate of business tax or the rate at which the obligatory loan is levied by the republic in which the collective in question is situated. The return accruing to the collective from borrowed resources is measured by the vertically shaded area rI_2-iI_2, the amount arising from the difference between the rate of return on capital and the rate of interest.

To the extent that a collective appropriates a return from one or both of these forms of financing, the cost of labour will be raised relative to the cost of capital. On exactly the same principles as are applicable to entrepreneurial profit, there will be a corresponding propensity towards more capital-intensive modes of production in the future. The perpetuation of a situation in which the marginal productivity of business assets exceeds the rate of interest and any levy on Business Funds ensures both continued excess demand for investment resources and the encouragement of greater capital intensity.

Social agreements. The introduction of social agreements may have aggravated the problem of capital intensity. These agreements compelled those firms with relatively high incomes, themselves partly the return from monopoly rents, to plough back a relatively higher proportion of them. To the extent that these extra savings were invested in business assets, and that their investment did not lead to a corresponding fall in the demand for borrowed funds, this would have led, at prevailing costs of capital, to the accumulation of even higher monopoly rents. This, in turn, implies higher labour costs and even more capital-intensive modes of production.[9]

The incidence of taxation. A further factor biasing the self-managed firm in the direction of more capital-intensive modes of production was the incidence of direct taxation, whose main burden fell on the personal income funds. *Doprinosi*, or Contributions out of Gross Personal Incomes, were fixed percentage taxes levied by the socio-political communities on the value of the appropriation made by firms to their Gross Personal Income Funds. Their yields were used, almost exclusively, to defray the expenses of the social welfare system. The actual percentages charged varied from republic to republic and, within republics, from commune to commune. Typically, their total burden amounted to between 30 and 35 per cent. The choice of gross personal income as the tax base for contributions was intended to deter excessive personal income allocations and to encourage larger appropriations to the Business Fund.

New entry. The adverse effects of capital intensification on social sector employment could, to some degree, have been offset by the establishment of new social sector firms by the unemployed. However, the absence of a venture capital market and the very strict rules that surrounded company promotion effectively prevented such a practice developing on any scale. In effect, the unemployed were not allowed to compete for available capital. This problem and the question of new entry are discussed in more detail in Section 2 below and in Chapter 5.[10]

Social control. It is ironic to note that the interference by socio-political communities in the affairs of local enterprises, one of the main targets of the 1965 reforms, may have counteracted some of the suboptimalities and inefficiences that Western commentators believe to be inherent in the operation of the Yugoslav enterprise. For example, pressure on enterprises by their respective local authorities to retain or adopt labour-intensive technologies would oppose the capital-intensive bias flowing from 'entrepreneurial' labour. Equally, discouraging excessive inter-firm personal income differentials by persuading or compelling successful enterprises to plough back a substantial portion of their earnings, would offset the anti-saving bias foreseen by Furubotn and Pejovich as the logical result of the enterprise property rights structure. If this were the case, intervention for social or ideological reasons could be said to have had beneficial economic effects.

Following the reactivation of the Party and the introduction of contractual planning, firms became more susceptible to official pressures to increase the numbers employed. These pressures intensified in the wake of the oil crisis. Annual employment targets became the subject of social agreements. The 1976–80 Plan set a number of longer term employment objectives to be realized through such agreements. Indeed, one of the main themes of the Plan was that employment should be consciously directed. The Plan was the first coherent attempt by the post-reform authorities to try and influence the relationship between the growth of labour productivity and the growth of the labour force.[11] Firms were set employment and accumulation targets, through the contractual planning system, to encourage them to use more labour-intensive methods. Unfortunately, many of the sectors singled out for priority financing during the Plan period were remarkable for their especially high capital cost per job created.

Theory and practice. It is tempting to say that the lower rate of employment growth in post-reform Yugoslavia is due to the tendency of worker managed firms to maximize personal income growth per worker by opting for high productivity and low employment growth. However, the statistical evidence for this assertion is, at best, inconclusive. The disproportionately low rate of growth of social sector employment, and correspondingly high rate of growth of social sector productivity, between 1965 and 1968 was probably due to the adjustments to new product demand patterns in more open markets and to the severe monetary squeeze imposed by stabilization policy.[12] From 1968, the lower growth rate in employment compared with the years 1956–65, is explained entirely by the lower growth rate in Social Product. Had the pre-reform link between employment and Social Product growth been restored in the early 1970s, at the time of the introduction of social agreements and the reassertion of Party authority, then the circumstantial evidence would have been more suggestive.

It has also been observed that employment output elasticities in post-reform Yugoslavia compare favourably with most other OECD countries. However, there was, equally, a general tendency for fixed assets per employee to increase and the capital cost per unit of output was high. Since this tendency coincided with rather low capacity utilization, the economy may simply have given the impression of good employment output elasticities. In the less developed areas, where the employment output elasticities were higher than the national average, investment rates were higher, capital costs per unit of ouput higher and capacity utilization lower than the national average.[13]

The growth of the labour force[14]

Population and participation. Despite the slower rate of growth of employment opportunities in the social sector after 1965, it was still well in excess of the rate of increase in the labour force. At the time of the 1981 Census, the total population of Yugoslavia was about 24m. In the decade 1961–71 it had increased at a modest annual aggregate growth rate of about 1 per cent. The rate of aggregate growth from 1971 to 1981 was even lower at about 0.8 per cent. However, global statistics are not very instructive in the Yugoslav case because there are wide regional differences in the annual rates of population growth. The regional rates for 1961–71 ranged from 0.5 per cent in Vojvodina to 2.6 per cent in Kosovo with all the so-called developed areas averaging below 1 per cent and all the less developed areas averaging above it. The increases for 1971–81 exhibited the same trends at slightly lower rates. Because of declining participation rates, the rate of growth in the labour force was, and is projected to be, even slower than the rate of growth of population. It was 0.7 per cent during 1961–71 and 0.6 per cent during 1971–81. But again the regional pattern varied greatly. Between 1961 and 1971, for example, the range was from 0.3 per cent in Croatia and Vojvodina to 2.0 per cent in Kosovo.

Dualism. Because of the rapid rate of growth of output in the social sector in the years before reform there was a massive shift of the active labour force out of private farming and into the social sector. Between 1953 and 1965 this migration from agriculture to industry involved over a million workers.[15] At first the movement was forced;[16] but later, as the attractions of urban living and social sector employment grew, it acquired a momentum of its own which was in full flood by the middle of the 1960s. Nevertheless, in 1965, 54 per cent of the active labour force was still employed predominantly in peasant agriculture. By 1980, the comparable proportion had dropped to 30 per cent. But this still represented a pool of nearly three million peasant farmers whose productivity and earnings were very low by comparison with those of the social sector.[17] Thus, although the social sector still created far more new jobs than the growth in the total labour force produced new workers, the dualistic nature of the Yugoslav economy ensured an excess of supply in social sector job applicants.

Registered social sector unemployment as a percentage of the active labour force is shown in Annex 9. These statistics are misleading as a measure of the size of excess demand for social sector employment in Yugoslavia because a significant proportion of the workers employed in private agriculture were either underemployed or dissatisfied with their rural way of life. They represented a potential immediate source of demand for social sector work since they could, at any moment, decide to enter the market for a social sector job. During 1970, for example, the social sector and foreign labour markets together provided about 358,000 extra jobs, 200,000 of which were abroad. During that year the growth in the active labour force was about 287,000. If it is assumed that the total work-force consisted of those employed plus registered job applicants this should have reduced the numbers registering for work by about 71,000. In fact the numbers registered declined only by about 11,000, implying that 60,000, not initially registered, either entered employment directly or became registered job applicants during that period.[18]

The dimensions of the problem varied sharply from region to region. Rates of registered social sector unemployment were much higher in the less developed areas and these, as we have seen, under-estimated the true extent of excess demand. For example, at the end of 1973 there were 65,055 persons seeking employment in Macedonia amounting to 21.6 per cent of social sector employment. The average rate of unemployment had increased by 6 per cent per annum over the previous three years.[19] By contrast, at the end of the same year the Slovenes reported an acute shortage of labour of all types in their republic. So much so that an estimated 150,000 persons from other republics were currently employed there, amounting to a quarter of the republic's social sector labour force.[20] It is interesting to note that, at that time, Macedonia had the highest birth-rate, 23.2 per thousand, and the lowest death-rate, 7.6 per thousand, in Yugoslavia; the comparable figures for Slovenia were 16.3 and 10.5 per cent.[21] Moreover, in Macedonia only 44 per cent of the population were employed in the social sector compared with 70 per cent in Slovenia.[22] The dimensions of the problem also depended upon the particular skill category concerned. The Serbian Employment Institute, which recorded overall for 1973 an excess of job seekers over available work, reported that for 1973 there was a severe shortage of qualified labour in the republic.[23] It reported 959 graduate job applicants in 1973 compared with 4,849 openings for personnel at graduate level. By the end of the decade, the return of skilled workers from abroad following the recession had either eliminated these scarcities altogether or substantially alleviated them.

It is not possible to measure with any degree of accuracy the size of the excess demand for social sector employment or, indeed, its regional distribution. What can be said with confidence is that the decline in demand for foreign labour in Western Europe after 1973 has substantially enlarged it. During 1976, the net increase in social sector employment opportunities was about 89,000 extra jobs, the increase of 169,000 in the domestic sector being offset by 80,000 returning migrants. In that same year the active labour force grew by about 104,000. Had the total work-force consisted of those employed plus registered job applicants, the numbers registering should have increased by about 15,000. In fact they increased by 95,000.[24] It is also true that migrants originating in the Northern republics and returning from abroad displaced some of those who migrated from the Souhern republics to take up their jobs in the North. So the problems posed in the areas of severe unemployment in the South by returning external migrants, were aggravated by returning internal migrants.

Migration. The removal of restrictions on those seeking employment abroad at the time of reform provided an alternative to social sector employment by which the demand for an urban life style could be satisfied. It led to a massive outflow of workers seeking temporary employment abroad, especially in West Germany, where there was a strong demand for foreign labour.[25] Workers in the South, the area with the most serious employment problems, were slow to take advantage of these new opportunities.[26] In the early years of the external migration boom they tended to migrate internally in order to take up the jobs vacated when their Northern brethren travelled abroad. From the early 1970s, however, there is evidence that an

increasing proportion of those who sought work abroad came from
the less developed areas.[27] By 1971 there were 478,000 Yugoslav
workers employed in Germany, but this underestimated the total
number temporarily employed abroad.[28] The 1971 Census recorded
672,000 persons said by their relatives to be temporarily abroad
during that year and it is probable that even this figure underestimated the true number.[29]

There is little doubt that external migration brought substantial
benefits to the post-reform economy. Indeed, in some respects it is
hard to see how reform could have survived without it. First, had the
migrants remained at home there would have been work only for the
more skilled amongst them. Apart from the added burden on the
welfare system, their presence may have led to a higher degree of
social unrest, although the authorities might have chosen to modify
their industrial policy so as to create more social sector employment.
Second, the balance of payments was immensely improved by the
hard currency remittances of migrants. These increased from
$US55m. in 1965 to $US1,379m. in 1974. In that year they amounted
to 36 per cent of total commodity export earnings. Given the
dimensions of Yugoslavia's post-reform balance of payments difficulties, it is hard to see how it would have achieved the rate of growth
that it did, in the absence of such support; and, with slower growth,
the unemployment problem would have been even worse. Third,
many of the unskilled migrants eventually returned with a proper
training. Thus the economy acquired, at no cost, productive workers
to improve its economic performance in future years.

In the short run, therefore, external migration was plainly in the
interests both of those that went and those that remained. However,
despite the value of foreign working experience, from a long-term
perspective it had its disadvantages. A significant percentage of
emigrants were highly skilled workers from the developed regions. A
comprehensive report based upon several surveys and the 1971
Census showed that up to the end of 1971 twice as many migrants
came from the developed as from the less developed areas.[30] Moreover, about 30 per cent of the migrants from the developed regions
were technically qualified as against 13 per cent of migrants from the
less developed regions.[31] Over half the agricultural worker emigration
came from areas of advanced farming.[32] Although the rate of increase
of emigration from the less developed areas picked up sharply in the
early 1970s the regional origin and skill structure of expatriates

became a matter of growing concern to the authorities. A high proportion of workers were departing whose skills were in short supply
and who came from regions which were beginning to complain of
labour shortages.[33] Even the departure of unskilled peasant labour
began to be questioned in the light of worsening dependency ratios in
the poorer areas. Moreover, the authorities saw little likelihood of the
voluntary return of many workers, in view of uncertain employment
prospects and the substantial wage differentials between Yugoslavia
and the countries to which the workers were emigrating.

   In April 1973 a resolution of the League of Communists was passed
proposing that some restrictions be imposed upon worker emigration.[34] It was felt that the exodus had reached its permissible limit.
It was suggested that each republic should draw up a plan establishing the desirable rate and skill composition of annual departures.
Later in the year legislation was passed enabling registration procedures to be established for those seeking foreign employment; and
those registered were to be offered alternative employment at home
where it was available. Those who had not completed military
service, were reserve officers, or had not made proper provision for
their dependants, were not allowed to depart. In other cases the
question of limits on numbers or skill groups were to be matters for the
republics. It was hoped, however, that they would co-operate to
produce a co-ordinated inter-republican social agreement which
would, *inter alia*, encourage greater internal mobility by first directing
workers to available work in other republics before allowing them to
go abroad. Early in 1974 representatives of the republican and
provincial governments signed such an agreement;[35] but it was
drafted in broad terms and it was not clear to which occupational
groups the restrictions would apply. Policies were also to be formulated to encourge the return home of workers already abroad. But
by 1974, in the wake of the recession initiated by the international oil
crisis, the demand for expatriate labour in Western Europe was
falling off rapidly and the need for such measures grew less urgent.
Suddenly, the issue was transformed into the problem of how to
employ returning emigrants whose jobs in Western Europe no longer
existed.

   One of the interesting facts to emerge from the sample surveys on
external migration is that the lack of employment opportunities at
home was not the major motivating factor for departure.[36] The desire
to earn foreign currency in order to buy or build a house, buy

agricultural equipment or start a private business appears to have been an important influence. But more than 60 per cent said that they were seeking higher earnings. Since the prospects of achieving these objects were greater for the better educated, better qualified and more sophisticated Northerners, it is not surprising that the effect of external migration was to exacerbate inter-regional disparities in labour supply conditions. These disparities were, to some extent, offset by internal migratory movements. The 1971 Census shows that there had been a strong movement from the less to the more developed regions during the previous decade.[37] This net internal transfer was of the order of 250,000 people. The main movements appear to have been from Bosnia, Kosovo and Montenegro to Serbia, Croatia and, to a lesser extent, Slovenia.

The motive seems to have been chiefly economic though it was somewhat modified by ethnic and linguistic considerations. For example, the richer areas of Slovenia, with its own language, and Vojvodina, with its strong Hungarian culture, did not attract as high a proportion of migrants as Croatia, despite labour shortages. On the other hand Macedonia, with its distinct language and culture, provided relatively few internal emigrants. Prospective emigrants from Kosovo, with their Albanian links, were faced with similar difficulties, though in their case the economic pressures to move were much stronger. Bosnia provided the largest number of emigrants, most of whom went to Serbia or Croatia. In the 1950s and early 1960s, Serbia was the most important immigration area with its numerous centres of rapidly growing industrial activities. However, in the second half of the 1960s and in the early 1970s, the two richest republics, Croatia and Slovenia, became important immigration regions; more than 300,000 workers emigrated from them during that period. Much of their deficit in unskilled and semi-skilled labour was made up from Southern workers, especially, its seems, from Kosovo.

2 The private sector

One obvious way of alleviating the pressure on the social sector to create more job openings would have been to encourage the development of a vigorous and productive private sector. Apart from agriculture itself there were a variety of activities, mainly in the tertiary sector, which social sector firms were either unwilling or unable to undertake and which were eminently suited to a private sector approach. Tourism was perhaps the clearest example. The role of the private sector proved a lively source of debate in post-reform Yugoslavia. But, despite some early concessions to expediency, the weight of official opinion was against major institutional initiatives.

Under the 1946 Constitution private enterprise was permitted in agriculture, on a maximum land area of ten hectares, and in handicrafts, where no more than five workers were employed. Family members employed by an artisan counted towards the limit of five, but hotels could employ three people in addition to members of the family. Although these cases were tolerated, they were discouraged by discriminatory fiscal and monetary policies. They were regarded as a remnant of capitalism, redolent of exploitation and alienation, to be contained if not eliminated. No attempt was made to expand the sector during the pre-reform period though its status was confirmed in the 1953 and 1963 Constitution. Article 22 of the 1963 Constitution included a general prohibition on contractual employment, setting out the above-mentioned exceptions to this general rule in subsections (2) and (3).

Beginning in 1963, a number of concessions to private ownership were made, in particular to handicraft, hotel and agricultural employers, and generally in matters of social security and pensions. In each case there was a practical motive behind the legislation. The authorities were anxious to expand the output of those sectors in which the rules were changed. For example, the Hotel Law of 1965 and its Amending Law of 1967 were both designed to expand the capacity of the tourist sector to meet the unprecedented demand for temporary summer accommodation which the social sector proved quite unable to match.[38] Equally the Law on the Purchase and Use of Farm Implements by private farmers was designed to foster productivity in a sector which, given the fiscal and monetary handicaps under which it operated, could do little else but stagnate.[39]

This spate of measures provoked a move to clarify the role of the private sector in the post-reform economy. At the end of 1967 the Socio-Economic Sub-Committee of the Central Committee of the League of Communists, together with leading members of the Socialist Alliance,[40] drafted a Thesis on the topic which formed the basis of the Resolution adopted at the beginning of 1968 by the Socialist Alliance. It was during the formulation and drafting of the Thesis, in the second half of 1967 and the first half of 1968, that a serious debate on the whole subject took place in the pages of *Gledišta*. Perhaps the most significant factor which emerged from this debate was the widely held view that capitalism and private property were not necessarily synonymous; nor was the one a pre-condition of the other. Indeed, that capitalism could exist in proprietorial forms other than private ones was essential to the ideology of market socialism. The preferred definition was not to link it to any particular legal form but to classify it more generally as exploitation. Yet, if this were so could the converse be true? Was it conceivable that private property could exist in the absence of exploitation? Both Bajt and Lavrac distinguished between the legal form of private property and its economic content and considered that much of the opposition to private property had been engendered by confusing these two aspects.[41] Having made this distinction both adhered to the view that there was no inconsistency between socialism and the legal institutions of private property. The title adopted for the Thesis, 'Individual Work with Personal Property,' avoided altogether the term private property.

Not everybody agreed with the Thesis or with the views of its chief supporters. Cerne would not accept that, even in circumstances in which the private owner ploughed back all his wealth into the business and employed nobody on a contractual basis, there was no element of exploitation.[42] Others considered that the essence of exploitation lay not in the existence of private property or personal endeavour but in the contractual employment of labour.[43] There were also those who were opposed on more pragmatic grounds. They argued that a modernized private sector would be more dangerous to socialism than a backward sector.[44]

One of the difficulties of resolving the debate lay in the different meanings ascribed to the word exploitation. In his 'Essay on Yugoslav Society',[45] Horvat sought to resolve this debate by distinguishing between exploitation and power over labour. Exploitation, he argued, was a factor common to all proprietorial systems:

What answer shall we give to the following question: who is exploiting—a private person or a socialist enterprise—if the private person pays a worker 100,000 dinars and the enterprise pays him only 80,000 dinars? . . . Such exploitation exists wherever there are monopoly situations. As a result economic theory in the West frequently proposed to take the degree of monopoly as the only objective measure of exploitation. In that sense, because of their greatly differing operating conditions, economically privileged workers collectives exploit others, arbitrary decisions by the state and by banks lead to exploitation, and, of course, taking advantage of or creating monopoly situations on the market means exploitation of some collectives by others.[46]

To Horvat the essence of capitalism, whether in the form of private property or state bureaucracy, was not exploitation but power over labour.

Power over labour seems to me to give the essence of [capitalism] better and more precisely than the usual concept of exploitation . . . It signifies the specific social relationships in which one class of individual, by means of private ownership or state power, subordinate another, and larger, class economically. The latter class is that of wage workers. The former has power over labour.[47]

The elimination of private property, therefore, did not necessarily exclude either exploitation or power over labour from an economic system. But does all private property necessarily imply power over labour?

Horvat posed this question in a practical way for his readers:

Does a farmer who works ten hectares with his family, or an electrician who goes around with his son repairing our home electrical system, achieve power over others' labour? Of course not . . . And if he works with a helper? Probably not even then. How many helpers can be tolerated? That depends upon a practical evaluation, the criterion being as follows: as long as the proprietor works himself and that direct work is his basic function, there is no danger of capitalist development. As soon as his primary function becomes entre-preneurship, i.e. the organization of the labour of others, then even by definition he is no longer a worker but is a capitalist.[48]

This did not mean that Horvat was prepared to accept all forms of private ownership that did not lead to entrepreneurial and therefore capitalist relationships. There were some fields of economic and social endeavour in which not only were capitalist relationships intolerable but also 'commercial commodity money relationships in general'.[49] He cited as examples, health, education and culture. Here distribution had to be 'according to needs and not according to ability to pay'. For that reason he was opposed, for example, to the in-stitution of private medicine.

He believed, moreover, that there was a further problem. In a period of automation, the absence of entrepreneurship was an insufficient condition for the absence of power over labour. A trucker who systematically uses his savings to purchase more trucks, which he then rents out, or a farmer who behaves likewise with land or tractors, 'does not employ labour directly, but still practises power over labour indirectly via the market'.[50] Therefore, the prohibition on entrepreneurship had to be supplemented by limits on the size of production resources that private businesses could employ. The magnitude of such limits, he believed, was a practical policy matter. He, himself, seems to have seen them as being fairly narrow. It might be that individuals could own one or two more houses besides their own for commercial renting, but owners of trucks and tractors should only work them themselves and not rent them out.[51]

The policy issues invariably concerned the extent to which any individual could control one or more of the three factors of production, land, labour and capital. For example, one of the most discussed matters was whether or not peasant farmers should have the right to purchase modern agricultural equipment.[52] During the pre-reform period such purchases were forbidden. In the course of 1965 and 1966 many commentators questioned the wisdom of maintaining the prohibition on tractor ownership in particular. Those opposed to any change argued that the purchaser would be obliged to rent his tractor out to other smallholders since it could not possibly be profitable to buy such an expensive machine to develop a mere ten hectares of land. Those supporting change asserted that such practices could be easily controlled by fiscal penalties; and, moreover, a countervailing incentive to renting out could be provided by expanding the area of land that the peasant was entitled to cultivate. In 1967 the right of peasants to purchase agricultural machinery, including tractors, was recognized. But the question of the right to use the tractor on the property of other peasant farmers was not resolved, and nor were restrictions on the area of cultivable land relaxed.

Another controversial area of potential endeavour was the provision of medical services. In the immediate post-reform period there was considerable concern about the inadequate facilities of the social health service. A Slovenian law of 1967, dealing with the organization of the republic's health services, included a clause giving each commune the discretion to allow private services if local circumstances so dictated.[53] Surprisingly, perhaps, for the most private-enterprise-minded republic in Yugoslavia, the majority of communes were as opposed to this innovation as were the health services themselves. A few took advantage of the clause but even then their motives may have been to bring out into the open what had, hitherto, been a clandestine practice. Despite its rather lukewarm reception in May 1969, the Federal Assembly adopted a new federal law on public health which foresaw exceptional circumstances in which health services might be provided outside the social sector.[54]

The Resolution on the role of private property, adopted by the Federal Conference of the Socialist Alliance in February 1968, was based upon the Thesis drafted by the Socio-Economic Sub-Committee of the Central Committee.[55] In general terms it declared a positive approach to the role of the private sector in Yugoslav society.

The Federal Conference emphasizes that private work is a social necessity as a supplement to social labour with social means of production both in tertiary sectors and in agriculture . . . Being a socially necessary activity it should be encouraged and developed.[56]

It asserted that working people engaged in the private sector should have the same rights and obligations as those working with socially owned means of production.[57] To that end it recommended that private sector workers should be integrated into both the social sector system of health and the social sector insurance and pension arrangements.

The Resolution accepted that, in addition to the labour of members of his family, an individual working in the farming, craft, catering or related branches could employ, within limits, extra labour. However, it expressly declined to recommend an extension of this practice beyond the limits imposed by existing state law unless the employment relationship was governed by self-management norms. If, therefore, a private employer wished to expand his work-force beyond the statutory limits then his business would automatically become a social sector firm. The owner, in view of his private rights, would be entitled to receive an annual sum fixed in proportion to the value of the business at the time it changed its status. Otherwise he would be in exactly the same position as any other member of a workers' collective, though he would be likely to become director. This arrangement would provide an incentive for the private business to expand since its owner would not be 'expropriated' once he had hired labour beyond the legal limit.[58] The Resolution also recommended some alleviation of the fiscal burden on private enterprise. And it gave particular prominence to the development of co-operative arrangements between the social and private sectors.[59] This particular suggestion was subsequently incorporated into Article 66 of the 1974 Constitution.

Unfortunately, the Resolution appeared at a time when the private sector was under heavy attack from the media for excessive profiteering. Accusations of commodity speculation, employment in excess of the norms, fiscal fraud, extortionate rent from weekend property and foreign exchange regulation evasion, were daily occurrences in the press.[60] Some of these allegations were justified. But many were based on a misunderstanding of the economic role played by property owners or by middlemen. The Resolution, to some extent, reflected this mood:

The Federal Conference considers that the various forms of middlemanship, entrepreneurship, usury, etc. which are a kind of appropriation of the results of the labour of others and an expression of old outdated relationships, are incompatible with our socio-economic relations.[61]

Particularly harsh criticism was reserved for the *Grupriogradjansko preduzece* or GGs as they were usually called. These were social sector firms promoted by groups of private citizens. Strictly speaking they had nothing to do with the private sector, as Section 3 of Chapter 5 explains, yet they were popularly regarded as being part of it.

Popular concern about the activities of the private sector reached such a pitch that the federal authorities felt compelled to introduce restrictive measures in the summer of 1968. Although the Resolution had recommended further devolution of private sector regulation to the republics, the new measures were a move in the opposite direction. In transport, any individual was limited to owning one lorry of not more than five tonnes and one car with not more than five seats,[62] whereas hitherto the rules had differed from republic to republic, some imposing no tonnage or seat limits. In tourism, families were now limited to one hotel,[63] where, previously, republican rules had varied. Some, like Slovenia, had particularly favoured the development of private initiative in tourism. Others, like Montenegro, had preferred to develop their tourist industry under tight communal control.

The radical changes in the social sector that took place in the early 1970s overshadowed the debate on the role of the private sector, which was anyway muted by the campaign against liberalism. However, the 1974 Constitution contained an important section on the role of private enterprise, now referred to as 'Independent Personal Labour with Resources in Citizens Ownership'. First, by Article 66,[64] independent workers were allowed to co-ordinate their business activities with social sector firms in co-operative arrangements. Within the framework of such arrangements the independent worker could share in the management of joint affairs and receive income proportionate to his contribution to its generation. The Article, therefore, permitted independent workers and social sector firms to conclude agreements similar to the industrial co-operation agreements discussed in the next chapter[65] and already well established in the social sector domain. In fact such arrangements were already on foot in the tourist and, in particular, the agricultural sectors and Article 66, more than anything else, served to confirm their legality.

Second, Article 67 authorized independent workers to pool their means of production and their labour with the labour of other workers to form a Contractual Organization of Association Labour (COAL). The organization of a COAL was based on a contract entitling the independent worker to be its director and to receive a rate of return independent of his labour and proportionate to the net value of his business assets at the time the COAL was created. It also provided that the director 'shall retain the right of ownership and other contractual rights regarding the resources he has pooled in this organization'. Once these resources were withdrawn or repaid, the special right he enjoyed by virtue of their presence in the COAL automatically terminated.

The substance of both these articles reflected and developed recommendations which had appeared in the Resolution of the Socialist Alliance some six years previously. In framing the new rules the authorities adopted many of the techniques they had employed in an exclusively social sector context. The COAL, for example, had a strong affinity with the investment partnership. However, the Constitution also recognized that there would be circumstances in which neither Article 66 nor Article 67 would be appropriate. According to Article 68:

It shall be regulated by statute in which activities, consistent with their nature and social needs, and under what conditions a working man who independently performs activities with his personal labour and privately owned resources may, exceptionally and to a limited extent, make use of the additional labour of other persons by employing them without forming a contractual organization of associated labour.

On the thorny question of hired labour, therefore, the authorities continued to be wary of laying down any general principle.

The straightforward hiring of labour by independent workers was still regarded as a matter to be dealt with on an *ad hoc* basis as and when the need arose. Article 68 did, however, go on to require that any private sector contract of employment should conform 'with the collective contract entered into between the appropriate trade union and the chamber of economy or other association representing working people who independently perform activities with their personal labour and privately owned resources'. The effect of this provision was to ensure that hired labour would have similar social security, sickness and pension benefits to those of members of a collective. Moreover, the authorities retained the right to convert any surplus earned by the private entrepreneur into social property, presumably in circumstances of their own choosing. In the words of Article 68, 'it may be regulated by statute that the part of income which is the result of the surplus labour of workers employed by a working man who independently performs an activity with his personal labour and privately owned resources shall become social property and shall be used for development needs.'

Information on the private sector in Yugoslavia is rather sketchy. Roughly speaking, about 360,000 were employed in the non-agricultural private sector in 1975.[66] Of those, 42 per cent were employed in handicrafts and 37 per cent in construction. The remainder were involved in transport services or catering. Handicrafts were declining, and transport and catering increasing, in importance. The absence of job security, discriminatory employment, fiscal, credit and foreign exchange rules and, above all, the fluctuating attitude of the authorities towards private enterprise, combined to contribute to the sector's modest role.

The 1976–80 Plan stressed the importance of small scale social and private sector industry in Yugoslavia—primarily as a means of encouraging labour intensive technologies to alleviate the problem of unemployment. It contained assertions about the need for improved fiscal, social security and credit conditions in the private sector. A social agreement was concluded in May 1976 underlining, in particular, the value of ancillary enterprise such as rural workshops[67] and urban service facilities. However, the restrictions on the number of employees remained and, by the end of the decade, there was no evidence of an increase in the attractiveness of private enterprise to Yugoslavs. The COAL had some success in establishing itself, especially in Slovenia. It did not suffer from the same disadvantages as the purely private firm with respect to tax and credit—though the Slovenians limited the number of owners to ten.

3   The structure of incomes

By international standards Yugoslavia has enjoyed a relatively equitable income distribution, the share of the top 5 per cent of the population in total household income being roughly twice that of the bottom 25 per cent at the beginning of the 1970s.[68] The main reason for this was the absence of any private ownership of productive assets on any scale and the corresponding absence of large *rentier* incomes. Nevertheless, significant differences did exist between the private agricultural sector and the social sector, between the developed and the underdeveloped regions, and, within the social sector itself, both within and between skill categories.

Private agricultural and social sector incomes

Sample surveys of peasant household income levels were conducted annually, though on a small and rather selective basis. These, together with the quinquennial Household Budget Surveys, convey a picture of slow growth in the average real income of peasant households.[69] After the demise of collectivization in 1953, the authorities used as the medium for their agricultural development strategy the *kombinats* which were the social sector successors to the state farms. Unlike the private sector they had no restrictions on size of holdings and generous access to social sector finance. It is likely that a high proportion of peasant households suffered either a stabilization of, or even a decline in, real income. Moreover, most of the growth that did occur appears to have derived from non-agricultural sources, either from work in social sector firms or from second jobs in the private sector.[70]. In 1970, for example, only 32 per cent of peasant household income was earned from private agricultural activity; 25 per cent of the balance was earned in social sector employment.[71] Although it is only measurable on a sample basis it appears that the average per caput income of a member of a peasant household was about half that of a member of a household engaged in non-agricultural activities.

Developed and less developed regions[72]

The aggregate per caput income differentials between the richer and the poorer regions widened during the inter-censual years from 1953 to 1971. During this period the per caput income of the less developed republics fell from 65 to 50 per cent of that of the developed republics. This was the result of both slower growth in Social Product and more rapid growth in population. Each of these factors explains about half of the decline for the less developed area as a whole. Had the rate of growth of population in the poorer regions been the same as in the richer areas there would still have been a decline in their per caput incomes of about 8 per cent.

Although the less developed regions had about 35 per cent of the total population during the post-reform period, they had only 28 per cent of the active labour force. The fall in their share in national income per active member of the labour force during the years 1953–71 was about half that of the fall in their share in per caput income. It dropped from 80 per cent of the level of the developed areas in 1953 to 69 per cent in 1971, and the differential stabilized from the early 1960s onwards at around the 70 per cent mark. Dependency ratios, therefore, were an important factor in per caput income differences. Nevertheless, the economically active members of the population still produced and earned relatively less. This was partly because a relatively larger slice of the labour force was engaged in private agriculture in the less developed republics. But labour productivity in their social sectors was also lower. In the post-reform period the capital–labour ratios of the developed and less developed areas were barely distinguishable, being 46.9 and 45.9 thousand dinars respectively in 1965, and 64.6 and 64.1 thousand dinars respectively in 1970. The difference lay in the higher capital–output ratios of the poorer areas, too widespread to be wholly accounted for by different structures.[73]

The social sector

Intra-skill differences. There is convincing evidence to show that since 1965 there were considerable differences between the net personal incomes of workers in identical skill categories who were employed in different parts of the social sector. This may be illustrated by the example of the industrial sector. In 1972, the year of the introduction of social agreements, the range of earnings of unskilled workers in twenty of the twenty-one major industrial branches was a multiple of just under 2.0. If the twenty-first branch, the film sector, is included then the range increased to 3.7.[74] Moreover, the greater the disaggregation of the sector the greater the range.[75] A substantial portion of these differences probably result from the unique employment relationship and property structures of the self-managed social sector firm.

In a capitalist economy there is, in principle, a simple mechanism for ironing out the differences between the wages of workers possessing similar skills. If the marginal product of labour in a firm, that is the income yield of the unit of labour it employs, exceeds the market price of labour, then it will bid for more labour, if necessary by offering to pay a higher wage. It will go on bidding until the productivity of the last person it employs equals the wage it pays him. Equally, unemployed workers can bid down their price thus fostering demand for labour in firms where, hitherto, the marginal product of labour had equalled its price. If, therefore, the income yielded by the last unit of labour employed differs from firm to firm, or if there is a body of unemployed workers, then the bidding mechanism that operates between potential employers and employees will relocate labour from relatively low to relatively high income yielding activities. Apart from its impact upon output, employment and the allocation of resources, bidding will tend to equalize the wages of persons with similar skills. Of course, the process has become distorted in the capitalist economies by the intervention of trade unions. But the principle remains intact.

In the self-managed economy, however, it is not possible for collectives, on the one hand, or potential members, on the other, to communicate in this way. The net income per worker of the firm is determined *ex post* operations and not known in advance. No commitment, therefore, can be entered into by a firm with respect to the level of future personal incomes. Equally, prospective members cannot offer to accept lower remuneration because they would be bound to receive a pro rata share of whatever personal income turned out to be after they joined. In principle, market forces can operate indirectly through a manipulation of skill categories. Prospective employers might offer to place work seekers in higher skill categories; and work seekers can make themselves more attractive by being prepared to accept a lower skill classification. But such practices, when they did occur, created bad feeling and were generally frowned upon.

Not only was it impossible for employers and employees to enter into binding contractual undertakings about future levels of remuneration. It was also rather difficult to make an accurate estimate as to what these levels were likely to be. The difficulty arose because of the absence of property rights in net worth. A worker gradually accumulated a non-transferable capital investment in his firm—a notional share in the Business, Reserve and Collective Consumption Funds. The longer he stayed, and the more senior he became, the greater the size of this notional share. On departure he lost his share. Equally, on joining another social sector firm he inherited, free of charge, a similar share in its net capital value. The rational social sector job changer, therefore, had to compare the expected net income streams for his particular skill category, discounted over his chosen time horizon, as between his present and prospective employment. If he thought he would inherit at least as good a right to future income and collective consumption levels as he would forgo, then he would be indifferent as to whether he stayed or went. The calculation was made more difficult by the intangible nature of the benefits that accrued from collective consumption assets. Indeed, the existence of collective consumption not only enlarged the difficulties inherent in making personal income comparisons. It also added a non-financial dimension to the employment decision; one which would have persuaded a member against moving in spite of the clear financial advantages that a particular move in his case offered. In short, the incentives to move from one job to another were not as clearly demarcated as they are in a capitalist system.

If intra-skill personal income differentials in Yugoslavia had been solely the result of differences in the skill and effort of workers within a particular skill category then the differentials in excess of these would probably have owed much to market distortions attributable to the factors just mentioned. However, it is worth reminding ourselves again at this juncture that the absence of a contractual wage meant that the returns appropriated by labour consisted of more than just the return to its own skill and effort. Entrepreneurial profits, where positive, and the failures to price capital or land in accordance with their relative scarcities[76] ensured, as we have already noted,[77] that labour also appropriated returns to entrepreneurship including monopoly, capital and land. Since social sector firms operated under varying degrees of capital intensity, market structure and pricing arrangements, they were bound to generate different per caput incomes for each skill classification, even had the skills and efforts of labour of equal qualifications been identical throughout the social sector.

As Chapter 5 will show, in certain sectors concentration ratios were high, entry and exit sluggish and foreign protection considerable. Despite the progressive toughening of price controls, these factors suggest a potentially strong propensity within these sectors towards monopolistic practices. In their case the return to entrepreneurship was likely to have included, in addition, a substantial return to monopoly power. Equally, the greater the capital intensity of a firm, in conjunction with access to underpriced financial resources, the larger the return to capital appropriated by the collective. The rational collective would only have been prepared to share these returns with a work seeker if his employment raised the income per worker for the entire collective. On this basis it would have taken on extra members up to the point at which the income per worker yielded by an extra unit of labour was equal to the average income per worker earned in the firm in question. The greater the appropriation of returns to entrepeneurship, land and capital in any firm, the greater the average income per worker. As this rose the rational firm was likely to hire fewer workers because the income per worker yielded by the marginal worker would have to be higher to match the higher average income per worker.[78]

A study on social sector income differentials in Yugoslavia by Sofia Popov,[79] which ends in 1970, compares the rank order of unskilled personal income levels in twenty-two industrial branches with the rank order of fixed capital per worker and concentration ratios. Her results show that the eight industries recording the highest average unskilled income payments for the period 1961–9 also had amongst the highest capital–labour and concentration ratios. While her results were not subjected to econometric analysis, they do suggest that capital and product market imperfections contributed to the remarkable income differentials to be found within skill categories in Yugoslavia. A more recent and sophisticated study for the years 1967–73, made by Saul Estrin, shows that capital intensity and concentration significantly explain more than 70 per cent of the inter-industry earnings dispersion. Regional factors appear to have made a negligible contribution. Although inter-republican earnings differentials for workers of identical skills were substantial, *intra*-republican differentials for such workers were even greater.[80]

The attitude adopted, in the main, by those supporting the reforms was that earnings inequality, provided it accurately reflected differing levels of efficiency, was a necessary and even desirable part of the new system.[81] While such a view had some persuasive merit in respect of inter-skill differentials, reinforced a little later when the better qualified began to migrate in large numbers, it had less force in the face of intra-skill dispersion which sometimes exceeded 200 per cent. Moreover, it contravened a strong tradition of egalitarianism deeply engrained in Yugoslav society.[82] The whole ethos and structure of self-management to some degree reflected this tradition. And it lay comfortably alongside the Marxian ethic, 'from each according to his ability to each according to his need'. The tradition received support at a number of levels. The press, and especially the popular press, was quick to spot and admonish those who appeared to be appropriating more than their fair share.[83] Indeed there was no easier issue in Yugoslavia on which to arouse a sense of outrage. In December 1967, for example, the authorities placed limits on the earnings of workers in the electric power industries, foreign trade organizations and banks following repeated attacks by the press on the excessive earnings of workers in these branches.

The indiscriminate linking of social sector differentials with private profiteering served to heighten the general unrest about them. The Belgrade student manifesto of 4 June 1968 called for the removal of social inequality by introducing a fairer system of personal income distribution—not least because it was an obvious way to gain the support of discontented workers.[84] Intra-skill income differentials also offended the socialist humanists who saw them as a symptom of the disintegration of social property into group property rights enjoyed exclusively by members of social sector firms and protected, to a greater or lesser extent, by the functioning of the market. The identification in social agreements of the personal income level of the average firm, combined with the concessionary treatment of those earning less and the penal treatment of those earning more than the averge, was *inter alia,* a deliberate attempt to erode intra-skill differentials.

Inter-skill. If the intra-skill earnings differentials in Yugoslavia were uncommonly high, the average inter-skill differentials were surprisingly narrow, reflecting the egalitarian ethos. A number of surveys conducted in the late 1960s suggest that, with the exception of executives, workers felt that differences between minimum and maximum incomes should be small.[85] In 1971, *Vus* commented that there was more wage egalitarianism in Yugoslavia than in China, and expressed the view that that was the main reason why over one-third of those working abroad were skilled.[86] Although there were some, usually well-publicized, examples of particular individuals within firms who were paid inordinately high incomes, workers in the highest skill categories in firms with low average earnings per worker sometimes earned less than the least skilled workers in firms with high average earnings per worker.

Before the social agreements, the number of skill categories within a particular firm, and the distribution of its membership between them, was entirely a matter for the representative organs in consultation with the administration. The usual procedure was for the Workers' Council to attach a certain number of points to each position in the firm based upon its difficulty, danger, skill required and so on. The available Personal Income Fund was then divided by the total number of points to arrive at the value of one point. Finally, that amount was multiplied by the number of points appropriate to his job in order to determine the share in the Personal Income Fund of any member of a collective.

The social agreements affected inter-skill as well as intra-skill differentials. The original Serbian agreement, for example, stated that within each firm in the republic, average earnings within any skill category must not exceed a stated percentage of the average earnings of unskilled labour in the firm. The relevant maxima laid down by the agreement fell between 135 per cent for semi-skilled workers and 390 per cent for those with postgraduate degrees. Administrators were entitled to receive up to 40 per cent more than the amount indicated by their skill maximum. Similar limits were adopted by other republican agreements.[87] The notions of the standardized worker, the average firm and the inter-skill maxima introduced by the social agreements, appear to have made some contribution to the reduction of both intra- and inter-skill differentials in Yugoslavia.

CHAPTER 5

THE GOODS MARKET

The transition from planned to market-induced growth implied a radical change in the pattern of demand and required a correspondingly radical reorientation in the production of goods and services. The ability to reorient, as Chapter 3 demonstrated, was severely hampered by deficiencies in the capital market. In spite of this, as Section 1 relates, certain industries succeeded in making progress, usually with the help of foreign partners. Generally speaking, however, the responses to the new environment were poor. Quite apart from capital market problems, the rate of inflation and the state of the balance of payments were often serious enough to require a high degree of administrative intervention in the form both of domestic price control and foreign trade quotas. The distorted incentive pattern led, as it had done before the reform, to patterns of profit and loss which bore little relation to relative degrees of genuine competitiveness. These distortions are discussed in Section 2.

Of all the defects, however, perhaps the most limiting was the absence of free entry to and exit from industrial markets. The absence of equity share or a satisfactory surrogate, together with the severe limits on the private sector, made it extremely difficult for companies to shift their resources into new areas of production. Moreover, the communal authorities were most reluctant to use their powers to liquidate loss-making concerns. Quite apart from the ideological difficulties of liquidating worker-managed enterprises, and the obvious added financial burden on communal budgets, the authorities were reluctant to discipline firms whose financial crises were often the consequence of macro-economically motivated state intervention in the market and not their own inefficiency.

1 Concentration and integration

In 1970 there were 2,374 industrial firms in Yugoslavia. This compared with 2,090 in 1952 on the eve of the first wave of decentralization. Annex 10 indicates their size structure. After 1971 the statistics became misleading because of the disaggregation of most firms with 250 workers or more into BOALs. However, since these disaggregated units almost invariably reintegrated on a contractual basis, the pattern disclosed by the 1970 statistics remained largely valid. What is so striking about these figures is the derisory role played by small firms in providing employment and generating social output. The structure of the manufacturing and mining sector manifests, by conventional statistical measures, a high degree of concentration. An analysis of concentration ratios for 103 industrial sub-sectors for the year 1968 revealed ratios of 100 per cent in 21 cases, 80 per cent in 41 cases, and 50 per cent or more in 83 cases.[1] A similar picture emerges from data published by the Federal Institute of Statistics on the number of firms producing each of several hundred products. Of the 684 products manufactured in 1968, 27 per cent were produced by 2 firms or less, 50 per cent by 5 firms or less, and 80 per cent by 20 firms or less.[2]

On the face of it, therefore, Yugoslav industrial market structure seems highly oligopolistic. But these ratios are rather misleading. It is true that many branches of industry were dominated by a few firms. But it is also true that, because of the policy of industrial diversification pursued by the authorities in the 1940s and 1950s, the total output for which each sectoral grouping of firms was responsible was very small. Yugoslavia manufactured almost all the major producer and consumer products. Moreover, the pattern of diversification tended to be intra-regional, with each republic having its own basic industrial complex. For example, six steel firms produced in 1970 less than two and a half million tons of crude steel per annum.[3] Given the small size of Yugoslav industrial markets it is not surprising that the number of firms was limited. Indeed, the striking factor is not that there were so few firms but that there were so many. One of the main reasons for this was, of course, the republican bias built into investment strategy.

The problem that the authorities had to face at the time of reform was that industrial structure was excessively concentrated yet insufficiently integrated. There were too few firms in most markets to ensure competitive behaviour, but too many for any single one to achieve optimum economies of scale. The problem first became an open issue at the time of the 1961 reform measures when a substantial liberalization of the foreign trade regime was undertaken. This made it vital to develop an industrial establishment which could compete in hard currency markets. The authorities believed that the most immediate task in this respect was to try and integrate the existing production, and future investment, programme of firms in the same industrial markets. The first official expression of this policy came from the Fourth Plenum of the Central Committee of the League of Communists of Yugoslavia, held in 1962.[4] Initially, the emphasis was on integration between domestic firms. But following the 1965 measures the authorities increasingly stressed the importance of integration with foreign firms.

Co-operation and competition

Co-operation. By far the most popular institutional vehicle of co-operation for promoting integration was the industrial co-operation agreement.[5] This involved the linking of one or more of the stages of the manufacturing cycles of two or more firms. The most common form comprised the joint production of particular end-products, sub-sequently marketed under joint or separate trade marks. These agreements might be purely domestic or might involve a foreign corporation. A domestic example involved FAP of Serbia, which made truck chassis, and FAMOS of Bosnia, which made heavy engines. They integrated their production and investment schedules to produce trucks and buses which were marketed under a joint trade mark.[6] The agreement between *Rade Koncar* of Zagreb and *Castor and Inel* of Turin, concluded in September 1966, illustrates a domestic– foreign agreement. This involved the joint manufacture of automatic washing machines. The Yugoslavs produced the electric motors and heaters and the Italians supplied the rest. The partners then exchanged components, assembled the completed product and sold it in the respective market areas set out in the agreement. The Italians supplied, on credit, the machinery needed for the Yugoslavs to fulfil their part of the bargain, together with the appropriate document-ation and know-how.[7]

The authorities were particularly concerned to encourage inter-national industrial co-operation agreements, either by themselves or in conjunction with investment partnerships. There were a number of reasons for this. First, given the variable technical, quality and design standards that characterized the output of most Yugoslav industrial firms, they were more likely to be competitive internationally by specializing in the less advanced sector of the industrial component market. For example, *Rade Koncar* could not have hoped to sell its own automatic washing machines in Italy, at least at anything remotely approaching a competitive and economic price. By concentrating on the simpler stages of the manufacturing cycle, firms secured guaranteed long-term hard currency markets. Moreover, this was achieved without incurring any marketing costs. Second, the agreements improved the operating efficiency of domestic firms, not only by transferring foreign technology and fostering economies of scale through specialization, but also by committing the foreign partner to ensuring that the Yugoslav component was manufactured to a standard appropriate to hard currency markets. Third, the agreements promoted closer ties with world markets, one of the major objects of reform. Finally, the arrangements were, at least partly, self-financing. This was because the resulting interdependence of the partners generated bilateral flows of complementary goods and services which reduced credit requirements from Western sources. By the end of 1972 about 340 industrial co-operation agreements had been concluded.[8]

Industrial co-operation agreements should be distinguished from both business associations and Economic Chambers. But the dividing line was not always clear-cut. Business associations were similar to trade associations in the United Kingdom and the tasks they undertook varied greatly from industrial branch to branch. Some merely provided a forum for an exchange of views; others dealt with standardization and product specification; yet others were responsible for joint marketing projects or research programmes. There were even associations, such as the steel producers, which allocated responsibilities for the production of particular end-products or, such as the shipbuilders, which purported to co-ordinate investment programmes. It was at this stage that the dividing line between industrial co-operation agreements and business associations blurred.

Both business associations and technical co-operation agreements were distinguishable from Economic Chambers.[9] In addition to their role in the drafting of federal economic legislation, the provision of a range of technical services and the formulation of business customs, Economic Chambers, composed of committees of business men at the local, republican and federal levels, provided a clearing-house for the exchange of information on industrial planning. It was believed that the practice of keeping interested firms informed on each others' investment intentions was a necessary means of avoiding the duplication of production facilities and wasteful competition. Until the introduction of contractual planning, the role of the Chambers, in this respect, was strictly confined to the exchange of information. Their meetings were not supposed to assign production tasks, though in some of the more concentrated industries, such as steel, the functions of Chamber and business association often overlapped. From the mid-1970s, of course, they played a central role in the investment planning process.[10]

Competition. Having determined upon a policy of integration and co-ordination of production and investment, the authorities were faced with the adverse implications that it might have for competitive behaviour. Here they were to rely upon two counterbalancing factors. The first of these was the presence of effective foreign competition. The 1961 measures had made several inroads into the system of protection that surrounded the industrial sector. But it was not until the measures of the mid-1960s that the authorities were able to introduce a comprehensive policy of inducing domestic competitive behaviour by opening up the home market to foreign competition. Indeed, foreign competition was regarded as both a spur to domestic integration and a guarantee of the competitive behaviour of integrated units. Unfortunately, as Section 2 relates, the deteriorating balance of payments, which characterized the post-reform years, meant that many of the pre-reform restrictive measures had to be reimposed.

The second counterbalancing factor was the role accorded to the economic courts.[11] In respect of business associations and co-operation agreements the position was set out in Articles 111 and 132 of the Basic Law on the Unified Chambers of Economy and Business Co-operation passed in 1965.[12] By Article 111:

It is forbidden to form a contract of industrial co-operation or to found a business association whose objects are contrary to the principles of a unified economic sphere, a planned orientation of the economy and other principles of the socio-economic system. In particular, a contract for industrial co-operation or the foundation of a business association may not contain clauses intended to limit the volume of production and the utilization of the plant capacity of producers, to prevent the economic survival in the market of other economic organizations, to divide the market and business zones, or whereby contracting parties make arrangements respecting sale prices on the internal market.

And by Article 132:

> A contract of industrial co-operation or clauses thereof providing for objects contrary to the principles specified in Article 111 hereof or to other provisions of the law shall be voided by a decision of the Supreme Court.

The implementation of those articles was helped by the obligation imposed upon firms by Article 114a to furnish their appropriate Economic Chamber with full information on the nature of the arrangements they had entered into. In practice, resort to the courts under these Articles was hardly ever necessary because the negotiations prior to the conclusion of an agreement or the establishment of an association were carefully monitored by the relevant Economic Chamber.

The Basic Commodity Trade Law of 1967, authorized by Article 30 of the 1963 Constitution, laid down more general prohibitions against discriminatory business practices which covered all kinds of commercial relationships between firms.[13] Section 52 prohibited inter-firm price fixing, market sharing and production limiting arrangements, though an exception was made for agreements which demonstrably led to an improvement in economic efficiency. This section was rarely relied on despite the widespread price fixing arrangements between members of business associations. Section 53 was directed against speculation, or any deliberate withholding of goods ultimately intended for sale on a market. Section 54 contained a blanket provision against unfair competition and this was the section most relied on in inter-firm disputes in the economic courts.

The oil industry proved especially litigious. For example, the long-standing quarrel between the Croatian group, INA, and the Serbian group, *Jugopetrol*, found its way into the economic courts in 1967.[14] *Jugopetrol* argued that INA was abusing its monopoly power to prevent the expansion of the *Bosanski Brod* refinery and the completion of the refinery at *Pancevo*. Concurrently a further contest was taking place within the *Jugopetrol* group itself. The provisional management of the future *Pancevo* refinery quarelled with their sponsor *Naftagas* about its support for the *Novi Sad* refinery. *Pancevo* feared that *Novi Sad* would compete unfairly with it despite the assurance of *Naftagas* that the processes and products of the two refineries would be entirely different.[15]

There was, in fact, no definition of 'unfair' in the law. Most cases concerned misleading advertising campaigns or unacceptable marketing techniques. There were instances of firms being accused of unfair competition through domestic price cutting in breach of business association price agreements which had escaped condemnation because they were deemed to enhance economic efficiency.[16] The law also forbade various monopolistic practices by communes, notably in the retail field. In December 1974 the Federal Assembly passed the Law on the Suppression of Unfair Competition and Monopolistic Agreements,[17] which was in most respects a consolidation of the 1967 legislation. The new law prohibited particular classes of commercial practice which inflicted damage on other firms or on consumers. Any kind of agreement which tended to reduce free competition or to acquire for a firm a monopolistic or even privileged position was condemned in general terms. Practices expressly condemned by the legislation were price fixing, market sharing and cartel agreements on the terms of purchase and sale.

The introduction of self-management agreements posed a new challenge to competition law. The authorities had decreed that the anarchy of the market was to be replaced by self-management agreements freely negotiated within the context of social agreements. To the extent that requirements with respect to price, quantity and market destination were obligations imposed upon firms by social agreements, issues of competition law did not arise. But in circumstances where such requirements were not binding, the dangers remained. In 1976 regulations were issued[18] stating that all self-management agreements must be published before they are implemented so that those adversely affected may raise objections. In the event of an objection, the parties to the proposed agreement must reconsider their position. If the objector still remains unsatisfied then he may go to the Court for compulsory arbitration.

Since the introduction of the BOAL, it is worth distinguishing between those self-management agreements which determined the terms upon which products were 'marketed', usually by a Work Organization (WO) as a result of 'arm's length' negotiations; and those which were concluded between intermediate production units, usually BOALs, which contributed to the manufacture of such products. Of course, the distinction is one of degree and the expressions 'marketed' and 'arm's length' are relative. On the one hand, the WOs were negotiating within the restrictive framework of production and price targets established by thirty republican sectoral social agreements. On the other, all manufacturing units which performed a separate function within the manufacturing cycle were, by law, BOALs; and since all BOALs were constitutionally independent, they themselves were negotiating with each other. But, as we have already learned,[19] the technological realities of advanced manufacturing left many BOALs with no alternative but to submit to a substantial degree of central planning by the WO of which they were a part. In effect 'transfer' prices were charged to allocate costs and benefits 'fairly' between BOALs, taking into account the extent to which the profitability of one depended upon the contribution of others.

Sectoral developments. Significantly, perhaps, the two industrial sectors which made the most rapid strides in the direction of improved efficiency, the electrical goods and transport sectors, concluded a number of major industrial co-operation and investment partnership agreements with foreign corporations. The electrical goods sector, consisting of about eighty firms, was particularly successful with a good productivity record, rapid expansion in employment and an increasing proportion of output sold as exports.[20] Throughout most of the post-reform period the industry enjoyed a buoyant and rapidly expanding domestic market for electrical products, both in consumer goods, such as TVs and washing machines, and intermediate products, such as components for the car and shipbuilding industries. The success abroad was achieved by widespread improvement in the quality and design of electrical equipment and was particularly marked in the Third World markets for electric power stations and transmission lines. Competitiveness was due to an amalgam of factors. The prices of domestically produced copper and lead were relatively low. Firms were, for the most part, situated in the North where the more sophisticated labour required was readily available. Above all, many firms had concluded industrial co-operation arrangements with foreign firms, similar to the *Rade Koncar* agreement just discussed, which had a favourable impact on their productive efficiency and marketing opportunities.

The transport sector[21] was the third largest employer in Yugoslavia after metal fabrication and wood processing and it was highly concentrated. It is true that in the private car branch at least five different makes of foreign vehicle were assembled under licence at one time or another: Citroens at *Tomos*, Renaults at *Litostroj*, Saabs at *Agrostroja*, Austins at *Novo Mesto* and Fiats at *Crvena Zastava*. But of these, only the *Crvena Zastava* assembly, situated in Serbia, was of any significance.

Its relationship with Fiat began in 1954 and became progressively more intimate, culminating in an investment partnership in 1969 whose objective was an annual output in excess of 150,000 units. All the engines for *Zastava* cars were produced by UMI, a holding company which also manufactured most of the country's tractors, agricultural combines and diesel engines. The relationship involved a substantial component exchange with a steadily growing proportion of the total value of the cars being produced on Yugoslav soil. Despite the tariff protection and favourable retention quota treatment that it received, the *Zastava* operation appears to have been reasonably competitive by international standards, though the concessions it received excited adverse comment from the other republics.

The manufacture of trucks was dominated by two firms. *TAM* was the sole producer of medium-sized trucks; and despite an annual output of less than 10,000 units, industrial co-operation with KHD of Germany enabled it to produce reasonably efficiently. *FAP-FAMOS,* an integrated firm producing both engines and chassis, was the only manufacturer of heavy trucks and the main manufacturer of buses. Its annual output was less than that of TAM and its productivity record less impressive. Eventually it switched its licence from Saurer of Austria to Mercedes of Germany and completed an industrial co-operation agreement with the latter.

Unfortunately, integration, whether domestic or international, was notably less in evidence in the so-called basic industrial sectors such as steel, oil, and chemicals, whose rationalization was regarded by the authorities as central to an improved industrial structure. Given the post-reform trend towards republicanism there was no chance of persuading a particular republic to close its steelworks or petro-chemical complex or even to merge it with another's. But it was hoped, at least, that progress could be achieved in the co-ordination of production and investment schedules.

The steel industry provides particularly good examples of the kinds of difficulty encountered.[22] The annual domestic production of just under three million tons at the time of reform was divided between six plants each situated in a different republic. Most production facilities were suboptimal and incorporated outdated technologies. This was particularly true of the blast furnaces which were too small and mainly operated by the costly open-hearth method. Moreover, although there were reasonably good medium-grade iron ore deposits in Bosnia, high-grade iron ore and coking coal had to be imported and then travel long distances over land to the various mills; *Jesenice* in Slovenia, *Scoplje* in Macedonia and *Niksic* in Montenegro were particularly badly placed in this respect. Together, these factors meant that the cost of domestic pig iron production was inordinately high. Moreover, the Second Five Year Plan had neglected investment in finishing capacity; so that by the early 1960s pig iron capacity substantially exceeded raw steel and rolling mill capacity.

The ideal solution at this juncture would have been to phase out all the plants and build one large one on the coast. However, such a course was politically impossible. Recognizing that the only acceptable solution to the industry's problems would be one consistent with the continued operation of existing facilities, the authorities launched a five-year modernization and reconstruction programme in 1964, in order to replace old plant and, in particular, to eliminate bottle-necks which had been the main cause of low capacity utilization, the greatest blight of the Yugoslav steel industry. Unfortunately, the programme achieved few, if any, of its objectives. President Tito summed up the position in the year after its scheduled conclusion as follows:

We have a large number of small steelworks which put together do not produce 3 million tons while the Rumanians built at the seaside a steelworks with a capacity of 3 million tons. Our steel producers should integrate themselves and undertake specialization, and should reach agreement on assortments of their products . . . The *Niksic* Steelworks had stocks of goods amounting to about 3 billion dinars which could not be sold to anyone. The situation was similar with the steelworks of *Jesenice* and certain others as well. Therefore, it is necessary that steelworks should also be integrated. Considering that we have already had them located at different places let them at least reach agreement on a division of assortments of production and specialization.[23]

Serious attempts were again made in the early 1970s to improve investment and production co-ordination, and a number of expert studies were commissioned to determine a national policy for the industry. Probably the best solution would have been to turn each existing plant into a specialist producer by means of a domestic industrial co-operation agreement. But the decentralized nature of economic decision-making in Yugoslavia prevented any binding agreement being reached on the future of this highly political industry.

Similar problems were experienced in the chemical industry, the fastest growing industrial sector in post-reform Yugoslavia.[24] This was true especially in the field of petroleum refining and petrochemicals. Yugoslavia relied heavily on foreign crude, much of which was high cost Russian crude imported on barges to inland refineries. There were five refineries; two, *Rijeka* and *Bosanski Brod*, were on the coast and three, *Novi Sad, Pancevo* and *Sisak*, were inland. None of them was of optimum size though their combined capacity exceeded domestic needs. The excess refining capacity strongly contrasted with the shortage of 'downstream' petrochemical facilities. Unlike steel, not all the republics had their own refining facilities and those without it, Slovenia, Montenegro and Macedonia, all had plans afoot to build their own. As with steel mills, so petroleum refineries were an important prestige item; moreover, in contrast with steel, the price and foreign trade regime conspired to make their operations very profitable. The picture was further complicated by the running battle for the domestic petroleum market between the Croatian Group, INA, controlling the *Rijeka* and *Sisak* refineries, and the Serbian Group, *Jugopetrol,* controlling the *Novi Sad, Pancevo* and *Bosanski Brod* refineries. Commenting on developments in this field in the late 1960s Tito said:

There should not only be plans for the integration of oil producers, but also an integration of manufacturers in the petro-chemical industry. Certain republics which at present do not have the capacities of this kind want to build their own oil refineries to process imported oil because they have seen that this industrial branch is very profitable. However, they do not bear in mind the consequences which may occur after the construction of a large number of small enterprises.[25]

His words match closely his remarks about steel.

It would be wrong, of course, to convey a picture of total gloom. There were some successful developments in the chemicals industry, notably in artificial and synthetic fibres and in nitrogen fertilizers. But the general pattern was of fractured development. Because of the growing gap between the demand for, and the supply of, downstream petrochemical production, the authorities appear to have taken the view that the certain delay entailed in getting inter-republican agreement on investment strategy was too high a cost to pay in terms of foreign exchange forgone meanwhile. In short, the proliferation of petrochemical projects in the post-reform period seems to suggest an attitude of 'anything better than nothing'.

There are a number of plausible explanations for the failure of integration policy in these cases, and many of these apply with equal force to difficulties faced in integrating other industrial sectors. The regional orientation of extra-budgetary funds and bank lending has already been discussed and takes pride of place. Foreign sources of finance were important for the basic industry investment projects; but there was no stimulus to industrial rationalization from that quarter either. Foreign suppliers extending credits were concerned with selling equipment and foreign banks with security for their loans. Neither took an overview of Yugoslav industrial strategy. Technological factors were also important. Because of the self-sufficiency mentality of republican authorities in directing investment policy in the 1950s and early 1960s, plants tended to be competitive rather than complementary and not easily susceptible to a policy of national production co-ordination. Moreover, the 'process' nature of steel production and oil refining made them weak candidates for industrial co-operation agreements, whether domestic or international. Some blame must also be attached to the protective elements in the price and foreign trade regimes and to the defective operation of entry and exit, which are discussed in Sections 2 and 3 below. Both tended to support the continuation of the status quo.

Problems of integration were not confined to industry. They also afflicted the infrastructure of the economy. Firms in infrastructure sectors were organized into so-called alliances.[26] These were an institutional arrangement especially designed to deal with economic activities which could not be conducted on a market basis and in respect of which a national policy was especially desirable. Alliances could only be established by federal legislation and membership was compulsory for all firms within the designated sector. The usual practice was to establish republican alliances to co-ordinate the activities of firms on a regional basis and a federal alliance to co-ordinate the policies of one region with another. However, despite their federal origins and obligatory membership there was no obligation on members to enter into binding agreements about their activities. Moreover, what influence the federal authorities could wield with respect to investment policy disappeared with the abolition of the Federal Investment Fund in 1963.

All infrastructure sectors suffered from poor co-ordination. Perhaps the most serious difficulties in this respect were experienced by the power sector,[27] which was badly fragmented. There were about eighty independent firms, over half of which were distributors and a further quarter hydro-electric stations. The remainder were thermal generating and transmission centres. In theory the regional alliances, established in 1959, co-ordinated the production of firms in their regions, and the federal alliance co-ordinated the production, consumption and exchange of electric power as between regions. In practice, each republic followed an independent policy with respect to its own power resources. The size and direction of investment, the level of production and the decision whether to buy from or sell to outside sources were matters for the republican authorities through their powers to raise financing levies and to fix prices.

In fact neither high cost nor low cost producers of power wished to cede their autonomy to a central body. Slovenia, a high cost, deficit producer, wished both to protect its own coal-mining sector and to have the option of supplementing its requirements from low cost foreign sources. Bosnia, a relatively low cost, surplus producer, feared that a centralized regime would not offer it a fair price for the transmission of power to other republics. The absence of a national policy in this area had two serious defects. First, many republics suffered serious power shortages which interfered with industrial production and inconvenienced consumers. Second, the prices charged for power varied from region to region having an important differential effect upon the profitability of business operations and perhaps on the location of investment.

After the 1974 Constitution, the role of the 'community of interest' was broadened to include the supply of infrastructure services such as power and transport.[28] Previously, as we have seen, they were confined to managing health, education and social services.[29] They were designed to cater for circumstances in which the market proved an inadequate indicator of social value. Socio-political communities could now recommend or indeed, require, that certain activities be organized on such a basis. Their managing bodies comprised representatives of both the suppliers and users of services in equal numbers. They were separate legal entities and responsible for their own management and financing. They were entitled to raise loan finance from banks or customers and could charge for their service by a mixture of price and tax. Socio-political communities consulted them on all relevant legislative proposals.

Mergers.[30] Annex 11 sets out the pattern of mergers from 1965 to 1972. After the introduction of the BOAL the statistics are misleading. The total divides almost exactly between those involving the amalgamation of two or more firms into a new firm with a new name and those involving the absorption of one existing firm by another. The most remarkable fact about these statistics is that 70 per cent of the mergers occurred between firms within the same commune and a further 13 per cent between firms in neighbouring communes.[31] Of the remainder, 16 per cent were between firms within the same republic. Therefore, only 1 per cent of the mergers since the reform have been inter-republican. This pattern emphasizes the regional bias in capital movements already discussed.[32] It indicates that the merger technique contributed almost nothing to the inter-republican rationalization of industrial structures which was one of the main objects of reform policy.

The remarkably high percentage of mergers that occurred between firms within the same commune suggests two points which are, at least partly, supported by the evidence.[33] First, the vast majority of mergers were between firms of modest or small size, usually employing less than 250 workers. Second, a significant proportion of mergers had little to do with industrial integration. Only 30 per cent of a large sample took place between firms in the same industrial group. There is, indeed, good reason to believe that a large number of mergers took place for purely financial reasons. Communal pressure seems to have been applied to the larger or more prosperous firms within the locality in order to absorb the ailing or unviable ones.[34] To the extent that this is true then mergers acted as a vehicle to sustain uneconomic units in production, thus contributing to a misallocation of capital resources.

2   The incentive system

Prices

An intrinsic part of the reform measures were the major price adjustments undertaken in July 1965 to correct the distortions that had developed in previous years between the prices of manufactured goods on the one hand and the price of agricultural commodities, raw materials and infrastructural goods and services on the other.[35] At the same time the dinar was devalued to $US12.50 to assist in aligning all domestic prices with those prevailing on the world market. The price freeze on 90 per cent of industrial products, introduced at the same time as the realignment, was regarded as a temporary measure to tide the economy over the initial shock of reform. Thereafter, it was intended to leave all prices free to find their own level according to the state of supply and demand. Unfortunately, owing to the severe inflationary pressures which continued to plague the economy after reform, these intentions were never realized. Because of the inadequacies of monetary and fiscal policy,[36] administered prices continued to play a central role in the fight against inflation.

Until 1973 the authorities persevered with the pre-reform system of control. The prices of certain 'necessary' goods and services such as electrical power, railroad freight, sugar, oil and salt were fixed by the Federal Executive Council, and of certain other essential services and food, by the communes. Wholesale and retail trade margins were controlled by the republics and communes respectively. As far as industrial intermediate goods were concerned, ceiling prices were set by the federal authorities for certain 'basic' industrial goods such as coal, petroleum and steel. A varying number of other industrial goods were controlled by a system of prior increase registration, first introduced in 1958. The system involved two stages; first, at least two-thirds of both the producers and the consumers of the product in question were required to agree to the increase. The agreement had to be authorized by the appropriate Economic Chamber—an important step since it virtually guaranteed immunity from suit in an action for price fixing under the Basic Commodity Trade Law. Second, the producers had to inform the Federal Price Office (FPO) of their intention to implement the agreed price increase at least one month in advance. If the rise was not prohibited by the FPO within that period then it took effect. For commodities not subject to price control, manipulation of import quotas was sometimes employed as a means of putting pressure on domestic prices regarded as excessive. The system was by no means watertight. One of its most obvious limitations was that it could not control 'new' products and it was frequently evaded by means of small changes in product design. *Ekonomska Politika* reported that between 1 January and 31 March 1971, the FPO registered 30,000 new products. It is inconceivable that the economy underwent structural changes of such magnitude in three months; for the calendar years 1967 and 1968 the number of new products registered were 5,700 and 6,000 respectively.[37]

Not surprisingly, the continued use of administered prices prolonged the serious distortions in the structure of relative prices that characterized the years before reform. This, in turn, generated a pattern of incentives to firms which often provoked a response contrary to the object laid down in the Social Plan. These distortions occurred partly because of the multitude of types of control whose scope and intensity varied over time, and partly because of the differing criteria applied to individual requests for price increases. Although the criteria applied by the FPO for setting a ceiling price or evaluating a prior registration have never been officially divulged, it seems that one or more of a variety of factors was taken into account—world prices, cost-plus, the monopoly power of the firm in question, the production costs of other producers and the effect of an increase upon the standard of living. The difficulties inherent in such an approach are not hard to see. To take a simple example, if one criterion, say cost-plus, were applied to an input price and another, perhaps the world market price, were applied to an output price, then their combined impact might have important implications for the financial viability of the output-producing firm which bore no relationship whatsoever to its productive efficiency or lack of it.

In establishing a price policy to assist in the transformation of the industrial sector, the authorities were confronted with three con-flicting objectives. First, the price of processed goods had to be low enough to be reasonably competitive both at home and in inter-national markets. Second, profit margins in the processing industries had to be sufficiently high to generate funds to finance productivity enhancing investment. Third, the price of raw material inputs and infrastructure services had to be high enough to enable those sectors to expand their deficient capacities. The problem was that the combination of underdevelopment and inefficiency in the industrial sector made it impossible to devise a price policy which simul-taneously met all three objectives. Either the primary goods and services sectors earned a reasonable rate of return and the processing industries were squeezed to the extent that their modernization programmes were delayed or curtailed, as illustrated from the example of the steel industry given below; or the primary goods and services sectors were squeezed for the benefit of the processing industries, as in the fixing of railway freight rates;[38] or both the primary and the processing sectors were allowed to make a reason-able rate of return behind foreign trade protection, as in the case of oil refining.

An illustration from the steel industry provides an interesting example of the dilemma.[39] In 1963 price ceilings were set for steel.

The ceilings were not raised at the time of reform, even though the joint effect of price realignment and devaluation was to increase the prices of all raw material inputs and freight charges to the industry. The very narrow profit margin earned on sales seriously impaired its ability to implement the 1963–8 modernization programme designed to increase and improve raw-steel and finishing capacities. In 1968 the steel producers finally succeeded in persuading the required number of their customers to agree to a price increase; but the FPO prohibited the increase on prior registration because, it argued, it would raise the Yugoslav domestic price above the EEC export price. Ironically, when the EEC export price, along with world prices generally, rose in 1969 the industry failed to reach an agreement on a 12 per cent increase with the required number of producers. As a last resort they appealed directly to the Federal Executive Council who awarded them a mere 5 per cent.[40] This inadequate award made it more attractive to the industry to export than to meet domestic demand and the metal fabricating industry was then faced with substantial shortages and obliged to import.

In April 1972 the Social Price Act was passed.[41] The intention was to bring the system of price fixing into line with the new doctrine of contractual planning. It stated that the criteria for establishing individual product prices would, in future, be determined by agreements between groups of firms producing and consuming identical products within the framework of an inter-republican agreement. It emphasized, in very general terms, the importance of the application of market criteria in price setting. However, since all industrial intermediate prices were subject to the new system and the price levels established by it *still* subject to FPO approval, it amounted, if anything, to an increase in administrative control. Moreover, the legislation expressly reserved to the federal authorities the right both to exercise control over unspecified key commodities and to intervene on a general basis when macro-economic conditions warranted.

In April 1974, exactly two years later, the first inter-republic agreement on price policy was ratified.[42] It was intended to provide a set of guide-lines for the conclusion of inter-firm self-management agreements. The importance of market criteria was again stressed and more useful guidance was given as to what these actually were. In particular, agreements were required to improve the rate of return in the raw material and infrastructure services sectors, a target which was in line with the objectives of the 1971–5 Plan. Prices of processed output were required to be based upon the prices of domestic raw materials and services rather than on the import prices of similar goods. The authorities therefore appeared to have opted for a cost-plus approach, combating its adverse implications for international competitiveness through a flexible exchange rate and a modicum of protection. Further inter-republican price agreements were concluded annually.[43]

In effect, the onset of contractual planning made very little difference to the realities of price control. The Federal Authorities, either directly or through the FPO, continued to intervene as before. The FPO was abolished in October 1980 and replaced by federal and republican 'communities of prices'.[44] The concept of a 'community of price' was similar to that of a 'community of interest'. The communities contained both producer and consumer representatives from each sector. They fixed prices after consultation with the relevant socio-political communities, Economic Chambers and trade unions. The main criteria for fixing were demand and supply, world prices, liquidity and profitability considerations and the promotion of priority sectors. Depending upon the item, firms either informed the competent community of proposed price rises or presented them for approval.

By 1980, Yugoslavia was experiencing inflation of unprecedented severity. Initially, of the prices formerly under FPO control, 47 per cent became the responsibility of the federal price communities and the remainder, the responsibility of the republican communities. This represented a considerable decentralization. Concern was expressed that the devolution to republican communities tended to exacerbate the fragmentation of the Yugoslav market. However, in July 1982,[45] with the situation deteriorating, temporary measures were introduced shifting most of the prices under their control back from the republican to the federal communities of interest. The annual Economic Resolution had placed an overall limit on price rises for 1982 which was not being observed.

Foreign currency and trade restrictions

The reformers placed considerable emphasis on the need for greater integration with the world economy. Yugoslavia had been a member of the IMF since its inception and became a full member of GATT in 1966. It also sought closer ties with the EEC. To complement the July

1965 price reform and devaluation a foreign trade and exchange reform was also prepared, though its implementation was delayed until 1 January 1967.[46] This involved the abolition of export premiums and tax subsidies, the introduction of a foreign exchange retention quota system for exporters, the reduction in the average level of customs duties from 23 to 11 per cent and a reduction in import quotas. These measures were regarded as a major factor in establishing competitiveness and encouraging structural reform. In terms of changes in regulatory techniques they were not as radical as the 1961 measures.[47] Nevertheless, their adoption was what finally assured Yugoslavian membership of GATT.

The highest tariffs still exceeded 20 per cent, falling mainly on metal products and electrical equipment. Duties on most other major industrial products ranged from about 8 to 13 per cent and export-oriented industries, like non-ferrous metals and shipbuilding, attracted very low duties. All products attracted additional border levies of about 4 per cent. Of course, the gross duty on the c.i.f. price of imports did not necessarily reflect the effective net protection accruing to the domestic value added of the industry in question though such evidence that exists on this matter suggests that there was some correlation.[48] Moreover, the lower rates of duty frequently underestimated the degree of protection because of the additional impact of the import licensing regime and various forms of domestic subsidy.

For the purpose of licensing, imports were divided into several catagories whose precise definition changed frequently.[49] Roughly speaking, they fell into one of five groups: liberalized, conditionally liberalized, global exchange quota, commodity quota and licensed. Commodities falling within the liberalized category could be imported without restriction and these accounted for about 17 per cent of the total number of imported products listed at the beginning of 1967. Conditionally liberalized commodities, involving an obligation to purchase a fixed number of them from clearing-currency areas before being imported freely, represented a further 24 per cent of the total. Goods falling within these classes consisted mainly of foodstuffs, especially fruit, raw materials, such as coking coal, scrap-iron, iron ore, wool, cotton, crude oil, and some consumer goods. Global foreign exchange quotas affected products whose import levels were determined by agreement between domestic producers and consumers. Moreover, these agreements had to be approved by the appropriate Economic Chamber. They sometimes led to the total exclusion of equipment produced in sufficient quantities in Yugoslavia. 55 per cent of total imported products fell into this group at the beginning of 1967; but its statistical significance is hard to assess because much depended upon the relative bargaining power of the parties concerned as well as on the attitude of the Chamber. Commodity quotas were officially-set value or volume quotas, and licensed imports, the most restricted class, required specific permission for each transaction. Commodity quotas accounted for almost all the remaining 4 per cent of products, the number falling into the licensed catagory being very small.

The one innovation at the time of reform was the introduction of retention quotas as the main instrument for export promotion. Export premiums and tax rebates were abolished almost entirely. Instead, exporters were allowed to retain and freely use, irrespective of the quota and licensing system, a proportion of their foreign exchange earnings, while the remainder had to be sold to the National Bank at a fixed rate. The basic retention quota rate was set at 7 per cent but it increased, both with the share of total production exported and the rate of increase of exports achieved, up to a maximum of 24 per cent. The system appears to have provided a substantially smaller stimulus to the majority of exporters than the combination of premiums and rebates that it replaced and may, in part, explain the substantial slow-down in the growth of industrial exports that occurred in the second half of the 1960s. Moreover, it encouraged a number of exporting firms to import goods, bearing no relation to their production cycles, which traded at handsome mark-ups on the domestic market. Equally, many importing firms sought Yugoslav products on the domestic market which foreign suppliers would accept in part exchange or for cash. This practice tended to make imports more expensive—either because the cheapest supplier wasn't interested or because he charged a premium for on-selling to someone who was. The main reason for this wasteful deployment of scarce funds was that no domestic foreign exchange market existed in which exporters could sell the funds to bona fide importers at their real value.

Since 1967 the authorities have sought to simplify and liberalize further the foreign trade and exchange regulations.[50] When the balance of payments position was strong they relaxed quotas, lowered tariffs and softened foreign exchange restrictions; when it was weak they relied increasingly on exchange rate flexibility. Where the deficit was such as to require additional restrictive measures they employed short-term expedients, such as import deposits or customs duties surcharges. Only reluctantly did they resort to a more restrictive quota policy; and then usually confined it to consumer durables. Generally speaking, therefore, the added restrictions were imposed for short-term, demand-side, macro-economic reasons and not for long-term, supply-side, structural reasons. It must, though, be added that the discriminatory use of purely domestic instruments, such as subsidized interest rates or tax concessions, often had important implications for the level of protection.

It is difficult to make a generalization about the overall picture at the end of 1971, in comparison with the beginning of 1967, after six years of balance of payments fluctuations culminating in particularly large deficits in 1970 and 1971. The average duty on all imports, exclusive of the border tax and surcharge, had fallen from 14 per cent to 12 per cent, and on equipment imports from 24 to 18 per cent. Liberalized imports had increased overall from 17 to 29 per cent of the total. Commodities covered by global exchange quotas had fallen from 55 to 45 per cent of the total. The category of conditionally liberalized imports had been abolished and, although commodity quotas and goods requiring transaction licences increased from 4 to 20 per cent and from less than 1 to 6 per cent respectively of total imported products, only one-fifth of equipment imports, one-quarter of raw material and semi-finished goods, and about 35 per cent of consumer goods fell into the two latter categories. However, the dinar had been devalued to 17.00 = $US1, an import deposit scheme requiring 50 per cent of the value of imports to be deposited three months in advance had been in operation since October 1970, various measures had been taken in order to check foreign borrowing to finance imports and a 6 per cent *ad valorem* subsidy for exports to hard currency areas had recently been introduced.

The year 1972 brought about a remarkable turn-around in the state of the current account which was sustained until the latter part of 1973, with surpluses in these years of $US419m. and $US485m. respectively. In July 1972 and again in December further measures were taken to control the volume of foreign borrowing and earlier, under heavy pressure from the Croatians who were the most important foreign exchange earners in Yugoslavia, the federal authorities had increased the basic retention quota rate from 7 to 20 per cent. In

January 1973 it was decided to devalue the dinar by 10 per cent in line with the downward movement of the dollar and, four months later, in May, legislation of the previous autumn came into effect, decentralizing and liberalizing foreign exchange operations.[51] This authorized a bi-weekly inter-commercial bank foreign exchange market to be organized by the Yugoslav Association of Bankers. The rates established through dealing applied to all subsequent bank to bank, or bank to customer, dealings until the next market day. Firms were entitled to trade in foreign currencies with authorized business banks at any time and to hold their own foreign currency deposit accounts. However, the float was in practice 'dirty' because the National Bank intervened in the market, buying or selling to maintain the rate roughly within a 5 per cent margin of sixteen dinars per dollar. In October 1973 the import deposit requirements were removed and in January 1974 quantitative restrictions were lifted on the import of nearly 200 product groups, mainly raw materials and investment equipment.

To many commentators in 1973, dinar convertibility seemed no longer just a distant prospect but an immediate policy option.[52] However, by the middle of 1974 the current account was again in serious deficit. In July, import deposits were reintroduced. In August a number of food and manufactured consumer goods were placed in the transactions licence category and the global foreign exchange quotas for consumer goods subject to them were reduced by about 15 per cent. In October the National Bank relaxed its intervention policy in the inter-bank foreign exchange market so as to allow the dinar to depreciate by about 7 per cent against the dollar. Despite these measures the current account deficit for the year 1974 was a massive $US1,218m. and the trend in the first three months of 1975 indicated that the measures taken were inadequate. In April the temporary import surcharge standard rate was raised. In June, most consumer durables and many intermediate and raw material products were placed in the transactions licensing regime and bank credit conditions for imports were also tightened. These measures appear, not surprisingly, to have bitten and to have contributed to the substantial reduction in the current account deficit in the second half of 1975, and to the surplus in 1976.

In 1977, the Law on Foreign Exchange Operations and Credit Relations with Foreign Countries was passed. The Federal Assembly, on the recommendation of the Federal Executive Council, established annual balance of payments and foreign borrowing targets for the federation. The targets were implemented by the Federal and Republican Communities of Interest for Economic Relations.[53] Like communities of interest in other spheres they contained representative earners and users of foreign exchange, members of the Economic Chambers and delegates from the socio-political communities. The Federal Community of Interest, within the framework of the Resolution by the Federal Assembly, decided how to distribute available foreign exchange resources, including those available from foreign borrowing, between the republics, bearing in mind their relative export capacities and import needs. Negotiations terminated in an inter-republican agreement. The Federal authorities were entitled to impose the Federal Assembly Resolution if either inter-republican agreement was not forthcoming or the agreement deviated significantly from it. Once the republican targets and foreign exchange allocations were established, the Republican Communities of Interest then provided the framework for negotiation between potential importers who competed for the available resources.

Apart from the funds available to importers from foreign loans, hard currency had to be earned by Yugoslav exporters. The law introduced a new system for distributing hard currency earnings. Self-management agreements were concluded to share out resources between direct exporters and those who were not direct exporters but who participated in the manufacture of exported products. Customarily, each indirect exporter received a sum proportionate to his share of value added in the total value of the exported commodity.[54] This was fairer than the retention quota system which benefited, exclusively, the direct exporter. After keeping an agreed proportion, the earnings of both direct and indirect exporters then had to be pooled and distributed to importers according to the requirements of self-management agreements negotiated within the framework of the Republican Communities of Interest. Fears were expressed that these arrangements, by encouraging export-import links at the republican level, would reinforce the compartmentalization of the Yugoslav economy.

From 1977 the economy again experienced serious balance of payments difficulties. Stabilization Policy, including the usual regime of import deposits, stricter import quotas, generous export premiums and devaluation, succeeded in reducing the current account deficit from $US3.6b. in 1979 to $US0.8b. in 1981 and $US0.5b. in 1982.

However, by then the burden of servicing the country's external debt had become severe and further changes in the foreign exchange regime were made. The Law on Foreign Exchange Operations of December 1982 gave greater emphasis to federal priorities in the allocation of foreign exchange. Debt servicing, the requirements of exporting firms, oil imports, and suppliers to exporters throughout Yugoslavia, were given first claim to the federation's foreign exchange earnings.[55] The remainder was sold to certain business banks who were intended to distribute it to importers on the basis of planned priorities.

3 Entry and exit

Entry

Jaroslav Vanek has concluded, on purely theoretical grounds, that new entry to industry is both more important and less difficult in a self-managed than in a capitalist economy.[56] It is more important, he argues, for two reasons both of which derive from a similar source—the absence of a contractual wage in circumstances where the entrepreneurial profit is positive and the corresponding behavioural rule that the rational collective will only employ a prospective member whose marginal value product, that is the addition to the total income of the firm as a result of his employment, is at least as high as the average income per existing member. These reasons have already been discussed in Chapter 4 in the different contexts of income inequality and capital intensity and need, therefore, no more than restating.

First, the presence of entrepreneurial profit in a self-managed firm means that, other things being equal, its collective will require a prospective employee to earn a higher marginal value product than would the entrepreneur of a capitalist firm earning a similar profit. This, in turn, means that, in the absence of new entry, the output of a sector earning positive entrepreneurial profits in a self-managed economy will be lower than the output of a sector in a capitalist economy earning similar profits. New entry would have the effect of increasing supply, reducing prices and ultimately driving down the marginal productivity of labour to the level prevailing in a capitalist system: that is where the value of the marginal productivity of labour equals the wage rate. Second, the existence of any inter-firm variation in entrepreneurial profit means that firms in a self-managed economy reach their equilibrium at different levels of income per worker or labour productivity. Without new entry, attracted by the market signal of high average earnings per worker, no force would exist to equalize the returns and productivities of labour, thereby inducing a more rational allocation of resources. On the other hand, Vanek believes that the tendency towards lower output levels by firms in a self-managed economy means that they will be smaller than their capitalist counterparts, making it easier for outsiders to finance entry to their product market.

A study of new entry in the Yugoslav economy in the 1960s,[57] by Sacks, suggests that the phenomenon was comparatively widespread, at least in the late 1960s. A number of incentives appear to have been at work. First, there was the desire of existing firms to reduce costs or enhance profits by supplementing deficient domestic capacity in a related branch. *Union-Gas* of Ljubljana, for example, was founded by ten firms in order to supply natural gas; *Tekstilni-Kombinat*, a weaving firm, founded a spinning mill to provide yarn; OKI founded several small plastic fabricators to create a market for its polyethylene and polystyrol.[58] Second, there were a limited number of conglomerate firms in Yugoslavia which sought to place their resources in any economic activities which yielded high returns. *Energoinvest*, for example, the Bosnian based conglomerate involved in the manufacture of a wide range of products in a number of republics, entered the aluminium industry in a major way in 1970 when it promoted the great export-oriented project at *Sibenik*. The best known firms in this category were *General-Export* (Genex) and *Inter-Export* (Inex), the two large organizations whose main business was foreign trade. They confined their activities chiefly to the tertiary sector, to areas such as international trade, hotels, airlines, travel agencies and department stores. Generally speaking, they kept clear of the traditional industrial sector, though *Genex* had interests in the construction industry and *Inex* in brewing. Even quite modestly sized firms were prepared to diversify if they had spare funds and a tempting profit margin to play for, as the car assembly business bears witness.[59] Third, new entry was sometimes inspired or encouraged by republican or communal authorities for prestige or employment reasons. This was particularly true in the airline, steel and petrochemical industries. But it is frequently hard to distinguish socio-political inspired from firm inspired entry because firms often entered a particular area as a consequence of fiscal or other concessions designed to encourage them to do so.

Almost all new entry was effected by the expansion of an existing rather than the promotion of a new firm, and this was hardly surprising. The promoter could retain no managerial or financial interest in a new firm, save a right to the return of its capital investment at a fixed rate of interest not exceeding the prevailing rate on bank time deposits. If it were expected that the new venture would yield a higher income per worker than its founder, therefore, it was in the interest of the founder that it be established as a division or branch. The passage of the 1967 investment partnership legislation, of course, provided a way around the legal restrictions on promoters;[60] but, in practice, the joint venture was usually established as a separate economic unit of one of the partners with no independent legal personality.

It is worth emphasizing that the benefits of new entry by existing firms accrued exclusively to the existing and new members of those firms. However, groups of citizens were also entitled to promote social sector firms, the so-called GGs.[61] Like existing firms, the only interest they were entitled to retain in their offspring was return of capital plus interest—though, in practice, they all became members of its collective. According to Stephen Sacks, virtually all citizen-founded social sector firms were established between 1965 and 1968,[62] and at the end of 1968 about 390 were operating.[63] Their rapid growth during these three years was accompanied by a sustained press attack on their 'profiteering' and they were regarded as indistinguishable from private enterprise.[64] Many of them were, in fact, performing a variety of intermediary and brokerage functions whose importance to a burgeoning market economy the press entirely failed to grasp.

Bowing to this public outcry, the authorities introduced a number of restrictions on the activities of GGs which came into effect in November 1968.[65] First, they were excluded from undertaking wholesale, agency or any other form of intermediary work. Second, a measure was reintroduced that had been the law before 1965, giving communes the power to determine whether there was any need for the proposed business activity. Third, republics were to be allowed to specify the minimum amount of capital to be provided by the promoters and a minimum time period before the capital began to be repaid. Fourth, it was required that a special appointments committee be set up by communes to hire the necessary workers, appoint the director and establish the size and a proportion of the composition of the Workers' Council. This was a particularly severe rule since the citizen founders were normally synonymous with the subsequent collective, a group of people who had a good idea and wanted to put it into practice to reap any benefits that accrued to it. Last, but not least, all existing citizen-founded firms had to get the approval of their commune in order to continue in operation.

The net effect of this oppressive legislation was that existing GGs either liquidated or merged. Once merged with a non-citizen promoted firm their certificate of registration was no longer tainted with the letters GG. It might have been thought that the ideological attractions of a free association of producers as a basis for the self-managed firm, and the economic reality of a chronic state of excess demand for jobs in the social sector, would have evoked a different response from the authorities. Moreover, had they been allowed to flourish, GGs could have filled an important gap in both the tertiary sector and in certain types of light industry. Unfortunately, their strong capitalist flavour placed too great an ideological strain on the system.

New entry promoted by existing firms seems to have been of mixed benefit. Where there existed deficiencies in the domestic capacities of industries which were potentially competitive, such as aluminium, new entry was clearly desirable. But, where new entry was effected for reasons of prestige, as for example in the airline business,[66] or where the incentive was sufficiently distorted in order to favour industries whose levels of efficiency did not merit the high profits they earned, such as oil refining, then it was counter-productive. But perhaps the major inhibition to successful and economically beneficial new entry in Yugoslavia was the failure of the system to exact the full market penalty for inefficiency—liquidation. The entry of a more efficient firm into a market will only have beneficial effects if the less efficient either become more efficient or go to the wall. But the authorities were unprepared to force firms of any size into liquidation. They preferred a policy of integration; that policy met with very modest success. Consequently, firms of widely varying efficiency coexisted within the same market; often a market which was capable of sustaining only one, or at the most two, firms of optimum size.

Exit

In setting out the ground rules for the functioning of competitive markets, economists sometimes overlook a legal prerequisite which is fundamental to their success—that is the enforceability of contracts. Markets can only operate effectively if firms, in so far as they enter into any legally binding arrangements in pursuit of a profit, are protected by the courts in the event that the other party fails to perform its part of the bargain. Either the defaulter will be compelled to perform or he will be required to compensate the innocent party for his failing to perform by making a money payment. In the latter case the innocent party may then re-enter the market and obtain what he requires from another source. These sanctions enable the hirer or supplier of labour, the lender or borrower of funds and the buyer or seller of goods and services to engage in a calculated economic risk. If losses are made, it is because the entrepreneur misjudged the potential profitability of the transaction and not because the buyer of his output or the borrower of his money defaulted with impunity. Enforcing contracts rewards the firm that predicts the development of scarcities correctly and penalizes the firm that does not. It is central to the operation both of market incentives, by guaranteeing that profits and losses lie where they fall; and of market adjustment mechanisms, by forcing those who cannot meet their legal obligations out of business.

Insolvency may occur either because a firm is making a loss or because, although profitable, it is unable to obtain sufficient cash to meet its pecuniary obligations. In principle, in a market economy, if a company becomes insolvent it is in some way inefficient and justifiably liquidated. The market fulfils its disciplinary and adjustment role by releasing factors of production for more profitable employment elsewhere. However, insolvency may be a symptom not of micro-economic inefficiency but of government policy in pursuit of macro-economic stability. For example, product price controls introduced to stem inflation may lead to losses by firms whose operations are highly competitive. Interest rate controls can result in the physical rationing of funds and the inability of firms, often those able to make best use of them, to obtain them at all. Foreign trade and exchange controls may prevent a firm from pursuing a profitable line of production by denying it essential raw materials. In these circumstances, large numbers of firms may be rendered insolvent irrespective of their relative efficiency. In short, where non-price methods of resource allocation are employed, the enforceability of contracts and the interests of market efficiency are not necessarily synonymous. The impact of interest, price, and foreign exchange controls in Yugoslavia have already been discussed. Suffice it to say here that the presence of these factors made it extremely difficult to identify the marginal firm.

But, even if it is assumed that a marginal firm could be properly identified, other factors militated against liquidation proceedings which were special to the Yugoslav economy. First, collectives were unable to dismiss any part of their number for purely economic reasons. Members possessed the equivalent of a property right in their job which they could only be obliged to forfeit in the event of a serious disciplinary offence. In difficult times this reduced the range of options at the disposal of a firm which wished to put its financial house in order. Second, the country had a chronic unemployment problem which could only have been aggravated by, in the short run at least, closing down firms. Third, the republican and local sociopolitical communities were responsible for both subsidizing loss-making firms through the Joint Reserve Funds and paying out unemployment benefits. In terms of the financial burden on them, it was usually cheaper to keep the firm going than to pay the whole work-force out of social insurance funds.

An added complication was, of course, the definition of loss itself. Members of a collective had no contractual relationship with their firms. In principle they were residual claimants sustaining the risks and reaping the rewards of their work in the combined capacity of worker, entrepreneur and capitalist. In particular, they had no right to receive personal incomes until these have been legally appropriated out of income realized in the current year of operations, an amount only capable of determination at the end of that year. The monthly payments made to members, the *akontacije*, or calculated wage, were no more than advances against the expectation of ultimate appropriation. If, at the end of the accounting year, the appropriation to the Personal Income Fund exceeded the total amount already paid out as calculated wages, then a *visak*, or surplus representing the difference, was distributed. If it became clear before the end of the year that such a surplus would be paid, then it was sometimes anticipated in the remaining monthly payments. Equally, if it was apparent that the *akontacije* was excessive in relation to the expected year-end appropriation, then it was usually adjusted downwards for the remaining months. But the downward adjustment may have been made at too late a stage in the accounting year to eliminate over-distribution entirely; or may have been so large as to prove unacceptable to the members, who continued to anticipate income that they knew would not be realized by the end of the year.

In financing an end-of-year loss the first line of defence was usually the voluntary Reserve Fund. A firm could allocate to its own Reserve Fund more than the amount required by law and draw on this, down to the compulsory level, for a wide range of purposes. At the same time it usually applied to the appropriate Joint Reserve Fund for a grant. All enterprises were bound to make a payment into the *zajednicke reserve prevrednik organizacije* or the Socio-Political Communities Joint Reserve Fund, created at both the republican and communal level in 1962 to assist firms in temporary difficulties. These could be called upon by any firm in their respective areas to supplement its own reserves. Thereafter, the options were less attractive because they all involved the repayment of resources acquired. The compulsory Reserve Fund could be deployed but it had to be replaced out of future profit. Loans were sometimes available; but they had to be repaid with interest. The most attractive source was a subsidized loan from a Joint Reserve Fund. Otherwise, unless the firm had access to some other budgetary or extra-budgetary fund, the only resort was to the banking sector. In practice, the larger firms in financial difficulties have been the beneficiaries of a wide variety of subsidized arrangements. This has been particularly true in the steel industry where extra-budgetary resources have been provided through the business banks and interest moratoriums have been declared.

If the loss could not be financed because the Reserve Fund was exhausted and because loan finance was not forthcoming, then the firm's accounts could be 'blocked' by the Social Accounting Service. In the case of a deficiency in tax payments the initiative to block was usually taken by the Service, since one of its chief functions was to ensure that these were met. In the case of a deficiency in debt servicing, creditors were entitled to require the Service to institute blocking. The commune was also entitled to do this where it had been called upon to supplement the personal income payments to members which had fallen below the statutory minimum. The blocking procedure involved a court order requiring that certain creditors be paid, following which the Social Accounting Service paid debts in a prescribed priority as and when money was forthcoming. In theory it might be thought that, since personal income payments were only advances on anticipated income, the firm would have had a right to a refund from its members of an amount equivalent to the loss. However, there appears to be no example of members being asked to repay sums already disbursed.

It was not uncommon for the accounts of a firm to be blocked for as long as a year; and there have been examples of accounts remaining blocked for a number of years. If performance failed to improve, then an application could be made by any dissatisfied creditor for the appointment of a Public Receiver. This appointment automatically entailed the dismissal of all representative organs and the administration, the Receiver henceforth exercising total managerial authority. The task of the Receiver was to reorganize the finances of the firm and then hand it back to the collective. If the Receiver failed in this task then a Liquidator could be appointed to dispose of the remaining assets. However, the appointment of a Liquidator has been unheard of except in cases of shops and very small firms. There has been no example of a firm of any size having been liquidated as a result of creditor pressure. The usual solution adopted by the communal authorities with respect to a confirmed loss-making firm was to merge it with a more profitable one in the same locality. This was, in effect, no solution at all unless the members of the loss-making collective were able to move to more profitable employment within the enlarged firm. It simply shifted the burden of subsidization from the socio-political community to the enterprise sector. The profitable firm, wishing to divest itself of the newly acquired financial burden by running it down, would be faced by the same barriers to liquidation as existed previously.

At the time of the stringent measures against illiquidity, at the beginning of 1973,[67] an attempt was also made to deal with the chronic loss-maker by restructuring the Joint Reserve Funds. They had played an important role in sustaining large loss-makers in the crisis period of 1966–8 and again in 1971–2 through their subsidized credits and grants and their operations had come to be regarded as perpetuating situations of illiquidity and loss-making rather than solving them. Henceforth, their resources could only be used either to sustain a minimum level of personal income payments or to retrain labour in order to assist in shifting it to more viable sectors in the economy. General subsidies were no longer available. Management of the funds was also taken out of the hands of the socio-political communities and vested in special self-management bodies recruited from the enterprise sector. It was hoped that the new arrangements would penalize the loss-making firm, without punishing its work-force, and, consequently, encourage inter-sectoral resource shifts. They do not, however, appear to have made much difference.

Part Three

CHAPTER 6

STABILITY AND GROWTH

Until the end of the 1970s, the periodic imposition of stabilization policy proved no more than a series of temporary checks to the growth of the Yugoslav economy. As soon as inflation moderated and the current account deficit improved, the authorities became expansionists again. Despite some sharp movements about the trend rate, therefore, the growth of the Yugoslav economy has been impressive. Successive five year development plans contained the same ambitious industrialization targets based upon high rates of gross fixed investment and gross domestic savings, which the country did remarkably well to sustain.[1] GDP grew at an annual average rate of over 6 per cent between 1955 and 1980. Apart from the late 1960s, growth was accompanied by a reasonably high annual rate of increase of employment.

Unfortunately, as the post-reform period progressed, instability increased and the authorities found it increasingly difficult to maintain the development momentum. There are a number of reasons for this. First, the macro-economic policy instruments at the disposal of the federal authorities were inadequate. In dismantling a substantial part of the budgetary apparatus in 1964, and in further diffusing what remained,[2] the authorities denied themselves a vital stabilization weapon. The legislation, simultaneously, created a demand determined economy and destroyed the best established instrument for demand management. The post-reform fiscal system was wholly unsuited to short-term macro-economic fine tuning. This task, therefore, fell exclusively to monetary policy.

Even if monetary policy had worked as effectively as it does in advanced capitalist economies, it could not have fulfilled the stabilization function unaided. But in the context of underdéveloped financial markets, constrained by a variety of ideologically motivated prohibitions and with official policy keeping rates of interest well below the scarcity value of funds, money management by market methods proved impossible. The main policy instruments used by the National Bank were selective rediscounting and credit quotas. The reaction of money supply to the application of these instruments was often sluggish, sometimes because the authorities failed to apply them with sufficient vigour and sometimes because they failed to anticipate the monetary implications of balance of payments movements. But even if money supply did respond, firms usually succeeded in evading its consequences by resorting to the inter-firm credit market which, itself, prospered because of the absence of normal financial disciplines on firms.[3] In short, monetary policy had little influence upon the investment behaviour of enterprises. Consequently, the authorities were compelled to resort to temporary direct measures—such as pre-investment interest free deposits—which, themselves, aggravated existing market distortions. As the 1970s progressed, and with the introduction of contractual planning, temporary direct measures came to assume a permanent role.

Even when excess demand was successfully mastered, it did not always have the desired effect upon the variables it sought to influence. Owing to the peculiar nature of the Yugoslav firm, neither employment nor inflation proved particularly responsive to changes in levels of real demand. The trading account of the balance of payments, by contrast, was responsive. Unfortunately, as the post-reform years passed, the underlying trend of the trade account deteriorated. An overvalued exchange rate, an excessive range of industrial products, two oil crises and a policy of import substitution all played their part. Each new bout of excess demand, therefore, provoked an increasingly serious trade deficit.[4] But the full effect of this deterioration did not really strike home until 1979. Until the first oil crisis, the dramatic increase in invisible earnings from tourism and foreign workers more than compensated for the fall; and between 1974 and 1978, while earnings from tourism and foreign employment stagnated, the volume of merchandise imports rose at an annual rate of less than 1 per cent, due to stabilization policy and the application of import controls.

The crisis that struck the economy at the end of the 1970s was peculiarly severe. The magnitude of the imbalance in the visible trade account that year and the massive increase in hard currency debt compelled the authorities, for the first time since the War, to subordinate their characteristic five year planning objectives to the requirements of stabilization policy.[5] The declared purpose of the 1981–5 Plan was to equilibrate the economy by removing the imbalances which were regarded as the causes of inflation and balance of payments deficits. The core of this strategy was to re-establish exports as the main source of economic growth.

The presence of the macro-economic factor enormously complicates the task of assessing the effectiveness of market mechanisms in Yugoslavia. It would be comforting to say that where inadequacies in macro-economic policy lead to direct interventions which impair micro-economic efficiency, blame cannot be levelled at markets for failing to fulfil the industrial objectives they were set. But while some defects in stabilization policy were due either to inadequate macro-economic policy instruments or to their faulty application, others were due to immaturities and inadequacies in the product and factor markets themselves. The absence of proper financial markets, and the corresponding inability to employ open market operations, limited the capacity to control the money supply. Even when money supply did respond, the illiquidity phenomenon diluted its impact on domestic demand. Finally, even when domestic demand was successfully influenced, changes in it did not affect inflation and the balance of payments to the extent that they themselves were attributable to sectoral imbalances in the structure of production. In other words, precisely those factors that gave rise to the need for a strongly applied stabilization policy also helped to undermine its effectiveness.

1 Making economic policy

Fiscal policy

Expenditure. The consolidated accounts set out in Annex 13 comprise the budgetary and extra-budgetary accounts of the federal and all republican and communal socio-political communities and communities of interest. Annual total consolidated expenditure was in the region of one third of GDP, large enough to exercise substantial leverage on the level and pattern of total demand. However, the authority to spend was highly fragmented. Not only were there three socio-political layers of authority, with the communal layer involving several hundred independent units; but within each socio-political unit there were several communities of interest. Every republic and commune had its own budget and several additional community of interest budgets; the latter possessed separate legal personality and their own self-management organs. Each socio-political community decided what kinds of communities of interest to establish and the way in which they could raise their resources. It also determined the maximum prices they could charge or rates of contributions they could levy. But, in every case, the allocation of the assets of those funds was determined exclusively by their respective representative organs.

These extra-budgetary funds performed a wide range of economic and social functions. For example, Joint Reserve Funds assisted ailing firms, Road Funds were responsible for road construction and maintenance, Water Funds exploited water resources and supplied water, Education Communities ran local schools and Social Insurance Funds provided health facilities and paid pensions. Thus, a firm, say in Belgrade, could be affected, in one way or another, by the federal budget and all the federal extra-budgetary funds, the Serbian budget together with all the Serbian extra-budgetary funds and the Belgrade commune budget together with all its communal extra-budgetary funds. Since the budget and extra-budgetary funds at each territorial level were independent, the chances of imposing a co-ordinated national public sector policy to serve a single federal purpose were extremely remote.

The problem would not have been so formidable had federal budgetary expenditure accounted for a substantial part of the total. But federal expenditure proper, that is exclusive of extra-budgetary expenditure, averaged out at only about one quarter of the con-solidated total. Moreover, most of that consisted of defence and public administration expenditure which was not susceptible to sub-stantial short-term variation. Indeed, even if the federal authorities had been able to influence the spending policies of those who managed federal extra-budgetary funds, it would have been difficult to vary them downwards because most of the monies were devoted to the politically sensitive task of regional aid. About two-thirds of the consolidated total consisted of republican and communal public expenditure. In turn, some two-thirds of this comprised social service expenditure by extra-budgetary units at both levels. Hence, about 45 per cent of total public expenditure was the responsibility of literally thousands of entities which were independent of each other *and* of the socio-political budgets, themselves numbering over five hundred.

In one sense the Constitutional Amendments of 1971 exacerbated the difficulties because the extra-budgetary financing role of the federation was abolished and the assets and liabilities of these funds decentralized to the republics. This was regarded as a further step in the process of returning resources to the economy. Greater partici-pation was also sought by the users of social services in the management of the funds—yet there was also a sense of unease that decentralization had gone too far, inhibiting the development of economies of scale and frustrating co-ordinated policy-making in the social services sector. Extra-budgetary funds, before the introduction of the BOAL, outnumbered enterprises by at least 3 : 1. Following the passage of the 1974 Constitution, attempts were made to improve co-ordination between communal communities of interest.

Revenue. Generally speaking, socio-political budgets were financed by indirect taxes whereas communities of interest were financed by direct taxes on personal incomes. Their relative yields are set out in Annex 13. Direct taxes consisted of income tax and Contributions levied at each of the socio-political levels. Income tax was raised on various classes of income earned in the private sector. The federal rates were standard throughout Yugoslavia but the republican and communal rates varied. There was, in addition, a progressive tax levied by communes on the total income of families, above a certain level, from whatever source. Contributions, a much more important source of revenue, were charged at a fixed rate on the distribution by firms to the Personal Income Fund.[6]

Indirect taxes consisted of customs duties and turnover tax. Customs duties accrued exclusively to the federation until 1978 when they were partially devolved upon the communities of interest to be used as export drawbacks.[7] Turnover tax, despite its name, became a sales tax in 1965, levied, at the retail stage only, by federal, republican, and communal authorities. Republican and communal rates were substantially lower than federal rates. The Basic Turnover Tax Law of 1965 changed the basis of the levy from a multi-stage tax on production to a single-stage retail tax. Henceforth, it was levied only at the point of retail sale or ultimate consumption. The federal tax was, for the most part, charged at a uniform rate, although some items, such as fuel, had higher ratings while others, such as food, had lower or zero rating. The change to a sales based tax and the uniformity in rates made the turnover tax a potentially useful instrument of macro-economic management. But the authorities were, for both political and ideological reasons, unwilling to use it for this purpose. There was strong opposition to any renewed active involvement of the federation in the economy.

The revenue structure mirrored, to a large degree, the decentralized expenditure structure. Many spending authorities at all levels had independent taxing powers. The republics and communes had possessed such powers since 1952. These powers were confirmed by the 1963 Constitution and set out in detail in the Basic Socio-Political Unit Finance Act of 1965.[8] Every socio-political community was entitled both to select the kind of taxes it wished to raise within its territory from a range of permissible categories set out in the Act and to determine the rate at which they could be levied. They were, however, subject to certain other restrictions or requirements which limited their power to set such rates as they wished. The federal authorities retained the power to establish maximum levels for certain levies such as republican and local turnover or social insurance contributions. All socio-political communities were also under a duty to equalize the burden of taxation falling upon workers in social sector firms in the interests of unified market conditions.[9] Moreover, the power to increase rates was offset by the concomitant duty to equalize inter-republican per caput budgetary income.[10]

Certain extra-budgetary funds also acquired independent taxing powers after 1965. From 1 January 1967 schools were financed from the funds of the Education Communities which were themselves financed from an independent contribution from personal incomes.[11] Similar arrangements were made for child care in the following year.[12] The maximum rates of contribution were fixed by the republican and local assemblies. Social insurance funds also had independent sources of revenue. However, by no means all extra-budgetary funds were self-sufficient. Those that were not, had their resources supplemented from a complicated network of revenue-sharing arrangements whereby surplus tax revenues raised by socio-political communities were shared out between them. Even some communal budgets were supplemented from republican funds.[13]

Balancing the budget. Apart from the problem of co-ordination, one other factor militated against the use of the fiscal weapon in Yugoslavia. Particular emphasis was placed upon the importance of balancing budgets.[14] All spending units were obliged to adjust their expenditure to ensure that they did not exceed their revenue yields. In addition, socio-political communities were required to establish reserve accounts to which they had to allocate 1 per cent of annual revenue until its resources reached 15 per cent of their average annual budget revenue for the three previous years. If the reserve fund was used to finance a deficit, then the socio-political unit concerned was obliged to step up its reserve allocation until the amount spent had been redeemed.[15]

Despite devolving the extra-budgetary expenditure of the federation upon the republics, the 1971 Constitutional Amendments left the main items of federal budgetary expenditure intact. But they took away from the federation most of its sources of revenue, including the federal turnover tax.[16] Only customs duties and a few other minor sources of revenue remained to it. The excess of expenditure over income which flowed from these changes was financed by republican contributions in proportion to their share in social product. Because these contributions were frequently insufficient to cover federal expenditure, the authorities were compelled to finance their budgetary deficit by the issue of bonds to banks and social sector firms. Republics were also entitled to make such issues to meet their obligation to contribute.

Subscribers were encouraged chiefly by incentives.[17] Some issues provided that any bond due to be redeemed within twelve months would be accepted as payment, at an appropriate discount, for any liability of the holder to the issuer. Social sector firms could also hold up to 30 per cent of their reserve funds in bonds, or more if the republic in which they were issued so determined, and could use them as guarantee deposits for loans raised to invest in fixed assets. Banks were permitted to hold up to 50 per cent of their reserves in bonds. To attract household purchasers bonds were allowed to be used as down payments for consumer credits.[18] Some bond issues also attracted tax concessions. For example, in December 1974 the Federal Assembly passed a Law on Federal Bonds authorizing an issue of 4b. dinars to meet part of the shortfall expected from the 1975 budget.[19] In addition to the above-mentioned concessions, any purchaser could either obtain a 6 per cent rebate on any taxes paid up to the face value of the bond, including turnover tax rebates; or receive an additional 3 per cent interest rate in addition to the face-value yield of 10 per cent.[20] A similar issue for 3b. dinars at the end of 1975, allowed social sector firm subscribers in financial difficulties to pledge the bonds with banks for up to thirty days in order to provide resources for personal income payments. A number of bond issues were also made to settle the liabilities of the Federation to business banks with respect to exchange rate differentials arising from changes of the par value of the dinar.[21] Respecting the two devaluations of 1971 the federal authorities issued five-year bonds yielding 8 per cent. The repayment of the first instalment on these bonds, which was scheduled for 1 July 1973, was postponed until 1 July 1975, and again until 1 July 1976.

In 1976, the federal authorities were obliged to rely much more heavily than hitherto on central bank borrowing and the issue of treasury bills and short-dated bonds, in order to finance their budgetary expenditure. A reconsideration of the changes introduced by the 1971 Constitutional Amendments led to the passage of new legislation designed to reintroduce an element of autonomy in the federal budget and remove its deficit; in particular, expenditure on domestic market subsidies were transferred to republican budgets, and 50 per cent of turnover tax revenues reverted directly to the federal budget.[22] Moreover, from the late 1970s, there was a concerted effort to reduce public expenditure. It had risen from 35 per cent of social product in the early 1970s to 43 per cent in 1978 and the authorities believed that its growth was contributing to inflationary pressures. By reducing real pay and by making substantial cuts in fixed investment, they succeeded in reducing the share of public expenditure as a percentage of Social Product in each year between 1978 and 1982.[23] In 1982, a system was introduced whereby increases of public sector revenues in excess of planned targets, at all levels, were frozen in special blocked accounts in the National Bank.[24]

Monetary policy[25]

Because of the inflexibility of the fiscal system and the reluctance of the authorities to use it as an active economic policy weapon, the main burden of managing the level of demand devolved upon the monetary and banking system. The task was a formidable one. Not surprisingly, perhaps, it proved unequal to it. This was partly because money supply and bank credit were slow to respond to the limited range of monetary instruments that the authorities had at their disposal; and partly because demand was slow to react to changes in money supply.

Monetary instruments. Monetary targets were included in the Federal Executive Council's annual Economic Resolution, approved each year by the Federal Assembly, which set out the economic policy objectives for the following twelve months.[26] These targets were expressed first, as a change in the annual rate of monetary expansion and, second, in the form of guide-lines as to the rates of expansion of credit in various sectors of the economy which would achieve that money supply figure. They were sometimes readjusted on a quarterly basis. Achieving these targets was the responsibility of the Yugoslav National Bank. In theory, the Yugoslav National Bank was free to choose whatever monetary instruments it wished. However, two factors limited the range of instruments available to it. First, interest rates were subject to legal, and later voluntary, ceilings which, in the context of prevailing rates of inflation, were far too low to influence the strength of demand for credit. In fact, the authorities never attempted to employ the rate of interest as a short-term economic regulator. Second, the lack of differentiation and depth in financial markets in Yugoslavia made it virtually impossible to conduct open market operations. The developing practice of issuing socio-political bonds may ultimately improve the chances of employing this policy option.

The main instruments deployed to control the money supply were selective central bank rediscounting ceilings, reserve and associated liquidity requirements and direct credit ceilings. Selective bank rediscounting ceilings established both a global rediscount ceiling and a breakdown of preferred treatment within that ceiling. Since the commercial banks relied on National Bank credit for about 20 to 25 per cent of their outstanding loans,[27] selective rediscounting was an important discretionary weapon in the hands of the federal authorities. Some such discretionary arrangement was, of course, necessary in the absence of market clearing interest rates at commercial and central bank levels.

Until the Constitutional Amendments, the federal authorities identified the sectors and branches entitled to use the National Bank rediscounting facility. At the time of the Amendments the former republican branches of the National Bank were converted into independent Regional National Banks.[28] The only practical difference this made was to the discounting arrangements. Thereafter, the Regional Banks were entitled to distribute, according to guide-lines laid down by the republican authorities, a proportion of planned total annual rediscounts. The move was made because of criticism that the National Bank monopoly over rediscounting favoured some republics at the expense of others.[29] For example, it was usual National Bank practice to give preferential treatment to exports and agriculture. Devolution of such powers to the republics was also consistent with the trend in other aspects of economic affairs at this juncture. The proportion of total annual discounts to be delegated to the republics and the share of each republic within it were determined by the Inter-Republican Committee on Monetary Questions, one of the five inter-republican committees established at the time of the Amendments to determine federal policy. As to the reserve and associated liquidity requirements, the Federal Assembly decreed, from time to time, a range within which the National Bank might, at its own discretion, vary them.[30] The Bank was required to pay interest on the amounts held as reserves. Usually neither the selective rediscounting nor the reserve requirement proved sufficient to restrict the increase in money supply to the target level. In those circumstances the authorities resorted to imposing direct ceilings on business bank lending.

Controlling money supply. The annual rate of increase of money supply was usually set at, or just below, the projected annual rate of increase of nominal Social Product. The actual rates achieved are set out in Annex 14. The first clear phase of post-reform monetary policy began in the last quarter of 1966 when the reserve requirement and rediscounting instruments were used to pursue a restrictive monetary policy. The policy was so effective that money supply actually declined during 1967. Indeed, so savage had been its effect upon employment and growth that the authorities, encouraged by an improvement in the balance of payments position, adopted a more expansionary approach from the middle of 1968. By 1970, the rate of growth of money supply was considered excessive in the light of the increased rate of inflation and the deteriorating balance of payments position. During 1970 and 1971 frequent changes were made in the minimum reserve requirement and in rediscounting practices.[31] Yet the combined impact of these measures was relatively slight. The authorities seem to have feared a repetition of the sharply recessive impact of the 1966–7 measures and were, in any case, reluctant to deny rediscounting facilities to priority economic sectors and regions. They resorted instead to a variety of direct restrictions on the volume of lending by business banks, mainly aimed at credits for low priority activities such as the purchase of consumer durables or foreign holidays.

The five years 1966–71, as Annex 17 indicates, were years of balance of payments deficits, when the state of the current account had a liquidity draining effect upon the money supply. An entirely different situation confronted the monetary authorities in 1972–3, years of current account surplus. During these two years, the money supply underwent a period of unprecedented growth. It almost doubled, far exceeding the projected rates of growth for the two years, 12 and 17 per cent respectively, which were based upon the expected rate of increase of nominal Social Product. The domestic monetary expansion caused by the current account surpluses was not offset by a corresponding reduction in domestic credit growth. The National Bank was inhibited in its use of the reserve requirement weapon by the existence of a legal ceiling above which it was not permitted to go; and it could not mop up the excess supply through open market operations. This meant that rediscounting restrictions had to bear the full weight of adjustment. But the Bank was unwilling to impose them. In the opinion of the OECD, the main difficulty faced by the Bank was knowing exactly where to make the cuts in the absence of information about the relative benefits that had accrued to the various priority sectors from the foreign account induced liquidity increases.[32] This factor simply exaggerated the reluctance that the Bank already felt in interfering with the flow of finance towards priority economic sectors. The problem was further aggravated by the absence of marketable financial assets which prevented banks with excess liquidity from transferring it to those with insufficient. Banks suffering shortages automatically knocked at the door of the central bank.

In 1974 a move was made to divorce the central banking system from the task of selective rediscounting.[33] It was proposed that the responsibility for selective credit policy should devolve upon the business banks themselves, the actual priorities being determined by inter-commercial bank arrangements similar in style to inter-firm self-management agreements on income and price policy. In the course of the next two years the National Bank and Regional Banks discontinued most, though not all, of their rediscounting activities. Such a move, it was hoped, would encourage the National Bank to be single-minded in its approach to controlling the overall rate of increase of money supply through the use of minimum reserve rates, uninhibited by countervailing sectoral considerations. The National Bank was also encouraged to develop open market operations in its own treasury bills and in commercial paper. The scope for doing so was enhanced by the appearance, after 1971, of a federal government deficit.

In contrast to 1972 and 1973, 1974 and 1975 were years of exceptionally heavy balance of payments current account deficits. In June 1974 the money supply and bank credit growth targets were both raised to counteract the effect of the adverse foreign trade balance on domestic liquidity. Nevertheless, the annual rate of growth of money supply threatened to be substantially less than that of nominal Social Product and had to be adjusted accordingly. The year 1975 followed a rather similar pattern. By June it was clear that the domestic credit targets set at the beginning of the year were inadequate in the context of the contractionary effects of the persistent balance of payments deficit. Accordingly, they were raised. This factor, together with the improvement in the foreign balance in the second half of the year, led to a marked acceleration in the growth of the money supply.

That acceleration continued in 1976. Indeed, the increase in money supply for that year was 53 per cent as against an estimated 18 per cent. A proportion of the excess was attributable to the unexpectedly good balance of payments performance. But the bulk of it appears to have been due to a deliberate policy to offset the adverse effects on enterprise liquidity of the new accounting rules. These rules[34] forced enterprises to reduce their reliance on trade credit and to increase their demand for bank credit. The authorities were prepared to accommodate the demand, partly because of their belief that the new measures implied a permanent increase in the level of demand for liquidity and partly because the increase was unaccompanied, at least initially, by an upswing in real demand. However, the increases in 1976 probably contributed to the strong rise in the demand for investment resources later in the year and in 1977. The total increase in money supply from 1977 was about 21 per cent, the rapid expansion of domestic and foreign credit being counteracted by a large external current deficit.

Monetary growth in 1978 was projected at 19 per cent. Strong domestic demand led to a rapid acceleration of domestic credit and, by the end of June, two-thirds of the planned rise had taken place. Despite new global ceilings of 3 and 4 per cent for the remaining two quarters, priority sector rediscounting exemptions led to these targets being exceeded. At the end of November, the National Bank stopped discounting all short-term bills.[35] With the current account deficit having a contractionary effect, money supply grew by 25 per cent. In the first half of 1979, the rate of increase in money supply fell, as the restrictive credit measures took effect in the context of a massive acceleration of costs both imported and domestic. The effect of the current account deficit was also contradictory. Consequently, credit ceilings were relaxed in the second half of 1979 and money supply grew at 19 per cent for the year as a whole. Credit restrictions and the contractionary effect of balance of payments deficits in 1980, 1981, and 1982 kept the growth of money supply at 23, 26 and 26 per cent respectively.

Direct intervention

Apart from their monetary and limited fiscal responsibilities, the federal authorities retained few powers to intervene directly in the economy after 1965. The two main exceptions were price and foreign exchange policy. Constitutionally, the only additional measures they could take were in circumstances where there was a threat to the unity of the market or the stability of the economy;[36] and, even then, the measures had to be temporary. When it became clear that monetary policy would need supplementing by rather more than price and foreign exchange measures to control the level of domestic demand, the authorities resorted to a number of other direct measures to manage the levels of real consumption and fixed investment.

Consumer credit restrictions were invariably imposed during phases of excess demand. Temporary earnings freezes were also used to control the level of real personal incomes. Naturally, these were extremely unpopular and were never imposed for longer than absolutely necessary. The onset of contractual planning, however, provided the authorities with an opportunity to influence the level of real earnings on a permanent basis. Guide-lines were introduced into the annual Economic Resolution indicating the desirable rate of increase in nominal earnings in a particular industrial sector in relation to the rate of increase of value added in that sector. Sectoral social and self-management agreements were supposed to be negotiated to conform with these proposals.

The most frequently used direct measure to control fixed investment was the requirement to lodge a pre-investment deposit with a commercial bank. This had the effect of increasing the cost of money to the investor and was a useful way of avoiding the disadvantages of low interest rates. Periodic assaults on the illiquidity problem were also launched with varying degrees of success. These entailed the introduction of stricter, and the stricter enforcement of, accounting rules by the Social Accountancy Service. During a credit squeeze, however the absence of any market penalties for financial delinquency, usually led to the rules being evaded.

In principle, the onset of contractual and social planning in the investment sphere, ought to have made the control of 'unnecessary' fixed investment much easier. However, the evidence of the late 1970s suggests otherwise. So much so that the authorities sought, for the first time, to impose physical controls on fixed investment. In the early 1980s, a freeze was imposed upon all socio-political community investments; indeed, many were halted in mid-construction. Percentage increase value limitations were also imposed upon 'non-economic' investments and upon Collective Consumption Fund expenditures. A system of pre-registration of investments with Economic Chambers was also introduced.

The 1980 Economic Resolution made an important break with the past. It made legally binding many targets and policies that had, hitherto, been guidelines.[37] The package of measures it contains demonstrates just how important direct intervention had become to the macro-economic management of the Yugoslav economy. The rise in the total personal income bill in any sector was to be at least 5 per cent less than the rise of total value added in that sector.[38] In the non-economic sectors, the corresponding figure was 8 per cent less than the rise in value added in the economy as a whole. Employees in socio-political communities and communities of interest received a maximum of 16 per cent. All social and self-management agreements had to be negotiated in conformity with these targets. Until they were, personal incomes were fixed at the September 1979 level.

A number of targets respecting fixed investment were also included in the Economic Resolution and reinforced by supplementary legislation. Down payments of 50 per cent of the value of non-economic[39] investments and 15–30 per cent of the value of business investments were imposed.[40] The amount was reduced to 15 per cent for investments which were mainly foreign exchange earning or saving. In addition, any non-economic investment which had completed less than 65 per cent of its total cost was stopped. It also contained vigorous price and foreign exchange control obligations.

Controlling domestic demand[41]

If the response of the level of money supply to the application of rediscounting and reserve level instruments was uneven, so, equally, was the response of the level of domestic demand to the changes in the levels of money supply that actually occurred, as illustrated in Annex 15. The slow growth in money supply between 1966 and 1967 induced a greater reaction in the level of domestic demand than the authorities had anticipated. The recessive impact of the restrictive monetary policy appears to have been compounded by the disorientation experienced by many firms in adjusting to the new decentralized institutional framework and product demand pattern. Money supply began to expand from the middle of 1968 and continued to do so in 1969. By 1970 domestic demand was considered excessive and monetary restrictions were gradually reimposed. Gross fixed investment increased by 17.5 per cent in the course of that year and ran at a similar level for the first half of 1971. Yet the percentage rate of increase in credit made available to firms during 1970 only slightly exceeded the level for the two previous years. The widespread employment of inter-firm credit, the illiquidity problem, played an important role at this time in defeating the moderating effect of money supply changes. It was not until the second half of 1971 that the imposition of further restrictions on the extension of credit facilities dampened the level of effective demand.

During the years 1972 and 1973, years of balance of payment current account surplus, money supply almost doubled. This time the position was reversed; its expansion was not matched by a similar increase in domestic demand. These were years of relatively subdued economic activity. The main reason was the success of both the measures taken against illiquidity and a wage freeze. The combination of direct restrictions on investment expenditure and wage payments together with an unprecedented increase in liquid resources, resulted in a substantial improvement in the liquidity of firms and a corresponding reduction in the volume of inter-firm trade credit. However, the accumulation of liquid balances posed a potential threat to the imposition of a more restrictive monetary policy in future years.

Towards the end of 1973 domestic demand strengthened substantially, responding to the easing of many of the measures taken to combat illiquidity[42] and to the abandonment of the wage freeze.[43] Despite indications of a reversal in the balance of payments position, the 1974 Economic Resolution was distinctly expansionary in tone.[44] The level of domestic demand remained very high in 1974, led by a boom in gross fixed investment which was financed out of accumulated liquidity balance and a resurgence of inter-firm trade credit arrangements. The rate of growth of money supply during that year, because of the monetary impact of the balance of payments current account deficit, did not even reach the rate of growth in nominal Social Product. Personal consumption was also strong due to the removal of the earnings freeze in the middle of 1973 and the corresponding increase in real incomes. Although the pressure from personal consumption fell off towards the end of 1974 the rate of growth of gross fixed investment ran at an even stronger rate at the beginning of 1975. In the course of that year the authorities were obliged to take a number of direct measures to control it, mainly by insisting on very high prior deposits on the cost of investment projects and introducing stricter accounting rules in the valuation of receivable and inventory accounts.[45]

The direct measures had a relatively restrictive impact on investment expenditure in the first half of 1976 despite the massive expansion in money supply in the course of that year assisted by a return to current account surplus. This was really a repetition of the pattern in 1973. But it seems that the accumulation of liquidity in 1976, as in 1973, helped to fuel the sharp upsurge in investment expenditure later in the same, and in the following, year when the direct controls were relaxed. Between 1977 and 1979, domestic demand rose at an annual rate of 9 per cent, much faster than the productive potential of the economy. As a consequence there were crippling balance of payments current account deficits in 1979 and 1980, exacerbated, of course, by the second international oil crisis. Restrictive credit policy, together with the package of direct measures centred around the 1980 Economic Resolution, succeeded in reversing the upward trends of both real personal incomes and real fixed investment. There was, as a result, a substantial transfer of resources from the domestic to the foreign sector leading to a marked improvement in the current account.

It is interesting to note that in 1981 and 1982, in the context of restrictive monetary policy, inter-firm trade credit, once again, expanded rapidly. This time, however, it did not lead to a corresponding rise in fixed investment because of the comprehensiveness of the package of direct measures.[46] However, it did help to accommodate the very high rates of inflation. For example, nominal Social Product increased at nearly double the rate of growth of money supply in 1981.

2 Employment, inflation and the balance of payments

If the links between changes in the application of monetary instruments and monetary supply *and* between changes in money supply and the level of domestic demand proved tenuous, so, in certain respects, did the connection between movements in domestic demand and the behaviour of the economic variables the authorities sought to influence, especially employment and inflation. This section is devoted to a brief review of the problems of employment, inflation and the balance of payments in the macro-economic context.

Employment

The structural problems of the labour market have already been considered in Chapter 4. Here the only concern is to add a brief comment upon the short-term movements of employment in response to changes in the level of economic activity. In the Western capitalist, or mixed, economy changes in demand for investment and consumption goods have usually been accompanied by changes in the short-run levels of output and employment. In a world of contractual wages and collectively bargained wage levels the tendency of these economies is to reduce output and fire workers in the face of falling demand and to hire workers and expand output when demand picks up. In other words, the short-run response of supply to demand is fairly elastic. In Yugoslavia the position was, at least with regard to the hiring and firing of workers, rather different. Because of the extremely elaborate legislative system which governed the employment relationship, it was virtually impossible to sack anybody unless they had infringed the disciplinary code set out in the statutes and subsequent decisions of the representative organs. Even then, there was an elaborate system of appeals to which the member in question could resort.[47] The member was, after all, not an employee but the member of a collective and had as much right to his job as any other member.

The maintenance of employment security is frequently spoken of as an important behavioural objective of the collective.[48] And so it is, if the alternative threatened is the liquidation of the firm. But the objective is not necessarily true with regard to any single member of the collective. It is often in the interests of some members to remove other members; but because of the legislative regime they are unable to do so. Downward employment adjustment in Yugoslavia, therefore, is likely to be a long-run phenomenon attainable, in the absence of liquidation, only through resignation or retirement. It follows, equally, that the inability to fire is likely to breed caution in hiring. Firms need to be sure that a prospective member has a permanent role to play—despite the temptation to take advantage of any short-run gain that might derive from adding to employment. In a sense, therefore, labour may be regarded as more of a fixed than a variable cost in the short-run production function.

The substantial degree of inelasticity in the response of employment to short-term changes in effective demand meant, in principle, that the brunt of the adjustment process had to be borne elsewhere. The most obvious candidate was workers' incomes. Given a fixed number of employees and a drop in demand for output the corresponding fall in income would have to be shared out between them. With employment fixed, the initial response of firms appears to have been to continue production and sales at as high a level as possible hoping, *inter alia*, to spread their fixed costs as widely as possible. Sales were, accordingly, made on very generous terms and unsold inventory accumulated and charged against the cost of sale in order to enable firms to continue to pay out personal incomes at previous levels.

To the extent that they were unable to shift the burden of falling demand through the medium of the inter-firm credit market, the illiquidity problem, or through a delay in meeting contractual obligations generally, the burden fell on the level of average real personal incomes. Accordingly, the value of *real* personal incomes might be expected to fluctuate to a much greater extent in Yugoslavia than in a trade union dominated capitalist system.[49] A comparison of the annual rates of increase in the cost of living and average personal incomes with the annual rate of growth of social sector employment suggests that the burden of adjustment was mainly borne by employment in the 1966–7 recession and by real personal incomes in the 1972–3 recession and in the recession which began in 1979.[50] Too much, of course, should not be read into this comparison. The structural readjustment to demand in the late 1960s, the wage freeze in 1973 and the compulsory incomes policy after 1979 have an important bearing on the interpretation of these figures.

Inflation[51]

The annual rates of increase in the main price indices are shown in Annex 16. It is very difficult to come to any firm conclusion about the reasons for the high rates of inflation that have prevailed in Yugoslavia since the reform. The problem of analysis is severely complicated by the presence, throughout the period, of a large number of administered prices. Many increases were granted by the Federal Price Office (FPO) some time after the conditions provoking them. Industrial branches might have had to wait for at least a year, and perhaps longer, before they were permitted to reflect an increase in raw material prices in their own price. For example, some of the 1972 and 1973 price rises may have been attributable to the excess demand prevalent during 1970 and the early part of 1971. All that is intended is a brief review of some of the factors within the system which were conducive to strong inflationary pressures. The topics mentioned do not claim to be an exhaustive list. To do justice to such an immensely complex theme would require far more space than can be allotted to it here.

The Yugoslav economy is a developing economy which, before the 1965 reform, had undergone a period of rapid but extremely uneven growth. In particular, investment in agriculture, infrastructure, and raw materials lagged seriously in comparison with the processing industries. An important reason for this, as explained in Chapter 1, was the pattern of price relativities that prevailed during the pre-reform era. One of the purposes of the reform measures was to restructure relative prices so that they could reflect, more accurately, the real pattern of scarcities in the economy. The process of restructuring, carried out in July 1965, was the main reason for the massive rate of inflation which occurred in that year.

The readjustment proved insufficient to reflect, truly, the underlying scarcities. Despite continued price regulation in these sectors there was continual upward pressure on the prices of agricultural products and raw materials. Indeed, the index of agricultural prices rose more rapidly than any other price index. It seems almost beyond doubt that this was due to supply constraints. Since over 80 per cent of agricultural production was in the hands of small, private producers any inflationary pressures ascribable to the peculiar institutional make-up of the social sector firm could not have been present. Moreover, since the demand for most agricultural products is relatively inelastic, the sector was less likely to be affected by excess demand rather than demand variations.

To the extent that the authorities permitted primary sector price increases, the profit margins in the processing industries were often reduced. This encouraged the latter to try and raise their own prices in order to retain their previous margins, irrespective of the demand and supply conditions that they themselves faced. Because most industrial processing markets were highly concentrated, with firms actively encouraged to engage in co-ordinated policy-making, and because the threat of insolvency was an unreal one, it was not difficult to achieve compensating rises; though where the product in question was subject to price controls the increases were sometimes delayed. The inflationary impact of supply scarcities in one part of the economy was, therefore, exacerbated by market structures in other parts.

Market structures also appear to have contributed to sympathetic movements between prices and wages. After the reform measures of 1965, when the remaining fiscal and other restrictions on income distribution were removed, firms were free to establish personal income payments at any level they wished. There was no element of exogenous control like a contract of employment binding in law or a trade union collective bargaining agreement. Where wages and, because of market structure factors, to some extent prices, were under the exclusive control of a single entity, the firm, it is hardly surprising to discover that movements in the two variables turned out to be closely linked. Most of the academic studies on inflation in Yugoslavia show good correlations between sectoral movements of prices and personal income payments.[52] The difficulty for those in search of causation is that the statistics are equally consistent with personal income distributions pushing up prices, as they are with autonomous price increases pulling up nominal value added and, therefore, personal income distribution potential. But, once the process was under way, the important factor to bear in mind is that pressure appears to have existed for one to follow the upward movement of the other.

When post-reform inflation became a serious problem at the end of the 1960s, the authorities took the view that excessive personal income distribution was indeed playing an important role. In the closing months of 1970, for example, average earnings in the social sector were running at nearly 30 per cent higher than a year earlier.

The new system of personal income control through the social agreement mechanism was put into practice in 1972. The agreements sought both to increase the proportion of earnings retained in the firm and to eliminate inter-firm earnings differentials by requiring those firms with personal incomes per standardized worker higher than the republican average to plough back a progressively higher proportion of their earnings. By increasing the resources available for investment purposes these agreements may have assisted in moderating excess demand pressures which derived from high personal incomes. But in other respects they did not provide any assurance of price stability. For one thing, acceptable personal incomes–savings ratios of firms were linked to the average income levels of all firms within a republic. Therefore, a general increase in the nominal income levels of all firms within a republic would not lead to a higher savings rate for the firm sector as a whole.[53] Moreover, there was nothing to prevent a firm from raising prices, unless it was subject to price control, in order to increase the income available for allocation between savings and personal incomes.

Increases in the share of real consumption in the value of Social Product were, it will be recalled, an intended consequence of reform. The idea was to compensate for the negative effect that a reduced rate of accumulation would have on the rate of growth, by improving the productivity of such capital investment that was made. The real value of consumption did in fact increase as a proportion of Social Product in the years after reform, and the effect of this was to reduce the proportionate share of fixed investment. Unfortunately, the authorities had considerable difficulty in keeping the level of demand by firms for investment resources down to the reduced amount of real resources available for that purpose. In the years immediately after reform, there was a substantial shift in the income distribution of firms away from retention and in favour of personal income distribution.[54] But the absence of a market clearing rate for bank loans meant that the demand for investment finance consistently exceeded its supply. Firms could never borrow enough. The adverse implications that this had for the allocation of resources has already been discussed.[55] But this chronic state of excess demand for credit need not have had inflationary consequences if the authorities had been able to limit the capacity of firms to spend through the effective application of monetary policy. This they had great difficulty in doing, as we have seen, partly because of the inadequacy of the monetary policy instruments available to them in controlling money supply, and partly because of the illiquidity phenomenon. Those deficiencies, particularly in the years 1970–1, 1974–5 and 1977–9 enabled firms to finance expenditures on investment goods and on personal income payments, expenditures which, taken together, exceeded the capacity of available resources to respond to demand at a stable price level.

One other important source of inflationary pressure in Yugoslavia derived from the foreign sector. Import controls caused shortages in some sectors and created scarcity values for certain domestic products, particularly manufactured consumer goods. Sometimes an increase in the export price of a product produced and supplied domestically had the same effect. The more attractive foreign price, relative to the controlled domestic price, diverted domestic supplies abroad and created pressures for domestic price increases. This happened, for example, in the early 1970s with meat. Again emigration generated or aggravated the scarce supply of many types of skilled labour. But probably the most important impact of the foreign sector was its 'cost push' role. Yugoslavia imported about 60 per cent of its capital goods requirement and more than 20 per cent of its raw material needs.[56] The increases in cost of these items was partly due to an increase in their dollar costs, reflecting inflationary pressures in the exporting countries. But it was also due to devaluation of the dinar. It will be recalled that the dinar was devalued twice in 1971, by 16.7 per cent in January and 11.8 per cent in December, and floated down with the dollar in February 1973. From the middle of that year it went on to a 'dirty' float. It was devalued on several occasions during the crisis at the end of the 1970s and the beginning of the 1980s. Indeed, such was the level of inflation by the middle of 1981 that the exchange rate was almost continuously adjusted to maintain competitiveness.[57]

The problems that confronted the authorities with respect to the control of inflation are well illustrated by the situation in 1980. In 1980 inflation was rising rapidly at a time when both real fixed investment and real personal incomes were falling. There are a number of explanations. First, during that calendar year, the dollar price of imported oil rose by 100 per cent. Second, there was a substantial dinar devaluation in June 1980. Third, overdue price increases in both the industrial and the agricultural sectors were finally granted by the pricing authorities. Fourth, the legally binding incomes policy introduced by the Economic Resolution sought to control movements in *real* wages, by requiring firms to increase their nominal earnings at a specified slower rate than the rate of increase of value added in their industrial sector. While this policy successfully reduced the rate of growth of real consumer demand, thus contributing to the reduction in excess demand pressures generally, it contributed nothing to encourage *nominal* wage or price stability.

Incomes policy continued to focus upon the control of increases in real earnings until the end of 1980. However, despite the successful control of real demand and a vastly improved balance of payments, inflation remained out of control. The Economic Resolution for 1983 introduced another temporary wage freeze. It required that the average earnings per worker in the first quarter of 1983 should not exceed average earnings per worker in the last quarter of 1982. At the same time, the authorities sought to devise a permanent scheme which would reward the collective for enhanced productivity and effort while denying it the freedom to increase nominal earnings independent of those factors. One proposal was to relate nominal income growth to the so-called social efficiency of capital.[58] Ratios of saving to the value of capital stock in each BOAL would be compared to the avergae ratio in each republic. A BOAL would be permitted to distribute higher nominal personal incomes only when its ratio is above the republican average ratio by a specified amount. Appropriate depreciation allowances would be charged to keep the value of capital stock constant.

Balance of payments[59]

The balance of payments performance is set out in Annex 17. Since 1965 there has been an increasing deficit in the balance of visible trade with convertible-currency countries. The change in economic policy brought about by reform led to an enhanced dependence on Western suppliers since they were the main source of the modern technology that Yugoslav industry sought. At the same time both the barriers to international trade in agricultural goods and the difficulties that new entrants faced in breaking into Western industrial goods markets limited the rate of expansion of exports. The strong emphasis that the authorities placed on foreign investment and industrial co-operation indicated that they were seeking ways to link import and export performance. But had it not been for the phenomenal growth in invisible earnings, mainly from foreign worker remittance and tourism, which was not foreseen at the time of reform, it is hard to imagine how the system would have survived at all.

Trade direction. Annex 18 summarizes the direction of trade as between the world's three main trading areas. The trade relations broken off with the Soviet bloc at the end of the 1940s were successfully resumed in 1955. Two factors tended to encourage a surplus in trade with the Eastern bloc, one technological, the other financial. Exports to this area consisted chiefly of industrial manufactures. Owing to Yugoslavia's relative sophistication in industrial production, derived from its widespread exposure to Western technology, its processed products were in considerable demand in Eastern Europe. By contrast the Comecon countries were not a good source for this type of output, for their products were rarely of sufficient quality, design or efficiency to attract Yugoslav purchasers. Yugoslavia's main imports from this area, therefore, were fuel and raw materials. Moreover, since the prices of both exports to and imports from the Eastern bloc were, on average, higher than in trade with the West, and since the same exchange rate prevailed in trade with both areas, exporters preferred to sell in the East and importers to buy in the West. The bias was to sell for soft currencies and to buy in hard currencies. The Yugoslav authorities sought, for this reason, to achieve an exact balance of payments with Comecon countries. The pattern of trade with Third World countries was similar in structure, though in volume of considerably less importance.

Since the first American foreign aid in 1949 the West has been Yugoslavia's main trading partner. But Yugoslavia has persistently imported far more from, than it exported to, the West. After 1965 it faced serious problems in expanding its industrial output to hard currency markets which placed such a high premium on quality and technological dynamism. The gap remained manageable, until the successive oil crises, because of the remarkable increase in invisible earnings. On the import side Europe, particularly the EEC, was the main source of supply, with Italy and Germany playing the predominant role. The destination countries for exports were also primarily in the EEC with Germany, Italy and the UK usually in the first four. This heavy dependence upon the EEC has been a cause of considerable concern to the authorities. The market was very competitive, in some areas highly protected and member countries were strongly biased towards trade relations with their partners. Though Yugoslavia was included in the general preference for developing countries, it was in nothing like as strong a position as a member or an associate member. Moreover, it was particularly badly hit as an outsider because of the importance of its agricultural exports. In this latter respect the position has been somewhat eased by a series of special agreements. In March 1970, a three-year agreement on trade in meat, tobacco, wine and corn was concluded between Yugoslavia and the EEC countries, according to which each party granted to the other MFN (Most Favoured Nation) privileges. Certain tariff concessions were also granted in the case of meat.[60] A further agreement was signed in June 1973 to replace the expiring one, this time for a term of five years. Like its predecessor it contained MFN status and special arrangements for certain classes of agricultural products, in particular baby beef.[61] A new agreement, in similar terms, was signed in February 1980. Agricultural quotas were revised upwards and free access to the EEC for about 70 per cent of its industrial products was obtained, though sensitive products, like textiles and non-ferrous metals, were still subject to restrictions.[62]

Commodity structures. The rapid rate of growth of Social Product in the pre-reform economy was accompanied by an even faster rate of growth in its foreign trade. The annual average rates of growth of exports and imports were 13 and 11 per cent respectively.[63] The growth in exports brought with it a marked change in the proportion of total exports shared by different commodity groups. Though food, drink and tobacco together registered little change as a proportion of the total of about 25 per cent, finished manufactures rose from below 5 per cent in 1952 to exceed 33 per cent by 1965. On the other hand, raw materials fell from over 15 per cent of the total to under 3 per cent for the whole period. Yet it is important to qualify the statistics on structure with those on direction. Exports to convertible-currency areas during this period were chiefly wheat, maize, tobacco, wood and wood products, and non-ferrous metals. Exports to soft-currency areas, therefore, included a substantial proportion of Yugoslavia's total industrial exports. Indeed, one of the factors that gave Yugoslavia's export structure a relatively 'developed nation' profile was the ease with which it was able to sell its manufactures in Eastern Europe. With regard to imports during the pre-reform period the pattern of growth was steadier and changes in composition much less dramatic. Capital goods to assist the concentrated investment programme, and raw materials to feed the rapidly expanding industrial sector, remained important throughout the period. Foodstuffs, tobacco, and drink declined from about 35 per cent of total imports in 1953 to a little more than 15 per cent in 1965.

Annex 19 sets out developments in the commodity structure of trade since 1965. The changes in structure must be viewed in the light of the remarkable fall in the share of exports to OECD countries since 1969. The largest manufacturing exports to OECD countries during this period were leather goods, clothing and textiles, and furniture. But exports of paper products, electrical and non-electrical machinery, and certain metal products also grew rapidly. In the latter case, especially, a substantial part of the increase was attributable to the development of industrial co-operation and joint venture agreements. But the vast majority of chemical, pharmaceutical and consumer durable exports went to the Eastern bloc. This area also accounted for more than half the total exports of non-metallic minerals, ships, iron and steel products, electrical and non-electrical machinery, clothing and footwear.

Perhaps the most distinctive characteristic of Yugoslavia's export performance during the post-reform period, given its level of economic development, was the diversity of the processed goods that it sold abroad. By the mid-1970s over 1,500 categories of manu-factured goods were being exported. This was partly the inheritance of the industrial growth strategy of the 1950s. It was also, however, in the opinion of some commentators, part of a conscious policy by the authorities to reduce susceptibility to adverse reactions by trading blocs. As a non-aligned nation the Yugoslavs were particularly vul-nerable in this respect. By making only modest incursions into any single market with their products they hoped not to attract too much attention to their marketing successes. The policy also insured them against adverse demand changes for individual products.

The growth in Yugoslavia was heavily import dependent. More-over, the import content of social output was growing, reflecting both increased import dependence within sectors generally and, in par-ticular, the relatively greater importance in industrial production of sectors with an above average import content of output.[64] In 1970, eleven industrial branches, accounting for two-thirds of total industrial production, had an import content which exceeded 20 per cent.[65] In addition, nearly three-quarters of imports of raw material and investment goods derived from hard currency nations.[66] It was only in supplying fuels and iron and steel products that the Eastern bloc countries were of any significance. Over 70 per cent of chemicals, machinery and transport equipment, and non-ferrous metals came from the OECD area.

The main factor in the high degree of import dependence of the Yugoslav economy has been its industrial development strategy. Directly, until the reforms, and in many respects indirectly thereafter, as to which the development of the petrochemical industry bears witness, the authorities have pursued a policy of import substitution. This had the effect of increasing rather than reducing import dependence; initially, because manufacturing equipment had to be purchased abroad and, subsequently, because foreign raw material and semi-manufacture supplies were necessary to the new production processes. An 'integrated' policy of import substitution might have led to a gradual reduction in the demand for foreign inputs. But the strategy adopted in Yugoslavia was an unbalanced one. The cost of heavy investment in the processing industries during the 1950s and the early 1960s was neglect of the primary industries which then did not grow to meet the increased calls on their output resulting from the expansion of manufacturing capacity. Added to this, the policy of trade liberalization and international integration that followed the reforms required a further bout of heavy investment in advanced capital equipment to enable existing industries to compete in hard currency markets. The policy of import substitution also affected exports adversely. It produced a very high proportion of finished industrial goods for an economy at its level of development which could not hope to compete in international markets.

In addition to the effect of development strategy there were other factors which, though less significant, served to aggravate the problem. The retention quota system, as already mentioned, encouraged the import of low priority, hard currency items. The generally tight domestic credit conditions, coinciding with a fairly liberal period of foreign suppliers credit lending, persuaded many firms to buy abroad simply because they could obtain more favourable credit terms in that way or because it was the only way that they could get credit at all. Another contributing factor was the overvaluation of the dinar for much of the period which ensured artificially low import prices. Finally, the economy has been susceptible to extremely sharp increases in imports at times of buoyant domestic demand, as the years 1970/71, 1974 and 1979 bear witness. During such periods, moreover, the quantity requirements of the home market proved a stronger attraction to potential exporters than the more rigorous quality standards of international markets.

Invisible earnings. Without the massive contribution of invisibles to the convertible-currency earnings of Yugoslavia, either the foreign trade and payments regime would have had to have been considerably more rigorous or the rate of growth substantially lower than it was. Tourism and workers' remittances were almost entirely responsible; net earnings from these two sources between 1965 and 1975 rose from $US63m. to $US700m. and from $US55m. to $US1,644m. respectively. At their peak, in 1974, they amounted to about 53 per cent of visible export earnings. Their importance has declined somewhat in the aftermath of the shocks to levels of employment and disposable incomes in the OECD countries, brought about by the successive oil crises. But, together, at the beginning of the 1980s, they still represented more than a third of the value of commodity exports. The other source of invisible hard currency earnings derived from net transportation receipts; by the mid-1970s about two-thirds of net transportation earnings derived from hard currencies.

The factors governing the dramatic rise in workers' remittances were discussed in Chapter 4. The growth of tourism was due, essentially, to three factors. First, the beauty, climate and proximity to central Europe of the Dalmatian coast. Second, the scale of the investment made in tourist facilities. The Croatians, in particular, invested substantial resources in the tourist industry. The construction of new hotels was very actively encouraged by republican and local governments and subsidized credits were given to firms for this purpose. Heavy investments were also made in highway routes. Tourist development has had, and will have, heavy infrastructure costs. Building roads and hotels and public utility facilities on the scale anticipated, was, of course, extremely costly. However, it appears to have been a sensible use of resources. The ultimate benefits have accrued in foreign exchange; the immediate costs were almost entirely domestic and incurred in highly labour-intensive activities, thus creating much needed employment for skilled and semi-skilled labour. The third factor was the rapid growth in demand amongst Western Europeans for foreign holidays. Fluctuations in tourist earnings tended to depend upon the rate of growth of disposable incomes in other OECD countries. Thus, they stagnated between 1974 and 1977 in the aftermath of the 1973 oil crisis, only picking up in 1978. In the longer run the relative contribution of net tourist earnings may decline because of increased competition from similar Mediterranean resorts and growing travel abroad by Yugoslavs.

Deficit and debt. The net effect of the above mentioned factors was that, since 1965, Yugoslavia's current account balance to hard currency markets deteriorated. The decline was particularly marked after 1973, exacerbated by the stagnation in invisible earnings, the impact of successive oil crises and an investment-led expansion of the economy during the mid and late 1970s, far exceeding the country's growth potential, which both increased imports and diverted resources from the export to the home market.

Substantial convertible currency debt was incurred to finance these deficits. From 1973 to 1982, as Annex 20 reveals, it increased from $US4b. to $US18.5b. About one-third of this amount was public, or publicly guaranteed, debt. The remainder consisted of a variety of commercial obligations to the private sector. The cost of hard currency debt servicing in 1982 was about $US4b. or 24 per cent of the value of total current account revenues in that year. More than half of the amount outstanding was contracted on an adjustable interest basis, and the prevailing high rates since the late 1970s aggravated the servicing problem. About three-quarters of the value of outstanding debt was denominated in US dollars.

Annexes

Annex 1. *Domestic Sectoral Savings as a Percentage of Domestic Aggregate Savings*

	1960–3	1966	1967	1968	1969	1970	1971	1972	1973	1974	1975	1976	1977	1978	1979	1980	1981
Firms	45	57	50	50	51	50	52	49	52	62	51	48	54	53	57	60	62
Socio-Political Communities	36	20	22	24	18	15	−5	9	6	4	1	3	−3	2	4	1	4
Households & Private Producers	9	24	25	25	31	27	36	36	35	28	32	33	31	35	31	30	29
Bank Credit & Social Insurance Funds	6	5	8	9	9	9	9	10	11	9	13	15	15	14	14	13	13
Unclassified	4	−6	−5	−8	−9	−1	8	−4	−4	−3	3	1	3	−4	−6	−4	−8
Total	100	100	100	100	100	100	100	100	100	100	100	100	100	100	100	100	100

Source: National Bank of Yugoslavia, Quarterly Bulletin: Volume 1, No. 3, 1973, Table 7; Volume 3, No. 3, 1975, Table 7; Volume 4, No. 3, 1976, Table 7; Volume 10, No. 2–3, 1982, p. 10.

Annex 2. *Domestic Sectoral Financial Savings as a Percentage of Domestic Aggregate Financial Savings*

	1963	1966	1967	1968	1969	1970	1971	1972	1973	1974	1975	1976	1977	1978	1979	1980	1981
1 Households	2	40	26	13	31	34	49	62	59	60	56	57	59	67	68	72	65
2 Extra-Budgetary Funds	79	49	59	65	51	52	19	25	20	15	9	10	7	5	5	9	9
3 Federal Government	2	—	—	1	—	—	—	—	—	—	—	—	—	—	—	—	—
4 Regional & Local Government	17	10	—	7	7	—	—	—	—	9	1	8	—	12	11	5	6
5 Bank Credit & Social Insurance Funds	—	1	15	14	11	14	8	13	21	16	20	19	21	16	16	14	20
6 Unclassified	—	—	—	—	—	—	24	—	—	—	14	6	13	—	—	—	—
Total	100	100	100	100	100	100	100	100	100	100	100	100	100	100	100	100	100

Source: National Bank of Yugoslavia, *Quarterly Bulletin:* Volume 1, No. 3, 1973, Table 8; Volume 3, No. 3, 1975, Table 8; Volume 4, No. 3, 1976, Table 8; Volume 10, No. 2–3, 1982, p. 11.

Annex 3. *The Savings of Firms expressed as a Percentage of their Distributable Resources*

	1963	1965	1966	1967	1968	1969	1970	1971	1972	1973	1974	1975	1976	1977	1978	1979	1980
1 Gross Value Added	100.0	100.0	100.0	100.0	100.0	100.0	100.0	100.0	100.0	100.0	100.0	100.0	100.0	100.0	100.0	100.0	100.0
2 Depreciation	9.8	8.8	8.8	10.8	10.9	11.1	10.8	10.5	11.8	12.2	12.2	10.8	11.9	10.7	10.5	10.2	10.5
3 Legal and Contract Liabilities	51.2	39.9	35.8	37.6	37.9	41.0	39.3	35.8	36.6	36.9	38.7	39.1	40.1	40.8	41.6	41.8	40.0
4 Net Personal Incomes	28.2	31.9	34.7	35.6	35.8	37.4	38.2	37.7	37.3	36.4	33.6	34.5	36.1	36.2	34.5	33.6	31.5
5 Allocations to Funds	10.8	19.4	20.7	16.0	15.4	10.5	11.7	16.0	14.3	14.5	15.5	15.6	11.9	12.3	13.4	14.4	18.0
Distributable Resources (2+4+5)	48.8	60.1	64.2	62.4	62.1	59.0	60.7	64.2	63.4	63.1	61.2	60.9	59.9	59.2	58.4	58.2	60.0
Savings (2+5)	20.6	28.2	29.5	26.8	26.3	21.6	22.5	26.5	26.1	26.7	27.6	26.4	23.8	23.0	23.9	24.6	28.5
Savings/Distributable Resources	42.2	46.9	46.0	42.9	42.4	36.6	37.1	41.3	41.2	42.3	45.0	43.3	39.7	38.8	40.9	42.3	47.5

Source: Statistički Godišnjak: Osnovni podaci o privrednim organizacijama društvenog sektora (Basic Data on Economic Organizations of the Social Sector), 1965, Table 106.9; 1969, Table 106.8; 1970, Table 106.6; 1971, Table 106.5; 1972, Table 106.4; 1973, Table 106.6; 1974, Table 106.6; 1975, Table 106.6; 1976, Table 107.5; 1977, Table 107.6; 1978, Table 107.6; 1979, Table 113.3; 1979, Table 113.1; 1980, Table 113.1; 1981, Table 113.4; 1982, Table 113.1.

Annex 4. *Sources and Deployment of Household Receipts (Percentages)*

	1964	1965	1966	1967	1968	1969	1970	1971	1972	1973	1974	1975	1976	1977	1978	1979	1980
Composition of Household Receipts	100	100	100	100	100	100	100	100	100	100	100	100	100	100	100	100	100
Incomes	83.8	83.4	82.7	83.5	82.7	81.3	79.8	78.1	75.7	72.8	73.7	74.6	74.6	74.9	72.1	71.7	69.6
Social Security Receipts	14.8	15.2	15.0	13.7	13.9	13.9	13.4	13.2	13.7	13.9	13.9	14.5	15.2	15.4	15.8	16.2	15.6
Other	0.1	0.0	1.2	0.4	0.4	1.0	0.7	0.7	0.6	1.6	1.6	1.7	1.8	2.3	2.8	3.8	4.0
Net Transfers from Abroad	1.3	1.4	1.1	2.4	3.0	3.8	6.1	8.0	10.0	11.7	10.8	9.2	8.4	7.4	9.3	8.3	10.8
Savings as a Proportion of Household Receipts*	8.6	9.5	14.0	9.7	9.4	11.9	12.9	13.7	14.1	14.5	13.0	12.2	13.6	13.8	13.9	12.2	11.4

	1964	1965	1966	1967	1968	1969	1970	1971	1972	1973	1974	1975	1976	1977	1978	1979	1980
Household Receipts as Percentage of Social Product	55.7	59.9	64.4	66.0	66.7	67.7	69.1	68.4	70.7	69.7	67.0	67.4	69.6	69.8	69.7	67.6	65.9

*These statistics do not include foreign exchange deposits in dinars. Accordingly they show a much lower saving rate. Contrast Chapter 3, n. 40.
Source: OECD, *Economic Survey of Yugoslavia*, Nov. 1970, Table E; Apr. 1976, Table E; May 1983, Table E.

Annex 5. *Financial Investments by Households*

	1964	1965	1966	1967	1968	1969	1970	1971	1972	1973	1974	1975	1976	1977	1978	1979	1980
Currency	54	42	36	28	32	36	32	22	35	27	22	20	17	17	21	18	21
Sights Deposits	31	29	38	30	28	33	24	18	16	23	23	27	30	30	30	23	21
Time Deposits	11	17	8	13	17	15	17	12	11	12	14	14	16	12	11	11	11
Foreign Exchange Deposits	4	12	18	29	23	16	27	48	38	38	41	39	37	41	38	48	47
Total	100	100	100	100	100	100	100	100	100	100	100	100	100	100	100	100	100

Source: National Bank of Yugoslavia, Quarterly Bulletin: Volume 3, No. 3, 1975, p. 26; Volume 4, No. 3, 1976, p. 26; Volume 10, No. 2–3, 1982, p. 19.

Annex 6. *Domestic Sources of Finance for Fixed Investment (Percentages)*

	1960–63	1965	1966	1967	1968	1969	1970	1971	1972	1973	1974	1975	1976	1977	1978	1979	1980
Banks	5	37	46	45	41	43	43	41	40	40	41	44	47	47	50	49	48
Firms	35	28	39	37	51	51	50	53	53	56	56	53	50	51	48	49	50
Fiscal	60	35	15	18	8	6	7	6	7	4	3	3	3	2	2	2	2
Total	100	100	100	100	100	100	100	100	100	100	100	100	100	100	100	100	100

Source: Statistički Godišnjak; Utrošak za investicije u osnovne fondove (Investment Expenditure Payments on Fixed Assets), 1967, Table 119.5; 1970, Table 1194; 1971–3, Table 119.2; *Izvršene isplate za investicije po osnovim oblicima finansiranja* (Effected Payments for Investment by Principal Sources of Finance) 1979, Table 110.3; 1982, Table 110.2.

Annex 7. Long-Term Liabilities of Business Banks (Percentage at Year End)

	1966	1967	1968	1969	1970	1971	1972	1973	1974	1975	1976	1977	1978	1979	1980	1981
Tied Resources																
1 Earmarked Resources	58	52	48	33	34	32	27	26	28	25	22	18	13	1	1	1
2 Housing Funds	12	11	11	16	16	14	12	12	14	12	11	11	8	8	7	7
3 National Banks	2	1	2	2	3	12	13	15	2	3	3	4	3	3	3	2
Free Resources																
4 Time Deposits	8	11	13	21	23	19	15	14	15	16	17	16	15	14	13	13
5 Bonds	1	1	1	—	—	1	1	1	2	2	2	2	2	2	1	1
6 Foreign Exchange Deposits	—	—	2	3	5	8	10	11	15	17	19	21	24	28	35	40
7 Other Long-Term Credits	9	13	12	8	6	5	10	11	13	14	14	17	26	36	33	29
8 Bank Credit Fund	10	11	11	17	13	10	12	10	11	11	12	11	9	8	7	7
Total	100	100	100	100	100	100	100	100	100	100	100	100	100	100	100	100

Source: National Bank of Yugoslavia, Quarterly Bulletin: Volume 3, No. 3, 1975 and Volume 4, No. 4, 1976, Table 11A; Volume 10, No. 2 and 3, 1982, Table 10A.

Annex 8. *Borrowed Resources of Firms*

	1968	1969	1970	1971	1972	1973	1974	1975	1976	1977	1978	1979	1980	1981
Short-Term Bank Credit	29	18	17	13	36	48	18	26	22	11	13	16	13	20
Long-Term Bank Credit	30	26	32	18	50	17	22	37	54	40	29	29	18	12
Other Long-Term Financial Credits	5	3	2	—	1	12	2	2	6	9	3	2	1	1
Foreign Exchange Credits	4	4	3	15	10	3	5	11	15	15	8	7	23	13
Trade Credits	32	49	46	54	3	20	53	24	—	15	30	27	33	28
Securities	—	—	—	—	—	—	—	—	3	7	10	7	4	5
Pooled Resources	—	—	—	—	—	—	—	—	—	2	4	6	5	8
Other	—	—	—	—	—	—	—	—	—	1	3	6	3	13
Total	100	100	100	100	100	100	100	100	100	100	100	100	100	100

Credits for Goods Purchased and Sold (Bn. Dinars)

	1968	1969	1970	1971	1972	1973	1974	1975	1976	1977	1978	1979	1980	1981
Credits for Goods Purchased	10.5	22.0	23.0	39.0	1.0	10.5	67.7	26.9	-53.7	27.0	98.8	113.5	234.5	263.3
Credits for Goods Sold	14.6	23.7	24.6	41.6	2.6	13.9	76.6	20.3	-45.9	30.3	108.2	119.4	228.7	279.2

Source: National Bank of Yugoslavia, *Quarterly Bulletin:* Volume 3, No. 3, 1975 and Volume 4, No. 3, 1976, pp. 26–27; Volume 10, No. 2–3, 1982,

Annex 9. *Proportional Deployment of the Active Labour Force*

	1965	1966	1967	1968	1969	1970	1971	1972	1973	1974	1975	1976	1977	1978	1979	1980	1981
Active Labour Force	100.0	100.0	100.0	100.0	100.0	100.0	100.0	100.0	100.0	100.0	100.0	100.0	100.0	100.0	100.0	100.0	100.0
Paid Employment	43.7	43.0	42.3	41.9	42.2	43.6	45.3	46.7	47.7	49.7	52.0	53.5	55.7	58.0	60.2	61.8	60.4
Registered Unemployment	2.7	3.0	3.0	3.5	3.6	3.6	3.3	3.5	4.2	4.9	5.9	6.9	7.6	7.9	8.2	8.4	8.2
Other Labour Force	53.6	54.0	54.7	54.6	54.2	52.8	51.4	49.8	48.1	45.4	42.1	39.6	36.7	34.1	31.6	29.8	31.4
of which:																	
Worker Emigration (net)	0.2	10.3	3.4	4.6	6.5	8.9	10.4	11.3	12.2	11.4	10.3	9.5	8.9	8.6	8.5	8.2	7.8
Yugoslav Workers employed in Germany	0.7	1.1	1.1	1.4	3.0	4.8	5.4	5.3	5.9	5.2	4.5	4.2	4.1	3.9	3.9	3.7	3.4

	1965	1966	1967	1968	1969	1970	1971	1972	1973	1974	1975	1976	1977	1978	1979	1980	1981
Employment Growth Rate	1.5	−2.2	−0.6	0.7	3.3	3.9	4.8	4.4	2.3	4.8	5.4	3.5	4.5	4.6	4.3	3.2	2.9
Productivity Growth Rate	0.1	9.0	1.6	2.9	6.7	2.1	4.2	1.1	6.7	−1.3	−1.5	4.2	2.6	2.4	−2.1	−1.8	−2.0
Output Growth Rate (S.P.)	1.6	6.8	1.0	3.6	10.0	6.0	9.0	5.5	9.0	3.5	3.9	7.7	7.1	7.0	2.2	1.4	0.9

NB. Over 90% of paid employment was in the Social Sector. The statistics of the employment of Yugoslav Nationals abroad are a best estimate derived by the OECD. Registered unemployment measures the difference between those officially registered as offering Social Sector employment and those officially registered as seeking it.

Source: OECD, *Economic Survey of Yugoslavia:* June 1973, Table G; April 1976, Table H; May 1980, Table H; May 1983, Table H.

Annex 10. *Size Structure of Industrial Firms in Yugoslavia as a % of their Total*

No. of Workers	No. of Firms	Employment	Fixed Assets	Social Product
Below 30	5.9	0.1	0.1	0.2
30–60	6.3	0.5	0.9	0.8
61–125	15.9	2.4	3.1	2.5
126–250	22.0	6.6	6.4	6.4
251–1,000	34.7	28.9	26.0	27.4
1,001–2,000	9.3	21.0	21.3	20.7
Above 2,000	5.9	40.5	42.2	42.0
Total	100.0	100.0	100.0	100.0

Source: *Statistički Godišnjak*, 1972, *Privredne organizacije prema broju zaposlenog osoblijd* (Economic Organizations According to the Numbers Employed), Table 106.9; *Privredni organizacije veličini osnovni sredstava* (Economic Organizations According to the Value of Foxed Assets), Table 106.10; and *Privredni organizacije prema veličini neto-produkta* (Economic Organizations According to the Value of Net Product), Table 106.11.

Annex 11. *Post-Reform Merger*

	1965	1966	1967	1968	1969	1970	1971	1972	1973	1974	1975
Manufacturing and Mining	88	68	46	28	73	144	105	81	75	46	72
Agriculture	237	230	136	137	151	270	147	149	74	90	107
Forestry	3	5	3	1	4	16	17	8	6	3	2
Construction	17	18	13	10	9	16	8	25	25	12	23
Transport	8	38	8	16	17	13	11	12	12	9	9
Trade and Catering	182	165	78	98	166	201	185	139	131	86	91
Arts and Crafts	111	137	48	50	50	89	87	79	79	37	57
Public Utility	36	48	14	15	28	40	22	45	38	16	36
Total	682	709	346	355	498	789	582	538	440	299	397

Source: Statistički Godišnjak, 1975: Integracije u Privredni (Integrated Economic Organizations), Table 107.3.

Annex 12. *Annual Changes in Selected Macroeconomic Variables*

	1965	1966	1967	1968	1969	1970	1971	1972	1973	1974	1975	1976	1977	1978	1979	1980	1981
Current Account Balance ($USm)	70	−39	−75	−95	−63	−348	−357	419	485	−1183	−1032	165	−1582	−1256	−3661	−2291	−750
Rate of Growth of Cost of Living	34.0	22.4	7.3	5.7	7.5	11.0	15.3	16.4	19.4	21.3	24.1	11.6	15.3	14.2	20.3	30.1	40.1
*Rate of Growth of Employment	1.5	−2.2	−0.6	0.7	3.3	3.9	4.8	4.4	2.3	4.8	5.4	3.5	4.5	4.5	4.3	3.2	2.9
Rate of Growth of Social Product	1.6	6.8	1.0	3.6	10.0	6.0	9.0	5.5	9.0	3.5	3.9	7.7	7.1	7.0	2.2	1.4	0.9

*Social Sector Only.
Source: OECD, *Economic Survey of Yugoslavia,* Apr. 1976, Tables E, H, I and M and May 1983, Tables E, H, I and M.

Annex 13. *Consolidated Budget of Socio-Political Communities and Communities of Interest*

	1968	1969	1970	1971	1972	1973	1974	1975	1976	1977	1978	1979	1980	1981	1982
Revenue	100%	100%	100%	100%	100%	100%	100%	100%	100%	100%	100%	100%	100%	100%	100%
Direct Tax	42.2%	42.7%	45.1%	48.6%	44.8%	50.1%	53.4%	52.9%	53.5%	57.6%	60.5%	59.4%	59.8%	57.5%	57.7%
Indirect Tax	22.2%	22.9%	24.7%	34.1%	40.3%	40.0%	37.3%	36.5%	34.3%	35.9%	32.9%	33.5%	32.4%	34.2%	33.9%
Other	35.6%	34.4%	30.2%	17.3%	14.9%	9.9%	9.3%	10.6%	12.2%	6.5%	6.6%	7.1%	7.8%	8.3%	8.4%
Expenditure	100%	100%	100%	100%	100%	100%	100%	100%	100%	100%	100%	100%	100%	100%	100%
Administration and Defence	25.6%	24.6%	23.4%	22.6%	21.2%	22.2%	22.1%	22.5%	21.8%	22.9%	21.5%	22.1%	23.6%	24.3%	24.3%
Social Services	40.4%	41.5%	43.7%	44.9%	43.7%	42.3%	42.5%	42.3%	43.2%	50.6%	52.3%	52.4%	50.6%	50.7%	50.6%
Gross Fixed Investment	11.8%	11.3%	11.5%	18.7%	16.1%	13.3%	11.5%	11.6%	11.3%	8.9%	9.8%	8.9%	8.9%	8.4%	8.4%
Other	22.2%	22.6%	21.4%	13.8%	19.0%	22.2%	23.9%	23.6%	23.7%	17.6%	16.4%	16.6%	16.9%	16.6%	16.7%
Surplus/Deficit	6.5%	4.9%	2.5%	2.5%	−0.5%	−0.4%	3.1%	−2.5%	−4.7%	−2.3%	−1.3%	0.1%	−1.8%	1.7%	1.8%

Source: OECD, *Economic Survey of Yugoslavia,* Text Tables 5, April 1976; 14, July 1982.

Annex 14. *Annual Changes in the Sources of Money Supply (M1) (Bn. Dinars)*

	1968	1969	1970	1971	1972	1973	1974	1975	1976	1977	1978	1979	1980	1981	1982
Bank Credits	20.5	24.9	33.0	36.7	36.9	43.2	68.6	93.0	129.3	154.1	213.1	258.4	350.7	359.4	328.2
Foreign Exchange Transactions	−0.2	−1.3	−4.1	−5.2	7.6	7.7	−9.8	3.8	15.0	−22.1	−19.4	−79.5	−147.6	−113.2	−212.8
Increase in Non-Monetary Deposits	−15.0	−20.4	−22.7	−26.0	−26.5	−28.7	−37.2	−54.9	−67.1	88.4	−129.5	−120.1	−116.6	−123.6	−40.1
Total Money Supply Increase	5.3	3.2	6.2	5.5	18.0	22.2	21.6	34.3	77.2	44.6	64.2	59.8	86.5	122.6	155.5
Percentage Change in Total	26.0	11.6	20.0	14.9	42.3	36.8	26.1	33.3	53.5	21.6	25.6	19.0	23.0	26.6	26.6

Source: OECD, *Economic Survey of Yugoslavia*, Text Tables 10, Nov. 1970; 6, June, 1973; 9, Apr. 1975; 11, Apr. 1976; 8, June 1979; 9, July 1982; 10, May 1983.

Annex 15. *Annual Percentage Changes in Final Domestic Demand*

	1965	1966	1967	1968	1969	1970	1971	1972	1973	1974	1975	1976	1977	1978	1979	1980	1981	1982
Private Consumption	5.1	1.5	6.6	6.5	7.5	8.5	9.0	5.5	2.7	7.3	3.4	4.4	7.0	7.0	5.2	0.7	−1.0	0.5
Collective Consumption	−3.6	1.9	6.5	6.0	10.0	5.5	8.0	5.6	4.1	7.2	9.2	9.2	7.4	5.0	7.9	2.7	−0.7	−1.6
Gross Fixed Investment	−11.6	4.0	−5.3	12.7	10.0	17.5	6.5	6.0	4.2	10.9	9.6	8.1	11.1	13.5	6.4	−1.7	−9.3	−6.2
Final Domestic Demand	−1.5	2.3	2.9	8.2	8.5	11.0	7.5	5.5	3.0	8.0	5.9	6.1	8.4	9.1	5.9	0.0	−3.9	−2.0
Stock Building, Foreign Balance, and Statistical Error	3.0	4.8	−1.6	−3.7	1.5	−4.0	2.0	0.5	2.5	0.5	−2.1	−5.5	3.7	−4.6	4.3	1.4	3.0	−3.1
Social Product	1.6	6.8	1.0	3.6	10.0	6.0	9.0	5.5	5.5	9.0	3.5	3.9	7.7	7.1	7.0	2.2	1.4	0.9

Source: OECD, *Economic Survey of Yugoslavia*, Apr. 1976, Table A; June 1979, Text Table 1; May 1983, Text Table 3.

Annex 16. *Annual Percentage Rates of Increase of Prices*

	1965	1966	1967	1968	1969	1970	1971	1972	1973	1974	1975	1976	1977	1978	1979	1980	1981
Agricultural Producer's Prices	42.4	16.6	−3.1	−4.3	9.9	15.0	26.0	24.1	25.0	14.2	13.2	14.4	12.0	11.7	25.6	35.3	53.3
Industrial Producers' Prices	14.8	11.2	2.1	0.0	3.1	9.0	15.6	11.1	12.9	29.7	22.0	6.4	9.4	8.2	13.3	27.4	44.6
of which:																	
Materials	4.3	16.6	11.9	2.1	4.2	12.0	17.9	10.6	13.0	40.6	22.8	5.6	8.9	7.9	15.8	34.1	44.1
Capital Goods	6.9	4.3	2.1	0.0	1.0	5.0	12.4	6.8	9.5	13.0	22.4	13.0	9.2	5.9	6.0	12.1	25.3
Consumer Goods	16.4	11.8	1.1	0.0	4.2	7.0	13.1	12.4	13.2	22.1	20.7	5.3	10.8	9.8	10.9	21.0	43.7
Export Unit Values	6.8	3.2	1.0	−2.1	4.2	9.0	4.6	6.1	19.0	32.6	8.9	4.3	12.4	9.0	14.6	19.3	8.5
Import Unit Values	5.6	1.1	0.0	0.0	5.3	8.0	3.7	56.3	20.3	45.7	5.3	2.8	13.8	4.7	19.1	19.8	10.4
Cost of Living	34.0	22.4	7.3	5.7	7.5	11.0	15.3	16.4	19.4	21.3	24.1	11.6	15.3	14.2	20.3	30.1	40.1
Average Personal Income (Social Sector)	37.8	37.2	12.9	10.1	14.9	18.0	22.9	16.5	15.9	27.6	23.6	15.5	18.7	20.9	20.2	20.5	33.7

Source: OECD, *Economic Survey of Yugoslavia*, Apr. 1975, Table H; Apr. 1976, Table I; May 1983, Table I.

	1965	1966	1967	1968	1969	1970	1971	1972	1973	1974	1975	1976	1977	1978	1979	1980	1981	1982
Trade Balance	−195	−351	−454	−532	−659	−1195	−1435	−992	−1658	−3715	−3625	−2489	−4380	−4317	−7225	−6086	−4828	−3089
Exports, fob	1094	1225	1253	1265	1475	1678	1817	2241	2853	3805	4072	4878	5254	5671	6794	8978	10229	10247
Imports, cif	−1289	−1576	−1707	−1797	−2134	−2874	−3252	−3233	−4511	−7520	−7697	−7367	−9634	−9988	−14019	−15064	−15757	−13336
Services and Private Transfers	235	301	367	426	594	847	1079	1412	2144	2532	2593	2654	2798	3061	3564	3795	4078	2625
Transportation	118	140	145	146	171	211	224	240	323	396	430	429	568	585	731	832	1044	980
Foreign Travel	63	82	95	136	168	144	141	219	589	644	702	725	750	930	1028	1515	1853	1415
Investment Income	−60	−70	−74	−80	−90	−119	−139	−155	−181	−198	−275	−279	−258	−300	−633	−1084	−1710	−1773
Private Transfers and Workers' Remittances	55	63	160	191	284	544	789	1049	1413 }	1379	1327	1415	1427	1745	1710	1539	2042	1255
Other Services	59	86	41	33	61	66	64	59		311	418	364	311	101	728	993	849	748
Official Transfers	30	11	12	11	2	1	−1	−1	−1	—	—	—	—	—	—	—	—	—
Current Balance	70	−39	−75	−95	−63	−348	−357	419	485	−1183	−1032	165	−1582	−1256	−3661	−2291	−750	−464

Source: OECD, Economic Survey of Yugoslavia, Apr. 1976, Table M; July, 1983, Table M.

Annex 18. *Annual Percentage Shares of Imports and Exports by Area*

	1965	1966	1967	1968	1969	1970	1971	1972	1973	1974	1975	1976	1977	1978	1979	1980	1981	1982
Imports																		
OECD Countries	57.3	56.2	62.9	63.9	64.6	69.0	65.8	65.4	62.5	60.5	60.8	54.8	56.9	59.0	60.8	52.8	53.3	51.2
of which: EEC	31.1	31.7	44.2	44.3	45.1	46.4	44.1	44.0	42.2	40.0	41.1	39.0	39.5	38.3	40.6	34.6	35.4	33.6
Centrally Planned Countries	28.8	31.7	26.9	27.2	23.9	20.6	23.9	24.8	24.8	23.3	24.8	30.7	28.9	25.0	25.3	30.1	31.5	34.7
Developing Countries	13.9	12.1	10.1	8.9	11.5	10.4	10.3	9.8	12.7	16.2	14.4	14.5	14.2	16.0	13.9	17.1	15.2	14.1
Total	100.0	100.0	100.0	100.0	100.0	100.0	100.0	100.0	100.0	100.0	100.0	100.0	100.0	100.0	100.0	100.0	100.0	100.0
Exports																		
OECD Countries	42.7	48.5	51.6	51.9	55.8	56.1	52.9	56.9	55.7	46.6	35.6	41.8	39.9	42.9	43.9	37.4	32.1	28.2
of which: EEC	28.9	31.9	33.7	33.1	38.2	39.0	35.6	36.2	35.7	27.4	22.8	27.2	26.5	23.0	28.3	26.3	23.1	20.4
Centrally Planned Countries	42.1	36.6	36.2	34.4	30.8	32.5	36.7	36.0	34.0	41.6	47.3	42.4	40.2	38.5	40.2	46.0	49.7	51.0
Developing Countries	15.2	14.9	12.2	13.7	13.4	11.4	10.4	7.1	10.3	11.8	17.1	15.8	19.9	18.6	15.9	16.6	18.2	20.8
Total	100.0	100.0	100.0	100.0	100.0	100.0	100.0	100.0	100.0	100.0	100.0	100.0	100.0	100.0	100.0	100.0	100.0	100.0

Source: OECD, *Economic Survey of Yugoslavia*, Apr. 1977, Table L; May 1983, Table L.

Annex 19. *Annual Percentage Shares of Commodity Groups in Total Imports and Exports*

	1965	1966	1967	1968	1969	1970	1971	1972	1973	1974	1975	1976	1977	1978	1979	1980	1981
Imports																	
Agricultural	14.7	15.0	10.6	7.1	6.9	7.2	9.1	9.5	11.3	8.8	5.5	8.7	8.2	6.2	6.9	6.6	5.0
Raw Materials	16.8	13.5	11.6	11.0	12.4	10.9	9.6	10.4	10.8	13.3	9.6	9.4	9.7	9.9	8.6	10.2	10.4
Mineral Fuels	5.7	5.2	5.0	5.5	4.9	4.8	5.9	5.4	7.9	12.6	12.3	14.7	13.4	14.3	16.1	23.5	24.1
Chemicals	9.1	9.4	9.8	10.5	10.3	9.3	9.1	10.8	9.9	10.8	10.7	10.7	10.3	11.5	11.8	12.2	12.8
Semi-Manufactures	21.6	23.5	23.6	23.8	25.5	28.7	28.2	26.1	24.0	23.9	22.7	18.5	18.3	17.0	15.9	15.7	16.5
Finished Manufactures	31.0	32.6	37.6	41.1	39.6	38.4	36.5	36.3	35.4	29.7	37.7	37.1	39.3	40.6	40.3	31.1	30.5
Other	1.1	0.8	1.8	1.0	0.4	0.7	1.6	1.5	0.7	0.9	1.5	0.9	0.8	0.5	0.4	0.7	0.7
Total	100.0	100.0	100.0	100.0	100.0	100.0	100.0	100.0	100.0	100.0	100.0	100.0	100.0	100.0	100.0	100.0	100.0
Exports																	
Agricultural	25.6	24.3	26.8	20.6	19.6	18.7	17.6	17.5	16.1	10.8	11.7	12.7	11.6	12.1	10.5	11.3	10.5
Raw Materials	10.1	8.9	8.5	10.0	9.6	9.4	8.2	8.2	9.6	9.5	6.9	8.8	9.7	7.9	9.2	7.5	5.2
Chemicals	5.4	5.7	5.8	6.1	6.2	5.8	7.1	6.4	6.2	10.1	9.4	7.2	6.3	8.4	9.4	11.6	12.6
Semi-Manufactures	22.7	23.1	22.4	25.6	29.2	29.3	27.2	26.9	28.6	32.8	28.9	27.4	22.9	22.3	23.6	22.1	22.1
Finished Manufactures	36.0	36.3	34.3	36.5	34.2	35.4	38.5	39.7	38.1	35.2	42.1	42.6	45.8	45.8	43.2	44.4	47.2
Other	0.2	1.7	2.2	1.2	1.2	1.4	1.4	1.3	1.4	1.6	1.0	1.3	3.7	3.5	4.1	3.1	2.4
Total	100.0	100.0	100.0	100.0	100.0	100.0	100.0	100.0	100.0	100.0	100.0	100.0	100.0	100.0	100.0	100.0	100.0

Source: OECD, *Economic Survey of Yugoslavia*, Apr. 1976, Table K; May 1983, Table K.

Annex 20. *External debt ($USb)*

	1973	1975	1977	1978	1979	1980	1981	1982
Total gross indebtedness	4¾	6½	9½	11¾	15	18¾	20	20
Less lending	¾	¾	1	1	1¼	1½	1¾	1¾
Total net indebtedness	4	5¾	8½	10¾	13¾	17¼	18¼	18½
of which:								
Public total		2¼	2¾	3½	3¾	4½	6	6½
IMF	¼	¼	¼	¼	½	¾	1¼	1¾
IBRD	¼	½	¾	1	1¼	1¼	1½	1½
Other	1	1½	1¾	2¼	2	2½	3¼	3
Business banks	½	¾	1½	2¾	4¾	6½	6½	6½
Interest payments	¼	¼	¼	½	¾	1¼	2	2
Capital repayments	¾	1	1¼	1¼	2	2¼	2	2
Debt servicing, total	1	1¼	1½	1¾	2¾	3½	4	4
(As a per cent of total current account receipts)	(19)	(19)	(19)	(18)	(20)	(20)	(21)	(24)

Source: OECD, *Economic Survey of Yugoslavia*, May 1983, Text Table 9.

NOTES

Introduction

1 D. Rusinow, *The Yugoslav Experiment*, C. Hurst and Co., London, 1977, p. 138.
2 OECD, *Economic Survey of Yugoslavia*, June 1979, p. 5.
3 Ibid.

Chapter 1

1 *Službeni List* (Official Bulletin), hereinafter *SL*, 6 Dec. 1946, and 28 Apr. 1948. And, see, G. W. Hoffman and F. W. Neal, *Yugoslavia and the New Communism*, Twentieth Century Fund, New York, 1962, pp. 89–91 and pp. 95–6.
2 *SL*, 4 June 1946. And see Hoffman and Neal, op. cit., p. 96.
3 A valuable account of the causes and consequences of the Soviet-Yugoslav conflict appears in A. Ross Johnson, *The Transformation of Communist Ideology: the Yugoslav Case*, MIT Press, London, 1972.
4 D. Milenkovitch, *Plan and Market in Yugoslav Thought*, Yale University Press, Newhaven and London, 1971, Chapter 4, provides an extremely useful analysis of the ideological debate.
5 E. Kardelj, *Komunist* 3, No. 4, July 1959, pp. 1–84. And see Milenkovitch, op. cit., p. 65.
6 *SL*, 5 July 1950.
7 Quoted in Hoffman and Neal, op. cit., p. 166.
8 B. Kidrič, *Komunist* 4, No. 6, Nov. 1950, pp. 1–20. See Milenkovitch, op. cit., pp. 77–80.
9 See D. Rusinow, *The Yugoslav Experiment*, C. Hurst & Co., London, 1977, pp. 74–7.
10 See, for example, Hoffman and Neal, op. cit., Part 4; R. Bicanic, *Economic Policy in Socialist Yugoslavia*, CUP, 1973, especially Chapters 3–8; F. W. Neal, *Titoism in Action*, University of California, 1958, Chapters 5–7; and S. Pejovich, *The Market Planned Economy in Yugoslavia*, University of Minnesota Press, Berkeley and Los Angeles, 1966, Chapter 1.
11 See, for example, Hoffman and Neal, op. cit., pp. 246–52.
12 Ibid., pp. 255–8.
13 Until the reforms, the standard rate of interest charged was 6 per cent but most industrial branches were granted concessions. During the years immediately preceding reform, the average rate paid was between 2 and 3 per cent. The 1965 measures reduced the maximum rate payable to 4.5 per cent though the actual burden imposed was somewhat higher because the book value of all fixed assets was revalued at the same time to allow for inflation and devaluation. But again concessions were made. The average rate actually paid appears to have stayed between the 2 and 3 per cent marks with some branches paying as little as 1.7 per cent. See Jan Vanek, *The Economics of Workers' Management*, George Allen & Unwin, London, 1972, pp. 257–9.
14 See, in particular, J. Djordjevic, 'Local Self-Government in Yugoslavia', *American Slavic & East European Review*, Volume XII, Apr. 1953, pp. 188–200.
15 See *Worker Management and Labour Relations in Yugoslavia*, ILO, Labour Management Relations, Series No. 5, 1958.
16 See 'Law on the Formation and Liquidation of Enterprises', *SL*, 24 Dec. 1953. And

237

238   MARKET SOCIALISM IN YUGOSLAVIA

S. A. Sacks, *Entry of New Competitors in Yugoslav Market Socialism*, Institute of International Studies, University of California, Berkeley, 1973.

17 See 'Economic Chambers & Cooperative Associations', *Yugoslav Survey*, Volume 1, 1960. And Hoffman and Neal, op. cit., pp. 243–4.
18 Ibid.
19 Ibid.
20 See, for example. Hoffman and Neal, op. cit., pp. 244–6.
21 See Neuberger, 'The Yugoslav Investment Auctions', *Quarterly Journal of Economics* 72, No. 1, Feb. 1959, pp. 88–115.
22 *SL*, 25 July 1956.
23 *SL*, 18 June 1952.
24 See F. W. Neal, op. cit., Chapter 6, pp. 144–5.
25 Ibid., pp. 146–7.
26 See, for example, R. Bicanic, op. cit., pp. 160–1, and Hoffman and Neal, op. cit., pp. 258–9.
27 'The Law on Wholesale & Retail Stores', *SL*, 17 Aug. 1955, which contained anti-monopoly provisions, was never effectively enforced.
28 *SL*, 16 Mar. 1961.
29 *SL*, 29 Jan. 1954.
30 The Foreign Trade Bank was founded on 29 June 1955, the Investment Bank on 18 July 1956, and the Agricultural Bank on 27 June 1958.
31 See Hoffman and Neal, op. cit., p. 257.
32 See Hoffman and Neal, op. cit., pp. 258–61.
33 See, for example, Bicanic, op. cit., Chapters 5 and 7, P. Shoup, *Communism and the Yugoslav National Question*, Columbia University Press, New York and London, 1968, Chapter 6; Milenkovitch, op. cit., Chapters 6 and 7.
34 See Milenkovitch, op. cit., p. 123.
35 See examples given by Shoup, op. cit., pp. 242–8, and by J. C. Fisher, *Yugoslavia: A Multi National State*, Chandler Publishing Company, San Francisco, 1966, *passim*.
36 Rusinow, op. cit., pp. 97–8. and Shoup, op. cit., p. 210.
37 See, for example, Bicanic, op. cit., pp. 79–80.
38 See, in particular, Milenkovitch, op. cit., Chapters 7 and 8.
39 See Rusinow, op. cit., p. 96.
40 The views here ascribed to 'liberals' are the characteristic views of liberal writers generally. They are not necessarily true of any one writer normally classified as a 'liberal'.
41 See, for example, K. Mihailovic, 'The Regional Aspects of Economic Development', in R. Stojanovic (ed.), *Yugoslav Economists on Problems of a Socialist Economy*, New York International Arts & Science Press, New York, 1964, pp. 29–45.
42 See, for example, E. Kardelj, 'The Principal Dilemma: Self-Management or Statism', *Socialist Thought and Practice*, No. 24, 1966, pp. 3–29.
43 See, in particular, M. Todorovic, 'Some Questions of our Economic System', *Socialist Thought and Practice*, No. 9, 1963, p. 41.
44 Supporters of reform differed widely on the meaning of the word discrimination in relation to taxes, prices and interest rates. See Milenkovitch, op. cit., pp. 153–8.
45 See, for example, Bicanic, op. cit., Chapter 9.
46 Shoup, op. cit., Chapter 6.
47 Ibid., pp. 234–40.
48 Ibid., pp. 250–2. An alternative economic theory, adhered to by some Slovenians and Croatians, was republicanism, or polycentrism as it was called by its great advocate, Rudolf Bicanic. The idea was that the power to regulate economic affairs reside with the republican governments and that national economic policy

should emerge as a kind of consensus between the various republican centres. This theory was rejected as a blueprint for the 1965 reforms but subsequent political developments suggest that it is more accurately reflected what actually happened. R. Bicanic, 'Centralističko, decentralističko ili policentrično planiranje' (Centralized, Decentralized or Polycentric Planning), *Ekonomist* 16, No. 2, 1963, pp. 456–69. See also Bicanic, op. cit., Chapter 3.

49   *The Constitution of the SFRY*, Institute of Comparative Law, Belgrade, 1965. And see Rusinow, op. cit., pp. 15–52.

50   Ibid.

51   Shoup, op. cit., Chapter 5, pp. 206–9 and 224–5.

52   Ibid, Chapter 6, pp. 255–6.

53   See 'Financing Socio-Political Units', *Yugoslav Survey*, Volume 9, May 1968.

54   See 'Reform of the Credit and Banking System', *Yugoslav Survey*, Volume 6, July–Sept. 1965.

55   Ibid.

56   See 'The Development of the System of Distribution of the Social Product and Net Income', *Yugoslav Survey*, Volume 11, Aug. 1970.

57   See 'Reform of the Credit and Banking System', *Yugoslav Survey*, Volume 6, op. cit.

58   The view, for example, of Milenkovitch, op. cit., p. 147.

59   Ibid.

60   See, for example, Shoup, op. cit., pp. 257–60.

61   'Prices after the Economic Reform', *Yugoslav Survey*, Volume 7, Apr.–June 1966, and 'The New External Trade & Foreign Exchange System', *Yugoslav Survey*, Volume 8, Nov. 1967.

62   'Economic Reform', *Yugoslav Survey*, Volume 7, July–Sept. 1966.

Chapter 2

1   Op. cit., Chapter 1, n. 6.

2   But this requirement was frequently not met.

3   Below that number the Workers' Council was synonymous with the collective.

4   The first to do so was *Rade Koncar* in 1955.

5   See, generally, G. Leman, *Stellung und Aufgaben der Ökonomischen Einheiten in den jugoslawischen Unternehmungen*, Duncker und Humbolt, Berlin, 1967.

6   The leading source was the sociological journal *Moderna Organizacia*.

7   The literature on this topic is vast. Useful surveys appear in M. P. Canapa, *Reforme Economique et Socialisme en Yugoslavie*, Armand Colin, 1970, pp. 67–90; Neuburger and James, 'The Yugoslav Self Managed Enterprise', in M. Bernstein (ed.), *Plan and Market*, Yale University Press, 1973, pp. 245–84; D. Granick, *Enterprise Guidance in Eastern Europe*, Princeton University Press, Yale, Newhaven and London, 1975, pp. 323–430.

8   N. Jovanov, 'Prelog razmatranju pojave štrajka u našem društvi' (A Contribution to the Study of the Strike in our Society), *Nase Teme*, No. 2, 1970, pp. 319–20, quoted in Neuberger and James, op. cit., p. 279.

9   See N. Jovanov 'Odnos Štrajka kao Društvenog Sukoba i Samoupravljanja kao Društvenog Sistema', *Revija za Sociologiju*, 1–2, 1973, (translated into French in *Participation and Self Management*, University of Zagreb, Zagreb, 1972 & 1973, Volume 1), quoted in Granick, op. cit., p. 389.

10   See Canapa, op. cit., p. 69, and examples, given in I. Adizes, *Industrial Democracy: Yugoslav Style*, The Free Press, New York, 1971, pp. 177–87.

11   *Obustave rada* (Work Stoppages), Centar za političke studije i obrazovanje, Belgrade, 1967, quoted in Canapa, op. cit., p. 70. N. Jovanov compiled the

240   MARKET SOCIALISM IN YUGOSLAVIA

documentary basis for this study by the Serbian Trade Union Confederation from
survey data for 1964–6. Over 85 per cent of the strikes in the sample concerned
personal income grievances.

12 See, for example, R. Supek, 'Some Contradictions and Insufficiencies of Yugoslav
Self Managing Socialism', *Praxis*, 8, Nos. 3–4, 1971, quoted in Granick, op. cit.,
p. 387, who believes that the majority of strikes at this time were of this type.

13 N. Jovanov, op. cit., n. 9, quoted by Granick, op. cit., p. 388.

14 For example, B. Kavcic, 'O protestnim obustavama rada' (Work Stoppages),
Gledišta, Volume 7, No. 2, Feb. 1966, and 'Voem je vzrok konfliktov v podjetjih?'
(What are the Causes of Conflicts within Firms?), *Teorija in Praksa*, Volume 6, No.
1, 1969, quoted in Canapa, op. cit., p. 70.

15 Z. Vidakovre, 'Dva priloza protestnim obustavama rada' (Two Approaches to
Work Stoppages), *Gledišta*, Volume 9, No. 1, 1968, p. 43, quoted in Canapa, op.
cit., p. 70. Adizes, op. cit., pp. 104–6, cites an example of a Workers Council
sending reports of its deliberations and decisions to economic units but, for the
most part, their being unread.

16 Jovanov, op. cit., n. 9, quoted by Granick, op. cit., p. 389.

17 Jovanov, op. cit., n. 11.

18 Jovanov, op. cit., n. 9, quoted by Granick, p. 388.

19 Ibid.

20 Jovanov, op. cit., n. 11.

21 See Granick and Neuberger and James, op. cit., for references to the literature.

22 The conclusion of Josip Zupanov in *Samoupravljanje i Društvena Moć*, Zagreb, *Naše
Teme*, 1969, the leading monograph on the subject, pp. 103–4, quoted in
Neuberger and James at pp. 275–6. His conclusions are echoed by most other
researchers in the field.

23 See, generally, Zupanov, 'Is Enterprise Management becoming Profession-
alized?', *International Studies of Management and Organization*, Volume III, No. 3,
1973. Extensively quoted by Granick, op. cit.

24 1963 Constitution, op. cit., Chapter 1, n. 49, Article 93.

25 Zupanov, op. cit., n. 22, p. 252, quoted in Neuberger and James, p. 276.

26 Granick, op. cit., p. 364, quoting Zupanov.

27 Zupanov, op. cit., n. 23, quoted by Granick, op. cit., p. 366.

28 See, for example, M. Korac, 'The Possibilities and Prospects of Freedom in the
Modern World', *Praxis* 4, Nos. 1–2, 1968. D. Hodges, 'Yugoslav Philosophers in
the Struggle Against Bureaucracy', *Florida State University Papers* 1, 1967. Useful
summaries of the humanist philosophy are found in Milenkovitch, op. cit.,
pp. 285–91 and F. Singleton, *Twentieth Century Yugoslavia* Macmillan, London,
1976, pp. 297–303.

29 D. Rusinow, 'Anatomy of a Student Revolt', Parts 1 and 2, *Field Staff Reports*,
American Universities Field Staff, South-East Europe Series 15, Nos. 4, 5, 1968.

30 See, *inter alia*, A. Dragicevic, 'Income Distribution According to Work Performed',
Socialist Thought and Practice, No. 26, Apr.–June 1967; E. Kardelj, 'What is the
Authentic Revolutionary Nature of the Working Class?', Ibid., No. 30, Apr.–June
1968; M. Todorovic, 'A Revolutionary Vanguard—The Abiding Need of our
Self-Managing Community', Ibid., No. 31, July–Sept. 1968.

31 'L'Autogestion yugoslave', *Notes et Études Documentaire*, 23 July 1973, Nos. 4008,
4009, 4010, La Documentation Francaise, contains an excellent survey of events
surrounding and following the passage of Constitutional Amendment 15.

32 *Borba*, 15 Oct. 1969, quoted in 'L'Autogestion Yugoslave', op. cit., p.26.

33 *Borba*, 16 Nov. 1969, quoted in Ibid., p. 27.

34 *Borba*, 28 Jan. 1970, quoted in Ibid., p. 28.

35 *SL*, No. 25, 1970.

36   For details of the 1971 Amendments see 'The Latest Changes (1971) in the Constitution of the Socialist Federal Republic of Yugoslavia', *Yugoslav Survey*, Volume 12, Nov. 1971.
37   'L'Autogestion yugoslave', op. cit., p. 29.
38   *Borba*, 17 Mar. 1972, quoted in Ibid., p. 32.
39   Five members from each republic, three from each autonomous province, three from the army, and Tito comprised the Presidency. The Executive Bureau, in effect the most powerful organ, had fifteen members, two from each republic and one from each autonomous province plus Tito.
40   See, for example, D. Rusinow, op. cit., Chapter 1, n. 9, pp. 227–8. The powers of the autonomous provinces of Vojvodina and Kosova were also substantially enhanced.
41   Ibid., op. cit., Chapter 1, n. 9, p. 215.
42   Ibid., pp. 222–4.
43   For example, against the editors of *Praxis*, the journal of the socialist humanists.
44   'The latest changes in the Constitution of the Socialist Federal Republic of Yugoslavia', *Yugoslav Survey*, op. cit., n. 36.
45   Amendment 28.
46   Rusinow, op. cit., Chapter 1, n. 9, p. 285.
47   Ibid., p. 323.
48   Ibid.
49   A number of cultural societies, led by *Matica Hrvatska*, wanted the Constitution to protect the Croatian language against Serbian.
50   Rusinow, op. cit., Chapter 1, n. 9, p. 312.
51   Ibid., p. 321.
52   Ibid., pp. 318–26 for an account of the purges in the other republics.
53   *The Constitution of the Socialist Federal Republic of Yugoslavia*, Merrick, New York, 1976.
54   J. Steele, *The Guardian*, 7 June 1974.
55   M. Connock, *Management Today*, Dec. 1975, p. 43.
56   Op. cit., Chapter 1, n. 54.
57   *SL*, No. 4, 1966. And see, generally, 'Investment Capital of Socio-Political Communities', *Yugoslav Survey*, Volume II, No. 4, 1970.
58   *Social Plan of Yugoslavia 1976–80*, Federal Committee of Information, Belgrade, 1976, p. 17.
59   *Borba*, 1 Aug. 1971.
60   *Ekonomska Politika*, 12 Mar. 1973, pp. 20–3.
61   See for example, T. Vlaskalic, 'Practice Breaks Ground for Self-Management Planning', *Socialist Thought and Practice*, Volume 15, No. 6, pp. 28–38; C. Strahinjic, 'Self Management Agreements and Social Compacts', *Socialist Thought and Practice*, Volume 16, No. 6, pp. 26–48.
62   *Socialist Thought and Practice*, Volume 14, No. 6, pp. 43–4, quoted in Singleton, op. cit., p. 284.
63   According to Article 72, 'If the social plan lays down . . . that the fulfilment of specific tasks is indispensable for social reproduction, and if the organizations of associated labour or other self-management organizations and communities have not yet been able to ensure by agreement resources and other necessary conditions for their fulfilment, an obligation to pool resources for the purpose can be introduced by legislation.'
64   The elections were also based upon the principle of delegation, another ideological innovation of the 1974 Constitution, designed to rid Yugoslavia of the disease of liberalism which was said to afflict Western democracies. Members of all socio-political communities were delegates not representatives, subject to immediate

242

MARKET SOCIALISM IN YUGOSLAVIA

recall and replacement should they act contrary to the wishes of their electors.
65 Rusinow, op. cit., Chapter 1, n. 9, p. 286.
66 Kardelj, 'The Principal Dilemma: Self Management or Statism', *Socialist Thought and Practice*, Oct.–Dec. 1966, pp. 5–29, quoted by Rusinow, op. cit., Chapter 1, n. 9, pp. 216–7.
67 Rusinow, op. cit., Chapter 1, n. 9, p. 152.
68 *Socialist Thought and Practice*, 1972, p. 10.
69 Rusinow, op. cit., Chapter 1, n. 9, p. 322.
70 Ibid., pp. 314–15.
71 Ibid., p. 327.
72 The League of Communists exercised considerable influence over the membership of socio-political communities by virtue of its influence over the Socialist Alliance. The Socialist Alliance drew up the list of candidates for election.

Chapter 3

1 *SL*, 26 Dec. 1953.
2 Article 17.
3 Jaroslav Vanek, 'Yugoslav Economy viewed through the Theory of Labour Management', *World Development*, Volume 1, No. 9, Sept. 1973, pp. 41–7.
4 Based upon Article 9 of the 1963 Constitution. See also Sacks, op. cit., Chapter 1, n. 16, pp. 82–3.
5 See *Laws on Joint Investment of Enterprises*, Institute of Comparative Law, Belgrade, 1967. The legislation is complex and hard to interpret. It consisted of amendments to five existing laws and the promulgation of a sixth.
6 *Laws on Joint Investment of Enterprises*, op. cit., pp. 114–15: *The Law Amending and Supplementing the Basic Law on Enterprises*, incorporating a new Article 133a into, and amending Article 211 to, *The Basic Law on Enterprises*, *SL*, No. 17, 1965.
7 Ibid., incorporating Article 211b.
8 Ibid., Article 211.
9 Ibid., Article 133a.
10 *Laws on Joint Investment of Enterprises*, op. cit., pp. 130–5, *The Law on the Assets of Economic Organization*, as amended Article, 64.
11 Ibid., Article 64.
12 Ibid., Article 64(i), though, exceptionally, the rule could be relaxed.
13 Ibid., Article 64(l).
14 Ibid., Article 64(k).
15 Ibid., Article 64(d).
16 Ibid., Article 64(n).
17 *SL*, No. 58, 1971. See, generally, M. Radivojevic, 'Securities in Yugoslavia', *Quarterly Bulletin*, National Bank of Yugoslavia, Volume IV, No. 1, Jan. 1976.
18 Radivojevic, op. cit., p. 24.
19 See, Singleton, op. cit., Chapter 2, n. 28, pp. 295–6, for an account of this debate.
20 *Komunist*, 3 Feb. 1972, p. 12, quoted by Singleton, op. cit., Chapter 2, n. 28, p. 295.
21 Originally by the *Law on Credit and Banking*, 1961, op. cit., Chapter 1, n. 28, modified by the *Decision on Implementation of Credit Policy Measures*, *SL*, No. 13, 1963.
22 If their balance sheet for the previous year recorded a combined value for the Business and Reserve Fund exceeding D20m, *SL*, No. 2, 1972, laid down even more stringent conditions for the issue of bonds to be subscribed and paid for in foreign exchange.
23 See Chapter 6, pp. 191–2.
24 See, for example, E. O. Furubotn and S. Pejovich, 'Property Rights, Economic

Decentralization and the Evolution of the Yugoslav Firm, 1965–1972', *Journal of Law and Economics*, Vol. XVI, 2 Oct. 1973; 'The Formation & Distribution of Net Products & the Behaviour of the Yugoslav Firm', *3 Jahrbuch de Wirtschaft Osteuropas*, 1972; and 'Property Rights & the Behaviour of the Firm in a Socialist State: the Example of Yugoslavia', *30 Zeitschrift fur Nationalökonomie*, 1970.

25 *Western Economic Journal*, Volume 7, 1969, pp. 193–200.

26 Ibid., p. 195, 'The employees annuity from investing one dollar in owned assets is $y = i(l+i)^n/[(l+i)^n - l]$ where i is the rate of interest paid on savings accounts. One dollar invested in non-owned assets must yield at least the same annual return. It follows that the rate of return from investment in non-owned assets is $r = i(l+i)^n/[(l+i)^n - l]$ where n stands for the time horizon of the collective.'

27 See, for example, *Development with Decentralization*, Johns Hopkins Press, Baltimore and London, 1975, p. 129.

28 Jan Vanek, *The Economics of Workers' Management*, op. cit., Chapter 1, n. 13, pp. 197–200.

29 Neuberger and James, op. cit., Chapter 2, n. 7, p. 270 quoting Zupanov.

30 Ibid., p. 261, footnote 20, quoting Zupanov.

31 See, for example, 'Property Rights, Economic Decentralization and the Evolution of the Yugoslav Firm', op. cit.

32 Neuberger and James, op. cit., Chapter 2, n. 7, p. 270 quoting Zupanov.

33 The authorities sometimes varied the required ratios in an attempt to influence aggregate investment. See Chapter 6, pp. 197–8.

34 See Chapter 4, pp. 145–50.

35 See Chapter 6, pp. 197 and 205.

36 *Development with Decentralization*, op. cit., Appendix D, pp. 351–3.

37 See Chapter 6, p. 205.

38 See Chapter 4, pp. 127–8.

39 See Chapter 6, p. 198.

40 Savings as a proportion of household disposable income were as follows:

1975	1976	1977	1978	1979	1980	1981
14.1	15.5	15.6	18.5	17.2	16.9	18.1

Source: OECD, *Economic Survey of Yugoslavia*, June 1979, p. 11; May 1980, p. 9; May 1983, p. 11.

These ratios differ from those in Annex 4 which do not include foreign exchange deposits in Dinars.

41 *Household Financial Savings as a Proportion of Total Household Saving*

1966	1967	1968	1969	1970	1971	1972	1973	1974	1975	1976	1977	1978	1979	1980	1981
62	32	14	30	27	46	45	43	37	39	40	42	48	43	45	50

Derived from *National Bank of Yugoslavia, Quarterly Bulletin*, Volume 1, No. 3, July 1973, Tables 7 and 8; Volume 3, No. 3, July 1975, Tables 7 and 8; Volume 4, No. 3, July 1976, Tables 7 and 8; Volume 10, Nos. 2–3, pp. 10–11.

42 See Annex 16 and Chapter 6, pp. 203–7.

43 *SL*, No. 58, 1971, and see M. Jovanovic, 'Changes in the Yugoslav Banking System', *National Bank of Yugoslavia, Quarterly Bulletin*, No. 1, Jan. 1973, pp. 39–47.

44 OECD, *Economic Survey of Yugoslavia*, July 1982, p. 33.

45 See, for example, *Statistički Godišnjak*, 1973; Table 119.2.

46 Occasionally, the rate of interest for commercial loans exceeded the rate of increase in industrial product prices.

47   The charge had been under constant attack since the reforms. The most important reason for its demise at this juncture was the strength of the prejudice, both ideological and political, against the involvement of the federal government in any aspect of enterprise self-management.
48   *Borba*, 24 June 1969, p. 10.
49   See Chapter 2, pp. 68–70.
50   This account is based upon a series of discussions with *Energoinvest* management, but represents the author's interpretation of events.
51   This was especially true of the steel sector.
52   See Chapter 2, p. 74.
53   OECD, *Economic Survey of Yugoslavia*, 1980, p. 10.
54   See, for example, the views of the OECD in *Economic Survey of Yugoslavia*, June 1973, pp. 13–15.
55   J. L. Rodic, *Problemi likvidnosti jugoslavenske privrede* (Problems of Liquidity in the Yugoslav Economy), Privredni Pregled, Belgrade, 1972.
56   See Chapter 6, pp. 191–2.
57   See Chapter 6, pp. 194–7.
58   *Delo*, 26 July 1971, p. 1.
59   See remarks of Finance Minister Smole, reported in *Nin*, 30 Apr. 1972, pp. 13–14.
60   *Privredni Vjesnik*, 14 Oct. 1971, p. 3.
61   His remarks in *Nin*, op. cit.
62   *Delo*, 27 July 1972, p. 1.
63   *Privredni Vjesnik*, 23 June 1972.
64   Ibid.
65   *Vus*, 30 Jan. 1974.
66   Smole, op. cit.
67   *Privredni Vjesnik*, 8 Feb. 1972.
68   *Privredni Vjesnik*, op. cit., n. 62 above, concerning the *Law on the Social Accounting Service*.
69   See, for example, remarks by director of the firm *Bratsvo* in *Privredni Vjesnik*, 12 Sept. 1971, p. 5.
70   *Privredni Vjesnik*, 24 June 1971, p. 3.
71   Reported in *Ekonomska Politika*, 11 Nov. 1974, p. 49. From about this time a new factor began to make itself felt. The introduction of the BOAL rapidly multiplied the number of inter-firm credit transactions.
72   See Chapter 5, pp. 178–82.
73   *Foreign Investment in Yugoslavia*, OECD, 1974; V. G. Scriven 'Yugoslavia's New Foreign Investment Law', *Journal of World Trade Law*, Volume 13, No. 6, 1979, pp. 95–107. The legal regime, which saw the light of day in 1967 in the shape of amendments to five existing laws, was consolidated in 1973 in the *Law on the Investment of Resources by Foreign Persons*, *SL*, No. 22, Apr. 1973 and again, with modifications, in the *Foreign Investment Law*, *SL*, No. 18, Apr. 1978.
74   Since the mid-1970s, the authorities have encouraged BOALs to adopt similar arrangements in developing domestic industrial co-operation.
75   See Chapter 2, p. 89 and pp. 91–2.
76   *SL*, No. 55, Dec. 1969, Article 3.
77   No special foreign exchange regime was established by the July 1967 legislation.
78   They could carry over any unused balance to subsequent periods. The transfer entitlement related to gross proceeds. Any foreign exchange component of the goods exported was not netted out.
79   Amendments to the Law on Foreign Exchange Operations, *SL*, No. 33, July 1971, Articles 16, 16a, 28, 28a, and 46.

80 Amendments to the Law on Assets of Economic Organizations, *SL*, No. 34, Aug. 1971, Articles 66–74 and 111–14.
81 In particular, the Federal Executive Council *Decree on Foreign Investment, SL,* No. 26, June 1976 supplementing the *Law on the Investment of Resources by Foreign Persons* of 1973, op. cit., severely limited the powers of the joint venture Business Boards.
82 Scriven, op. cit.
83 Ibid., for a summary of the main provisions.
84 See Chapter 5, pp. 153–5.
85 There is an immense literature on the subject of Yugoslavia's less developed areas. Good summaries of the main issues appear in two World Bank surveys of Yugoslavia: *Development with Decentralization,* op. cit., Chapter 8; and *Yugoslavia: Self-Management Socialism and the Challenges of Development,* The Johns Hopkins University Press, Baltimore and London, 1979, Chapter 11.
86 Except briefly, as we have seen, through the FFFI.
87 See Chapter 1, pp. 38 and 44.
88 See *Nin,* 14 May 1972, pp. 52–60 for remarks by the Bosnian Prime Minister on this subject.
89 *Development with Decentralization,* op. cit., pp. 232–3.
90 *Borba,* 24 June 1969, p. 1.
91 See Chapter 2, pp. 69–70.
92 *Development with Decentralization,* op. cit., p. 232.
93 Ibid., pp. 204–5.
94 Ibid.
95 Ibid., pp. 194–202.
96 Ibid., p. 233.

Chapter 4

1 Statistics derived from *Statistički Godišnjak,* 1975, Table 106.4 *Kretanje društvenog proizvoda i narodnog dohotka* (Social Product and National Income), 1966 prices; Table 1051.1, *Zaposlenost po Vrstama delanosti i sektoru svojine* (Employment by Kinds of Activity and Sectors of Ownership); Table 102.7 *Osnovna sredstva privrede društvenog sektora* (Fixed Assets of Economic Activities of the Social Sector), 1966 prices and Table 1028 *Investicije u osnovna sredstva* (Investment in Fixed Assets), 1966 prices. And see, *Development with Decentralization,* op. cit., Chapter 3, n. 27, pp. 59–61; S. Estrin, The Effects of Self-Management on Yugoslav Industrial Growth, *Soviet Studies,* Volume 34, No. 1, 1982, pp. 69–85.
2 The theoretical foundations for the study of the Yugoslav firm were laid by B. Ward, 'The Firm in Illyria: Market Syndicalism', *American Economic Review,* Volume 48, No. 4, Sept. 1958: 566–89; and E. Domar 'On Collective Farms and Producer Co-operatives', *American Economic Review,* Volume 56, No. 4, Sept. 1966: 734–57.
3 See, pre-eminently, Jaroslav Vanek, *The General Theory of Labour Managed Market Economies,* Cornell University Press, Ithaca, New York, 1970. See, also, Jaroslav Vanek, *World Devlopment,* op. cit., Chapter 3, n. 3.
4 Ibid.
5 See discussion in Jaroslav Vanek, *World Development,* op. cit., Chapter 3, n. 3.
6 See Chapter 1, n. 13.
7 In practice, the amount of self-finance forthcoming may be a function of the amount borrowed. See Chapter 3, p. 100.
8 See Chapter 3, p. 118.
9 Jaroslav Vanek, op. cit., Chapter 3, n. 3, p. 43.

10 See Chapter 5, pp. 174–7.
11 *Yugoslavia: Self-Management Socialism and the Challenges of Development*, op. cit., Chapter 3, n. 84, pp. 270–3.
12 See Chapter 1, p. 46.
13 *Yugoslavia: Self-Management Socialism and the Challenges of Development*, op. cit., Chapter 3, n. 84, p. 258–63.
14 See, for example, 'Population Changes in Yugoslavia', *Yugoslav Survey*, Volume 12, No. 3, 1971, pp. 1–9, 'National Structure of the Yugoslav Population', Volume 14, No. 1, 1973, pp. 1–23; and D. Brznik, 'Demographic and Other Aspects of Labour Force Formation in Yugoslavia for the Next Twenty Years', *Ekonomist* 1, 1969.
15 See 'Changes in the Structure of the industrial Labour Force, 1952–1972', *Yugoslav Survey*, Volume 14, No. 4, 1973, pp. 55–67.
16 Until its repeal in 1957, the authorities had the power to dispatch state functionaries to any part of the country. This power had little economic force after 1952 when the members of firms ceased to be state functionaries.
17 See, for example, 'Employment and Temporary Unemployment', *Yugoslav Survey*, Volume 15, No. 2, 1974, pp. 1–23, 'Employment 1971–1975', Volume 17, No. 3, 1976, pp. 49–63.
18 OECD, *Economic Survey of Yugoslavia*, May 1977, Table H.
19 *Komunist*, 7 Jan. 1974, p. 11.
20 *Borba*, 3 Dec. 1973, p. 3.
21 *Komunist*, op. cit., n. 19.
22 Ibid.
23 *Privredni Vjesnik*, 22 Mar. 1974.
24 See OECD, *Economic Survey of Yugoslavia*, June 1979, Table H.
25 'Yugoslav Nationals Temporarily Abroad', *Yugoslav Survey*, Volume 13, No. 1, 1972, pp. 17–31.
26 See 'Some Basic Features of Yugoslav External Migration', *Yugoslav Survey*, Volume 16, No. 1, 1975, pp. 1–17.
27 Ibid.
28 See OECD, *Economic Survey of Yugoslavia*, May 1977, Table H.
29 The view of the OECD, which provides a useful survey of external migration in the *Economic Survey of Yugoslavia*, June 1973, pp. 26–44.
30 See *Nin*, 12 Mar. 1972, pp. 32–5, and *Komunist*, op. cit.
31 See 'Yugoslav Skilled Labour Temporarily Employed Abroad', *Yugoslav Survey*, Volume 13, No. 4, 1972, pp. 51–73.
32 See 'Yugoslav Agricultural Labour Temporarily Employed Abroad', *Yugoslav Survey*, Volume 14, No. 2, 1972, pp. 15–39.
33 *Yugoslav Survey*, ibid.
34 *Privredni Vjesnik*, 26 Apr. 1973, p. 3.
35 *Borba*, 1 Feb. 1974, p. 1.
36 See *Nin*, 12 Mar. 1972, pp. 32–5.
37 See 'Internal Migration', *Yugoslav Survey*, Volume 17, No. 1, 1976, pp. 3–21.
38 See review of measures, and generally, in Canapa, op. cit., Chapter 2, n. 7, pp. 11–31.
39 Ibid.
40 See 'Tasks of the Socialist Alliance in the Development of Private Work', *Yugoslav Survey*, Volume 9, No. 2, 1968, pp. 11–19.
41 A. Bajt, 'Društvena svojina—kolektivna i individualna' (Social Property—Collective and Individual), *Gledišta*, Volume 9, No. 4, 1968, pp. 531–44; I. Lavrac, 'Lični rad i privatna svojina u socijalizmu' (Personal Work and Private Property in Socialism), *Gledišta*, Volume 8, Nos. 6 and 7, pp. 897–907, quoted in Canapa, op. cit., Chapter 2, n. 7, pp. 11–31.

42 F. Cerne, 'Otvorena pitanja privatnog sektora' (Pending Private Sector Problems), *Gledišta*, Volume 9, No. 4, 1968, pp. 559–66, quoted in Ibid.
43 See, for example, B. Horvat, 'Individualno i društveno vlasništvo u socijalizmu' (Individual and Social Property in Socialism), *Gledišta*, Volume 8, No. 3, 1967, pp. 335–48, quoted in Ibid.
44 See Cerne, op. cit.
45 International Arts & Sciences Press, New York, 1969.
46 Ibid., p. 134.
47 Ibid., p. 134.
48 Ibid., p. 137.
49 Ibid., p. 138.
50 Ibid., p. 138–9.
51 Ibid.
52 Canapa, op. cit., Chapter 2, n. 7, pp. 19–20.
53 Ibid., p. 22.
54 'General Law on Public Health', *SL*, 8 May 1969, Article 5.
55 Op. cit., n. 40.
56 Ibid., p. 12.
57 Ibid., p. 15.
58 Ibid., p. 13.
59 Ibid., p. 15.
60 See, for example, *Politika*, 8 Sept. 1967, p. 6.
61 Op. cit.
62 *Ekonomska Politika*, 9 Sept. 1968, p. 1269.
63 Ibid.
64 Op. cit., Chapter 2, n. 53.
65 See Chapter 5, pp. 153–5.
66 *Yugoslavia: Self-Management Socialism and the Challenge of Development*; op. cit., Chapter 3, n. 84, pp. 263–6.
67 Ibid., pp. 273–4.
68 *Development with Decentralization*, op. cit., n. 27, p. 102.
69 'Income of Agricultural Households', *Yugoslav Survey*, Volume 14, No. 1, 1973, pp. 69–79.
70 *Development with Decentralization*, op. cit., Chapter 3, n. 27, pp. 105–6.
71 Ibid., and see, for example, *Gledišta*, Volume 11, 1972, pp. 1388–99. Survey shows that 47 per cent of people on private holdings have permanent employment outside their farms.
72 *Development with Decentralization*, op. cit., Chapter 3, n. 27, pp. 193–200, for a useful summary of this issue.
73 The gross profit rates of social sector firms in each republic differed with Slovenia at the top and Kosovo at the bottom. It appears that these differences cannot be explained by the contrasting economic structures of these regions. Attributing actual profit rates of each industrial sector in Kosovo to the sectoral structure of Slovenia, barely changes their inter-republican profitability differential. See *Yugoslavia: Self-Management Socialism and the Challenges of Development*, op. cit., Chapter 3, n. 84, pp. 171–5.
74 S. Popov, 'Intersectoral Relations of Personal Incomes', *Yugoslav Survey*, Volume 13, No. 2, 1972, pp. 62–81. and *Statistički Godišnjak: Prosrečna Neto Lična Primanja prema stepenu Stovenog obrazovanja* (Average Net Personal Receipts According to Level of Professional Education and Branches of Activities), 1970–6, Tables 122, 123.
75 S. Estrin, *Economica*, Volume 48, 1981, pp. 181–94 and *Economic Analysis and Workers Management*, Volume 13, Nos. 1–2, pp. 175–99.

76 There does not seem to have been any move by communes to charge an economic rent for commercially occupied land.
77 See, above, pp. 123–8.
78 This is, of course, another way of illustrating the matters raised earlier in this Chapter at pp. 123–8.
79 Popov, op. cit.
80 Estrin, op. cit., n. 75. See also Estrin, 'The effects of Self-Management on Yugoslav Industrial Growth', *Soviet Studies*, op. cit.
81 See, for example, A. Dragicevic, op. cit., Chapter 2, n. 30.
82 See, for example, S. V. Rawen, 'Social Values and the Managerial Structure', *Journal of Comparative Administration*, Volume 2, No. 2, 1972.
83 See, for example, the attacks on the *Grupriogradansko Preduzeće* (Citizen founded Firms), in *Ekonomska Politika*, 8 July 1968, pp. 879–80.
84 Rusinow, op. cit., Chapter 2, n. 29.
85 See J. Zupanov, *'Egalitarizam i industrijaliza'* (Egalitarianism and Industrialism), *Nase Teme*, 1970, No. 2, pp. 259–62, quoted by Neuberger and James, op. cit., Chapter 2, n. 7, p. 282.
86 *Vus*, 6 Jan. 1971, p. 7.
87 See Furubotn and Pejovich, *Journal of Law and Economics*, op. cit., Chapter 3, n. 24.

Chapter 5

1 Sacks, op. cit., Chapter 1, n. 16, pp. 106–9.
2 Ibid., pp. 93–102.
3 OECD, *Economic Survey of Yugoslavia*, May 1977, Table G.
4 See Shoup, op. cit., Chapter 1, n. 33, pp. 244–6.
5 See, for example, C. J. Prout, 'Industrial Cooperation Agreements in Eastern Europe', *East European Trade Council*, 1972.
6 This subsequently became a joint investment partnership with Mercedes.
7 Example given in W. Friedmann and L. Mates (eds.), *Joint Business Ventures of Yugoslav Enterprises and Foreign Firms*, Columbia University, New York and Institute of International Politics and Economy, Belgrade, 1968, pp. 66–7.
8 See Analytical Report on *Industrial Cooperation among ECE Countries*, United Nations, Geneva, 1973, n. 110.
9 Op. cit., Chapter 1, n. 17.
10 See Chapter 2, pp. 73–4.
11 See, generally, Peter Feuerle, 'Yugoslav Economic Courts: Between Central Planning and Enterprise Autonomy', *Columbia Journal of Transnational Law*, Volume 12, No. 2, 1973.
12 Op. cit., Chapter 3, n. 5 for text of amended law.
13 *SL*, No. 54, 1967.
14 See *Borba*, 17 Jan. and 7 Feb. 1967.
15 See *Borba*, 10 and 13 Feb. 1967.
16 For example, the paper industry. See *Privredni Pregled*, 16 Feb. 1967, and the construction industry, *Borba*, 22 July 1969, p. 15.
17 See OECD, *Economic Survey of Yugoslavia*, Apr. 1974, p. 54.
18 *Yugoslavia: Self-Management Socialism and the Challenges of Development*, op. cit., Chapter 3, n. 84, p. 52.
19 See Chapter 2, pp. 66–7.
20 Useful summaries of industrial problem areas appear in *Development with*

Decentralization, Chapter 5, op. cit., Chapter 3, n. 27 and J. Dirlam and J. Plummer, An Introduction to the Yugoslav Economy, Charles E. Merrill, 1973, Chapter 5.
21 Development with Decentralization, op. cit., Chapter 3, n. 27, pp. 140–2.
22 Ibid., pp. 134–6.
23 Borba, 24 June 1969, p. 1.
24 Development with Decentralization, op. cit., Chapter 3, n. 27, pp. 149–50.
25 Borba, op. cit., n. 20 above.
26 'Law on Electric Power Organizations', SL, No. 21, 1958, and No. 1, 1959.
27 Development with Decentralization, op. cit., Chapter 3, n. 27, pp. 178–83.
28 Yugoslavia: Self-Management Socialism and the Challenges of Development, op. cit., Chapter 3, n. 84, pp. 59–60.
29 See Chapter 1, p. 41.
30 See, generally, Sacks, op. cit., Chapter 1, n. 16.
31 Statistički Godišnjak, Table 107.3, 1975, Integracije u privredi.
32 See Chapter 3, pp. 105–7.
33 Statistički Godišnjak, Table 107.3, op. cit.
34 See Granick, for example, op. cit., Chapter 2, n. 12, pp. 408–13 for case study material in support.
35 See 'Movements of Prices in the Course of Reform', Yugoslav Survey, Volume 10, No. 3 (1969), pp. 95–103.
36 See Chapter 6, pp. 187–97.
37 Ekonomska Politika, 3 May 1971.
38 See Privredni Pregled, 10 Mar. 1969, p. 4, for international comparisons, and Borba, 22 July 1969, p. 13 for the views on this topic of the managing director of Serbian railways.
39 See Dirlam and Plummer, op. cit., p. 135.
40 Ibid.
41 SL, No. 28, 18 May 1972. And see 'Price Systems and Policy', Yugoslav Survey, Volume 13, No. 3, 1972, pp. 15–29, and 'The Price System—Development and Problems', Yugoslav Survey, Volume 14, No. 3, 1973, pp. 141–55.
42 OECD, Economic Survey of Yugoslavia, Apr. 1975, pp. 44–5.
43 See 'Social Compact on the Implementation of Price Policy in 1975', Yugoslav Survey, Volume 16, No. 2, 1975.
44 OECD, Economic Survey of Yugoslavia, May 1981, p. 38, and May 1983, p. 44.
45 Ibid., May 1983, p. 16.
46 See, generally, 'Foreign Trade in the Yugoslav Reform', Yugoslav Survey, Volume 10, No. 3, 1969.
47 See Chapter 1, pp. 26–7.
48 See Development with Decentralization, op. cit., Chapter 3, n. 27, p. 122.
49 A comprehensive analysis of the licensing system appears in V. Pertot, Ekonomika Međunarodne Razmjene Jugoslavije, (The Economics of International Transactions by Yugoslavia), Informator, Zagreb, 1972. See also I. Rankov, 'Economic Problems of the Foreign Exchange and Customs System', Reforma 123, 1971.
50 The following account is based on information obtained from OECD, Economic Survey of Yugoslavia, 1970–82.
51 Boris Martinovic, 'The Yugoslav Forex Market', Euromoney, Mar. 1975.
52 Ibid.
53 OECD, Economic Survey of Yugoslavia, May 1980, pp. 38–9.
54 Ibid.
55 Ibid., June 1983, p. 36.
56 Op. cit., Chapter 4, n. 3, p. 272.
57 Op. cit., Chapter 1, n. 16.
58 Ibid., p. 54.

59 See, above, p. 158.
60 See Chapter 3, pp. 90–2.
61 See Chapter 4, p. 141.
62 Op. cit., Chapter 1, n. 16, p. 115.
63 Ibid., p. 114.
64 See, for example, *Ekonomska Politika*, 8 July 1968, pp. 879–80.
65 *SL*, No. 48, 1968. See Sacks, op. cit., Chapter 1, n. 16, pp. 18–19.
66 Sacks, op. cit., Chapter 1, n. 16, Ibid., Chapter 6.
67 See Chapter 3, p. 111.

Chapter 6

1   OECD, *Economic Survey of Yugoslavia*, June 1979, p. 5.
2   See Chapter 1, pp. 41–3.
3   See Chapter 3, pp. 109–14 and 178–82.
4   See Annex 12 and Annex 15.
5   OECD, *Economic Survey of Yugoslavia*, May 1981, pp. 26–32.
6   See Chapter 1, p. 41.
7   OECD, *Economic Survey of Yugoslavia*, June 1979, p. 32.
8   'Financing Socio-Political Units', *Yugoslav Survey*, Volume 9, No. 2, 1968, pp. 59–75.
9   Ibid.
10 See Chapter 1, p. 41.
11 'The New System of Financing Education', *Yugoslav Survey*, Volume 8, No. 1, 1967.
12 *General Child Care Finance Act*, cited in 'Financing Socio-Political Units', *Yugoslav Survey*, op. cit.
13 'Financing Socio-Political Units', *Yugoslav Survey*, op. cit.
14 Ibid.
15 Ibid.
16 'The Latest Changes (1971) in the Constitution of the SFRY', *Yugoslav Survey*, op. cit., Chapter 2, n. 36.
17 'Law on the Use of Securities for Particular Purposes', see also, *SL*, No. 60, 1972, and, for example, M. Radivojevic, op. cit., Chapter 3, n. 17, pp. 26–31.
18 See 'Law Amending the Law on the Issue of Federal Bonds', *SL*, No. 57, 1974.
19 See, Radivojevic, op. cit., Chapter 3, n. 17, p. 30.
20 Ibid.
21 *SL*, No. 39, 1971.
22 OECD, *Economic Survey of Yugoslavia*, 1978, for a commentary on the changes.
23 OECD, *Economic Survey of Yugoslavia*, May 1983, pp. 31–4.
24 Ibid.
25 The chief source for the following account is the OECD, *Economic Survey of Yugoslavia*, 1970–80, especially Apr. 1974, pp. 28–38, and the Annual and Quarterly publications of the National Bank of Yugoslavia.
26 See Chapter 2, p. 75.
27 OECD, *Economic Review of Yugoslavia*, 1974, pp. 31–2.
28 Amendment 27.
29 See Chapter 2, p. 63.
30 Introduced by the 'Law on the Reserve Requirements of Banks at the National Bank' in July 1956. The 'Law on Credit and other Banking Activities', effective from 1 Mar. 1963, drew attention to the desirability of co-ordinating changes in the money supply with expected fluctuations in economic activity and

recommended that changes in reserve requirement levels and interest rates—particularly the central bank discount rate—should be considered more readily.

31 OECD, *Economic Survey of Yugoslavia*, Mar. 1972, pp. 51–4.
32 OECD, *Economic Survey of Yugoslavia*, Apr. 1974, pp. 48–9.
33 OECD, *Economic Survey of Yugoslavia*, Apr. 1975, p. 44.
34 See Chapter 3, p. 113.
35 OECD, *Economic Survey of Yugoslavia*, June 1979, p. 28.
36 See Chapter 2, p. 62.
37 OECD, *Economic Survey of Yugoslavia*, May 1980, pp. 43–7.
38 Ibid.
39 Non-economic sectors comprise mainly service activities, such as culture, welfare, health, education, and financial institutions, such as Banks and Insurance Companies.
40 OECD, *Economic Survey of Yugoslavia*, May 1980, pp. 45–6.
41 See OECD, *Economic Survey of Yugoslavia*, 1970–82.
42 Ibid., Apr. 1974, pp. 48–9.
43 Ibid.
44 Ibid., p. 53.
45 Ibid., Apr. 1976, pp. 5–11.
46 Ibid., May 1980, pp. 43–7.
47 See D. Gorupic and I. Paij, *Workers' Self-Management in Yugoslav Undertakings*, Ekonomski Institut, Zagreb, 1970, pp. 216–24.
48 See, for example, Neuberger and James, op. cit., Chapter 2, n. 7, p. 262.
49 It is interesting to note that the surveys undertaken on this issue indicate strongly that Yugoslav workers prefer stability of income to maximization of income. See, for example, Bogdan Ilic, 'The Self-management organization of the enterprise', *Gledišta*, Dec. 1969, p. 1717.
50 Real average earnings fell by 8 per cent in 1980, 5 per cent in 1981 and 3 per cent in 1982. See OECD, *Economic Survey of Yugoslavia*, May 1983, p. 17.
51 OECD, *Economic Survey of Yugoslavia*, 1973, pp. 5–25 for a valuable analysis of the problem.
52 S. Popov, op. cit., Chapter 4, n. 74.
53 See *Development with Decentralization*, op. cit., Chapter 3, n. 27, pp. 351–3.
54 See Chapter 3, p. 97.
55 See Chapter 3, pp. 105–14.
56 See, generally, M. Sakulic, 'Import Dependence in the Yugoslav Economy', in *Aktuelni Problemi privrednog razvoja i privredna Sistem Jugoslavije*, Informator, Zagreb, 1972.
57 OECD, *Economic Survey of Yugoslavia*, May 1983, p. 36.
58 Ibid.
59 See OECD, *Economic Survey of Yugoslavia*, 1970–82, and *Development with Decentralization*, op. cit., Chapter 3, n. 27, Chapter 12.
60 OECD, *Economic Survey of Yugoslavia*, Apr. 1974, p. 48.
61 Ibid.
62 Ibid., May 1981, p. 14.
63 See *Development with Decentralization*, op. cit., Chapter 3, n. 27, pp. 396–7.
64 See Ibid., Chapter 3, n. 27, pp. 280–3.
65 Ibid.
66 Ibid.

INDEX

accounting system (generally) 25–6, 86–7, 110, 111, 113, 200
appropriations out of income 25–6
Business Fund 16, 26, 106, 117, 128, 147
Collective Consumption Fund 25, 109, 147, 198
Fixed Capital Fund 25–6
investment partnership accounts 91
Net Income 25–6, 32, 44, 97, 105
Personal Income Fund 25–6, 41, 42, 97–8, 128, 150, 179, 189
Realized Income 25–6, 110, 120
Reserve Fund 25, 68, 109, 147, 180
Reserve Fund, Communal see Joint Reserve Funds
Working Capital 25–6
Adizes, I. 240, 241
Adminstrative Socialism see Plans, Administrative
administrators 4, 13, 17, 49, 51, 52–5, 56, 57, 60, 68, 79, 150
agriculture:
  collectivization 12
  incomes 122, 144
  peasant economy 5, 122, 130–2, 136, 139, 140, 142, 144, 145
  prices see Prices
airlines 176, 177
Albania 1
aluminium industry 107, 175, 177
appropriations out of income see accounting system
Austria 159
automobile industry 30, 106, 116–17, 159, 175

Bajt, A. 137, 247
balance of payments generally 29, 45–6, 74, 133, 171, 172, 173, 207–13
  commodity structures 209–12
  convertibility 35, 172
  customs duties 26–7, 32, 46, 62, 169, 170, 171, 189, 191, 209
  deficit/surplus 2, 6–7, 19, 20, 22, 27–9, 45, 74, 151, 155, 171, 172, 186, 187, 194, 195, 196, 199, 200, 213

import quotas 165, 169, 170, 171, 172, 174, 186, 206
invisible earnings 6, 7, 133, 186, 207–8, 212–13
retention quotas see foreign exchange controls
trade 27–9, 75, 170
trade direction 208–9
worker remittances 6, 102–3, 133, 208, 212
bankruptcy see insolvency
banks:
  Business (Commercial) Banks 3, 5, 32, 43–4, 63, 68–70, 74, 85, 93, 103–9, 118, 149, 172, 180, 194, 195
  Communal Banks 18, 20, 24
  deposits 85, 103
  domestic 103–4
  foreign exchange 102–4
  inter-bank agreements 103–4
  mobilizing savings 102–5
  National Bank of Yugoslavia 20, 22, 24, 70, 75, 94, 95, 104, 105, 170, 172, 185, 192, 193, 194, 195, 196, 244, 251
  Regional National Banks 42, 70, 193, 195
  Specialized Banks 18, 20, 24–5
  The Yugoslav Agricultural Bank 24, 42
  The Yugoslav Investment Bank 24, 27, 41, 69
Basic Organization of Associated Labour (BOAL) 4, 48, 50, 59, 60, 65–7, 68, 71, 73, 74, 79, 152, 157, 158, 159, 163, 189, 207, 244
Bernstein, M. 239
Bicanic, R. 237, 238, 239
bilateral clearing areas see balance of payments, trade direction
bonds see securities
Borba 71, 240, 241, 244, 245, 246, 248, 249
Bosnia–Herzegovina 1, 29, 37, 107, 117, 120, 121, 135, 153, 159, 163, 175
Brznik, D. 246
budget:
  balance 190–2